...all around the world

Commercial Union has offices throughout the world and its principal areas of operation are the U.K. and Ireland, the United States, Western Europe, Canada and Australia.

As a multinational organisation we have extensive interests in reinsurance and property development and are, of course, one of the City of London's foremost institutional investors.

Commercial Union aims to do business everywhere in the world where suitable opportunities arise. Our offices are spread across five continents and our service covers a market of nearly 1,200 million people.

Commercial Union likes to think of itself as a responsible corporate citizen, caring for people and the environment in which they live. Business is the centre but not the circumference of our thinking and Commercial Union demonstrates its sense of social responsibility in many ways such as its support of the Arts and Medicine.

Principal Offices of Commercial Union and Associated Companies

United Kingdom
Commercial Union Assurance Co. Ltd.,
Leadenhall House,
100 Leadenhall Street, London EC3P 3HD.

Argentina
Commercial Union Assurance Co. Ltd.,
Bartolomé Mitre 335/41, Bueños Aires.

Belgium
Les Provinces Réunies S.A.,
Avenue des Arts 6, 1040 Brussels.

Canada
Commercial Union Assurance Company of Canada,
PO Box 441, Commercial Union Tower,
Toronto-Dominion Centre, Toronto, Ontario, M5K 1L9.

France
J. Eeckman S.A.,
104 rue de Richelieu, Paris 75002.

Holland
Delta Lloyd Verzekeringsgroep N.V.,
Postbus 1000, Spaklerweg 4, Amsterdam.

Italy
Liberty Società Anglo-Italiana,
Piazza S. Fedele 2, 20121 Milan.

Japan
Northern Assurance Company, Cornes & Co., Ltd.,
No. 6 Tori 2-Chome, Nihonbashi, Chou-Ku,
CPO Box 158, Tokyo.

Pakistan
Commercial Union Assurance,
PO Box 4895, 110–117 Qamar House,
M.A. Jinnah Road, Karachi 2.

South Africa
Commercial Union Assurance Company of
South Africa Ltd.,
Cnr. Rissik & Main Street, Johannesburg 2000.

Sweden
Commercial Union Assurance Svenska A.B.,
Linnégatan 5, S–114 47 Stockholm.

United States
Commercial Union Assurance Companies,
One Beacon Street,
Boston, Mass. 02108.

Australia
Commercial Union Assurance Co. of Australia Ltd.,
"Temple Court,"
428 Collins Street, Melbourne, Vic. 3000.

Brazil
Commercial Union do Brasil-Seguradora S.A.,
Rua Mexico 168, 3°–4° Andar,
Caixa Postal 3774, Riò de Janeiro.

Denmark
Forsikrings-A/S "Vidar,"
Christian IX's Gade No. 1,
1111 Copenhagen K.

Greece
Commercial Union Assurance Co. Ltd.,
7 Pal. Patron Germanou Street,
Athens 124.

Ireland
Hibernian Insurance Co. Ltd.,
Hawkins House, Hawkins Street,
Dublin 2.

New Zealand
Commercial Union Assurance Company of
New Zealand Ltd.,
142 Featherston Street, Wellington.

Far East Region
Commercial Union Assurance Co. Ltd.,
PO Box 3991, Commercial Union Building,
4 Robinson Road, Singapore 1.

Spain
Commercial Union Assurance Co. Ltd.,
Via Augusta 23, Barcelona 6.

Switzerland
Northern Assurance Company,
Rue Adrien-Lachenal 26,
Case Postale 286, 1211, Geneva 3.

THE TIMES 1000

1979-80

The indispensable annual review
of leading world industrial and financial companies

TIMES BOOKS

THE TIMES 1000 1979-1980

LEADING COMPANIES IN BRITAIN AND OVERSEAS

Edited by Margaret Allen

Advertisements: A. Tollworthy, Financial Advertisement Director, Times Newspapers Limited

Cover design by Ivan and Robin Dodd

© Times Books Limited 1979

Published 1979 by Times Books,
18 Ogle St., London, W.1.

ISBN 0 7230 0232 0

Contents

Daimler

ENTER OUR NEW DAIMLER.

Change for change's sake has never been part of the Daimler philosophy. And demonstrating once again that a superb design, unremittingly and painstakingly perfected over the years, is far superior to a constantly-changing concept, we today present the Daimler Series III.

To improve on motor cars which are considered by many to be the finest in the world has been no easy task; continuous refinement to the specification and subtle treatment of the styling have resulted in a Daimler range which is sleeker, more spacious and even more lavishly equipped than ever before.

The new cars: the Sovereign and Double Six, the Vanden Plas 4.2 and Double Six, combine sublime smoothness, effortless power and ultimate technical brilliance.

In the Series III is a beautiful blend of everything that Daimler has always stood for and everything that today's owner and driver will expect his Daimler to be.

Manufacturers of fine motor cars through five reigns.

The Times 1000

Rank	Rank last year	Company	Headquarters	Main activity	Sales £000
Europe's top twenty industrial groups					
1	1	British Petroleum	UK	Oil industry	17,559,800
2	2	Royal Dutch Petroleum	Netherlands	Oil industry	13,767,000
3	3	'Shell' Transport & Trading	UK	Oil industry	11,684,800
4	6	Veba AG	Germany	Holding co. (electricity, chemicals, transport)	8,403,600
5	4	Philips' Lamps Holdings	Netherlands	Electrical products	8,124,000
6	8	Siemens AG	Germany	Electrical and general engineering, electronics	7,819,000
7	*	Fiat	Italy	Motor vehicles, ships' engines, diesel trains and aeroplanes	7,772,200
8	10	Volkswagenwerk	Germany	Motor vehicle manufacturers	7,203,200
9	11	Compagnie Française des Pétroles	France	Holding co. (oil and petroleum)	6,625,100
10	5	ENI	Italy	Holding co. (petroleum, chemicals, engineering, textiles)	6,577,800
11	7	Daimler-Benz AG	Germany	Motor vehicle and engine manufacturers	6,532,600
12	12	Hoechst AG	Germany	Chemicals, dyes, plastics	6,520,400
13	9	BAT Industries	UK	Tobacco, retailing, paper, cosmetics	6,512,000
14	14	Renault (Régie Nationale des Usines)	France	Automobile production	6,470,600
15	13	BASF AG	Germany	Chemical products	6,267,900
16	15	Bayer AG	Germany	Chemical products	6,155,300
17	16	Nestlé Alimentana SA	Switzerland	Holding co. (chocolate, milk and food products)	5,920,600
18	17	Unilever NV	Netherlands	Food products, detergents, animal feedstuffs	5,794,300
19	19	PSA Peugeot-Citroën	France	Automobiles and engines	5,624,700
20	*	Electricity Council and Boards	UK	Electricity suppliers	5,445,100
* Not listed last year.					

British Petroleum is Europe's largest industrial grouping by a considerable margin. In the last edition of *The Times 1000* it was some 8 per cent ahead of its nearest rival, Royal Dutch Petroleum, with a total turnover of £14,712,200,000. Now it has increased its lead even further. According to last published accounts, which showed a total turnover of £17,559,800,000, it was over 12 per cent ahead of Royal Dutch Petroleum, the Netherlands-based oil company, and its sales were 50 per cent higher than those of its nearest British rival, 'Shell' Transport and Trading, the UK sister company of Royal Dutch. The table above, showing the twenty largest industrial groupings in Europe, including the UK, illustrates very clearly the dominance of the oil and chemical industries in terms of size in the European industrial scene. These industries, together with the automobile and electrical and electronic industries, account for seventeen of the top twenty industrial groups in Europe. The remainder represent the food and tobacco industries.

Of the top twenty, four are British, including the state-owned Electricity Council and Boards, an organisation which is much bigger than all but three public commercial companies in the UK in terms of sales. Even so, its turnover is about £1000m a year less than that of Renault, the state-owned French car company. Germany has seven companies in the top twenty, the Netherlands and France three each, Italy two and Switzerland one. The most startling change among Europe's leading companies since the last edition of *The Times 1000* has been the improvement in the fortunes of Fiat, the Italian-based motor vehicle manufacturer. It has moved up forty places to become the seventh biggest company in Europe in terms of sales. This represents an increase in sales over the year from £6,804,100,000 to £7,772,200,000, an improvement of some 14 per cent.

The top 1000 UK companies (pp. 30–69)
The turnover of companies which reach the top 1000 and therefore become eligible for the table has continued to grow. A year ago a sales figure of a little under £22m was enough to get a company into the list: this year the comparable figure is over £25m. But this does not indicate much true growth. Most, if not all, of the increase has been swallowed up by inflation.

Looking at the table overall, the only changes in the top ten positions are General Electric, up one place to ninth, and the entry of Shell UK for the first time, in tenth position, following the break-up some time ago of Shell-Mex and BP. With these changes Esso Petroleum has dropped out of the top ten. Although British Petroleum and 'Shell' Transport and Trading are much larger than their nearest rival, BAT Industries, the first forty-five companies in the list have recorded sales in excess of £1000m. The biggest rise in the top fifty is that of BOC International, which has moved up from sixty-second place to thirty-first. Allied Breweries, swelled by its takeover of J. Lyons and Co, has also moved up well from thirtieth to twelfth place. In the opposite direction, Cavenham has dropped from twelfth to twentieth place, following some years of rapid rises.

As usual, we have included (page 9) a table showing which companies have come into the 1000 and which have dropped out. This time there are seventy-five new entries, Shell UK being by far the largest, but the four next largest entries are all the results of company re-organisation or reconstruction. Of the seventy-five companies replaced, forty-eight have dropped out from positions below 800.

In terms of profits, British Petroleum, for the second year running, records the largest monetary increase (see Table A, **Changes in profit**), but its closest rival, 'Shell' Transport and Trading, reports the biggest monetary fall. This table includes many well-known British industrial names. That is not surprising in a survey of absolute changes in profits, but the big companies do not score as well when it comes to return on capital employed (Table C). It is the smaller, essentially service-based companies with low capital assets which show the highest return on capital. Last year's leader, CBS United Kingdom (648 in Table 1), has slipped to third place this year. Its place has been taken by Cocoa Merchants, which lies only 165th in Table 1. Lummus Co. (426th in Table 1) remains in second place.

The top ten UK profit makers

Rank	Company	Profit‡ £000	Rank in Table 1
1	British Petroleum	2,695,200	1
2	'Shell' Transport & Trading	1,495,200	2
3	The Post Office	1,281,100	*
4	Electricity Council & Boards	862,300	*
5	British Gas Corporation	618,200	*
6	Imperial Chemical Industries	588,000	4
7	BAT Industries	499,000	3
8	Unilever Ltd	367,400	5
9	General Electric	356,800	9
10	Rio Tinto-Zinc	334,300	13

*A nationalised industry.
‡Before interest and tax.

With Cocoa Merchants reporting a 201.3 per cent return on capital employed, Green Shield Trading Stamp, by contrast, records the lowest return of 0.6 per cent. But this company and Star Aluminium are the only two with a return of less than 1 per cent: in the last edition of *The Times 1000* there were nine such companies. As usual, there are a number of companies reporting losses —twenty-six this time as against twenty-five a year ago. Some names are appearing for the second or third year, and the biggest loss is that of Govan Shipbuilders, which

A Changes in profit

10 Biggest rises

Rank in Table 1	Company	£000	per cent change
1	British Petroleum Co.	+301,400	+12·6
23	Texaco	+82,565	+196·9
9	General Electric Co.	+64,800	+22·2
12	Allied Breweries	+56,900	+59·4
26	Marks & Spencer	+46,694	+36·0
87	Thomson British Holdings	+39,400	+36·8
71	Rolls-Royce	+31,000	+333.3
54	Distillers Co.	+30,499	+21·1
91	Harrisons & Crosfield	+29,516	+118·9
3	BAT Industries	+27,000	+5·7

10 Biggest falls

Rank in Table 1	Company	£000	per cent change
2	'Shell' Transport & Trading	−252,000	−14.4
483	Elf Aquitaine UK (Holdings)	−55,703	−90·3
4	Imperial Chemical Industries	−54,000	−8·8
55	EMI	−37,239	−48·0
39	Rank Xerox	−29,900	−10·3
820	Total Oil Marine	−26,485	−82·5
73	Mobil Oil Co.	−26,065	−81·5
94	Massey-Ferguson Holdings	−22,847	−42·7
105	Ocean Transport & Trading	−21,484	−41·6
11	Esso Petroleum Co.	−19,656	−14·1

B Money losers

Rank in Table 1	Company	Loss £000
466	Govan Shipbuilders	13,261 p.a.
469	Alcoa of Great Britain	8,789
109	Chrysler United Kingdom	8,231
476	Firestone Tyre & Rubber Co.	5,457
764	Short Brothers	4,929
308	Borregaard Industries	3,941
568	SKF (UK)	3,704
432	Henry Boot & Sons	3,647
925	Armstrong Cork Co.	3,355
169	Amoco (UK)	2,980
434	Associated Fisheries	2,247
569	Alfred Herbert	1,569
868	Audiotronic Holdings	1,357 p.a.
276	Gulf Oil (Great Britain)	1,190
184	Tampimex Oil	1,129
795	Hardy & Co. (Furnishers)	1,094
446	Singer Co. (UK)	946
406	Internl. Synthetic Rubber	826
363	J. H. Rayner & Co.	812
259	Westland Aircraft	770
1000	Peek Holdings	607 p.a.
726	Polygram Leisure	601
936	Titaghur Jute Factory Co.	570
816	Luncheon Vouchers	516
634	R. H. Thompson Group	231
683	Favor Parker	168 p.a.

Behaviour + Communication = Reputation

Charles Barker City

Specialists in corporate and financial communication

For details on how CBC could help your company
make the most of its communications opportunities, please
contact George Pulay or Alan Bayley at 30 Farringdon Street, London EC4A 4EA.
Telephone 01-236 3011; Telex 883588

# Schroders

International Merchant and Investment Bankers

J. Henry Schroder Wagg & Co. Limited

120 Cheapside, London EC2V 6DS
Telephone 01-588 4000

J. Henry Schroder Bank & Trust Company

The Schroder Building,
One State Street, New York 10015
Telephone (212) 269-6500

J. Henry Schroder Bank A.G.

Central 2, 8021 Zurich
Telephone (01) 47 50 00

Group Companies, Associates and Representative Offices in

Argentina	Hong Kong
Australia	Japan
Belgium	Lebanon
Bermuda	Saudi Arabia
Brasil	Singapore
Cayman Islands	Switzerland
Colombia	United Kingdom
France	United States of America
Germany	Venezuela

Newcomers and departures in the Top 1000

Ins

Rank in 1979/80 1000	Name	Rank in 1979/80 1000	Name	Rank in 1979/80 1000	Name
10	Shell UK	859	Horizon Travel	957	Barretts & Baird (Wholesale)
74	George Wimpey	867	Clifford's Dairies	958	Superdrug Stores
87	Thomson British Holdings	868	Audiotronic Holdings	959	Johnson Group Cleaners
113	John Laing	872	Status Discount	961	Sandell Perkins
127	Costain Group	880	Kiril Mischeff (Holdings)	962	Norton Abrasives
292	Hunting Petroleum Services	881	Blyth, Green, Jourdain & Co.	963	Bernard Wardle & Co.
328	Wormald International Hldgs (UK)	884	Walkers Crisps	964	Transparent Paper
392	Bowater-Scott Corpn	887	George Ewer & Co.	965	British Midland Airways
483	Elf Aquitaine UK (Holdings)	894	HTV Group	966	Eva Industries
592	Harris Queensway Group	896	Lancia (England)	967	Fiat Allis UK
640	Manor National Group Motors	898	General Mills UK	974	Willett & Son (Corn Merchants)
668	OCS Group	900	Scotcros	975	Wilson (Connolly) Holdings
682	J. Soufflet (UK)	912	Hyster	981	Jessups (Holdings)
766	WGI	916	Minories Garages	983	J. Marr and Son
767	Sun Valley Poultry	917	Comben Group	984	Jones, Stroud (Holdings)
776	IDC Group	919	Geers Gross	986	J. B. Holdings
803	Brown & Jackson	920	Siemssen, Hunter	987	B. H. Blackwell
806	Bartella	927	Young & Rubicam Holdings	992	National Car Parks
813	Habitat Design Holdings	938	Wander	993	Playboy Club of London
820	Total Oil Marine	939	Western Motor Holdings	994	Alpine Holdings
830	N. G. Bailey & Co.	941	IAS Cargo Airlines	995	R. & G. Cuthbert
834	Arthur Bartfeld Group	944	Nacanco	996	United Scientific Holdings
840	London Export Corpn. (Holdings)	946	Williamson Tea Holdings	997	A. Goldberg & Sons
841	Carron Company (Holdings)	952	John Wood Group (Aberdeen)	998	Erith & Co.
846	Wigmore Holdings	955	Constantine Holdings	999	Shaw Carpets

Outs

Rank in 1978/79 1000	Name	Rank in 1978/79 1000	Name	Rank in 1978/79 1000	Name
53	J. Lyons & Co.	742	Swan Hunter Group	940	Clark Equipment
69	George Wimpey & Co.	746	Sena Sugar Estates	941	Kyle Stewart (Contractors)
103	Richard Costain	810	Fluor (England)	946	Warren Plantation Holdings
111	John Laing & Son	849	Reardon Smith Line	952	Francis Parker
135	Thomson Organisation	856	Cee-N-Cee Supermarkets	954	R. H. Cole
187	British Aluminium Co.	858	Pork Farms	956	Gomme Holdings
224	Charringtons Industrial Holdings	862	Crane	962	Manchester Ship Canal Co.
242	J. B. Eastwood	866	Office Cleaning Services	963	Stern Osmat Group
266	Matthews Holdings	873	R. Hostombe	965	Expanded Metal Co.
279	Hunting Gibson	880	Blackwood, Morton & Sons (Hldgs)	966	Elliott Group of Peterborough
307	Rudolf Wolff & Co.	882	Edwards Williams Hldgs.	969	Stocklake Holdings
318	Mather & Platt	898	Oliver Rix	970	William Pickles & Co.
482	Allied Polymer Group	902	Turner Manufacturing Co.	971	Linotype and Machinery
484	A. J. Mills (Holdings)	903	Macpherson, Train & Co.	975	Grundig International
504	Pride & Clarke	906	McConomy & Co.	978	Londis (Holdings)
539	Dentsply	907	J. Saville Gordon Group	979	Randalls Group
552	Scott Lithgow	910	United Continental Steels	980	Minter Investment Co.
587	Federated Chemical Holdings	912	Gambia Produce Marketing Co.	982	Murco Petroleum
590	Cosmos Air Holidays	914	Morgan Edwards	988	Yorkshire Chemicals
609	Staflex International	924	Fein & Co.	995	Ridpath Brothers
646	Harland & Wolff	926	Morgan-Grampian	996	Buitoni
650	Mears Bros. Holdings	931	Leisure & General Holdings	997	Dart Industries
663	Pontin's	932	Camrex (Holdings)	998	Norton Villiers Triumph
674	Samuel Osborn & Co.	936	Glass, Glover Group	999	Pitman
729	John M. Henderson & Co. (Hldgs)	939	Sanyo Marubeni (UK)	1000	S. W. Wood Group

You name it, Lex lease it.

Lex Vehicle Leasing is backed by the full resources of the nationwide Lex Service Group. Using our special Vehicle Locator Service, we are in a position to quickly source any make or model our customers demand. Lex leasing has special arrangements with the major motor manufacturers and purchases competitively from them all.

If you currently own your vehicles you may find that the cash released by their sale could be usefully employed in other company enterprises. Lex will purchase some or all of your vehicles and lease them back to you.

If you simply wish to start leasing there are other benefits which may interest you. A Lex leasing package allows you to optimise the company's cash flow by paying regular, fixed, inflation-proof instalments.

Lex Service

Lex leasing will remove from you the administration and maintenance worries connected with vehicle ownership. Our 'Pre-Delivery Inspection' checks ensure that your cars are delivered fault-free and fully road taxed. The Lex 'mobility guarantee' keeps you on the road by supplying a loan vehicle when you have

a breakdown, and offers the AA Relay service.

Flexibility

Lex Leasing specialises in advising their customers about the most economical method of running company cars. In some cases customers choose to lease only part of their fleet. In every case Lex is pleased to offer the option of leasing some vehicles enabling customers to compare Lex against current fleet arrangements.

For further details please contact Lex at any of the addresses listed below.

Lex Vehicle Leasing
Lower Glory Mill
Wooburn Green
Nr. High Wycombe, Bucks
Tel: 062 85 24942

Lex Vehicle Leasing
208 Western Avenue
Acton, London W3 6RW
Tel: 01 992 8706

Lex Vehicle Leasing
999 Chester Road
Stretford
Manchester M32 0RB
Tel: 061 865 2441

Lex Vehicle Leasing
Mill Walk, Northfield
Birmingham B31 4HL
Tel: 021 477 3110

Lex Vehicle Leasing

(A member of the Lex Service Group)

lost money at the rate of £13,261,000 a year, compared with a loss of less than £3,000,000 a year previously. Tampimex Oil makes an appearance among the losers this year: it is not many years since it was leading the list in terms of return on capital employed.

The average return on capital employed throughout the list has fallen since the last edition from 24.6 per cent to 23.3 per cent, with the top fifty trailing below the average, as is customary. Their return on capital employed has dropped from 21.1 per cent to 18.8 per cent over the year.

C Return on capital employed*

10 Highest

Rank in Table 1	Company	per cent
165	Cocoa Merchants	201·3
426	Lummus Co.	194·9
648	CBS United Kingdom	187·9
682	J. Soufflet (UK)	129·6†
859	Horizon Travel	127·9
909	Leigh & Sillavan Group	122·6
993	Playboy Club of London	116·7
947	Mills & Allen International	112·5
537	Saatchi & Saatchi Company	107·3
994	Alpine Holdings	104·1

10 Lowest

Rank in Table 1	Company	per cent
456	Green Shield Trading Stamp	0·6
705	Star Aluminium Co.	0·9
886	National Carbonising Co.	1·0
244	Chevron Oil (UK)	1·2
483	Elf Aquitaine UK (Holdings)	1·2
564	Roche Products	1·2
416	J. E. Sanger	1·4 p.a.
178	Nestlé Company	1·9
411	Andrew Weir & Co.	1·9
60	Western United Inv. Co.	1·9

*At beginning of year.
†On capital employed at end of year.

The two oil companies, British Petroleum and 'Shell', have the highest equity market capitalisation, but General Electric has replaced Imperial Chemical Industries at number three. Marks and Spencer has moved up to fifth place and BAT Industries has dropped from fifth to seventh. At the other end of the table Titaghur Jute has trebled its market capitalisation over the year, but remains the smallest, with its total equity valued at £300,000 on 13 July 1979, the date on which all the market capitalisations were calculated. The fall in the number of companies with an equity quoted on the Stock Exchange continues: this year 414 have reached the 1000 table without such a listing. Some are private companies, some unquoted public companies and still others subsidiaries of foreign (particularly American) companies.

D Equity market capitalisation

10 Highest

Rank in Table 1	Company	13 July 1979 £ million
1	British Petroleum Co.	4,783·2
2	'Shell' Transport & Trading	2,009·9
9	General Electric Co.	1,921·2
4	Imperial Chemical Industries	1,872·9
26	Marks & Spencer	1,455·6
5	Unilever Ltd.	951·9
3	BAT Industries	941·2
33	Great Universal Stores	895·2
56	Beecham Group	857·9
54	Distillers Co.	789·9

10 Lowest

Rank in Table 1	Company	13 July 1979 £ million
936	Titaghur Jute Factory Co.	0·3
1000	Peek Holdings	0·3
991	P. Panto & Co.	0·9
657	Charles Hurst	1·2
868	Audiotronic Holdings	1·2
706	Joseph Stocks & Sons (Hldgs)	1·3
752	J. E. England & Sons (Wlgtn)	1·3
915	Brunning Group	1·8
981	Jessups (Holdings)	1·9
212	Danish Bacon Co.	1·9

The total turnover of the 1000 companies is £233,366,591,000. The dominance of the top fifty companies is quite clear: with a combined total of £111,626,622,000, they account for 48 per cent of the total. In terms of capital employed, they take up 50 per cent, and of profits before interest and tax, as much as 53 per cent.

The top ten UK exporters

Rank	Company	Exports £000	Rank in Table 1
1	British Petroleum	1,259,000	1
2	BL	910,000	7
3	Imperial Chemical Industries	856,000	4
4	Ford Motor	775,000	8
5	General Electric	665,000	9
6	Unilever	468,042	5
7	Courtaulds	425,000	18
8	British Aircraft Corporation	410,587	85
9	Massey-Ferguson	363,800	94
10	Hawker Siddeley	361,000	45

The above figures do not include C. T. Bowring & Co. (Number 28 in Table 1), whose total export figure of £639,939,000 included £634,887,000 premium income earned overseas.

It is only when it comes to exports that smaller firms make a showing among the leaders (see the table of the top UK exporters, page 9). Even there, British Petroleum is in its familiar first place, followed this year by BL (formerly British Leyland), which was third last year. Imperial Chemical Industries has slipped from first to third place. What is interesting among the main exporters, however, is the appearance of the British Aircraft Corporation in eighth place, as against its eighty-fifth position in Table 1. It is followed in ninth place by Massey-Ferguson (ninety-fourth in Table 1) and finally by Hawker Siddeley, which is forty-fifth in Table 1. The table shows clearly Britain's dependence on vehicles, chemicals and oil for the big thrust of overseas sales.

The nationalised industries are by far the biggest employers of labour in the UK. The Post Office leads with more than 400,000 employees, and the private sector is represented only in fourth place by General Electric, which has 191,000 employees, a fall of 1000 over the year. Five of the top ten employers are nationalised industries, and the National Enterprise Board, which is a state-owned holding company, is another huge employer, though of its total of 278,514 employees (which makes it the third largest employer) 191,853 work for BL alone.

The top ten UK employers

Rank	Company	No. of employees	Rank in Table 1
1	Post Office	410,977	*
2	National Coal Board	300,000	*
3	National Enterprise Board	278,514[1]	‡
4	British Railways Board	243,264	*
5	General Electric	191,000	9
6	British Steel	190,000	*
7	Electricity Council & Boards	159,825	*
8	BAT Industries	153,000	3
9	Imperial Chemical Industries	151,000	4
10	Lonrho	128,000	30

*A nationalised industry.
‡A state holding company.
[1]Includes 191,853 employees of BL.

The leading advertisers (p. 28)
Once again, Unilever leads the table of top advertisers. It is in fifth position in Table 1. In 1978 the company increased its advertising by 9.5 per cent to a total, for press and television, of £32,036,000. At this level it spends 50 per cent more than any other advertiser in the country. Moving into second place from fifth is HM Government, which in 1978 spent £21,535,000 on advertising, a massive 62 per cent more than in 1977. As might be expected, the biggest advertisers are those companies which serve the public—the food, tobacco and retailing businesses. The nationalised industries are well represented, too. British Gas, the Electricity Council and the Post Office are among the top fifty advertisers. (For details of how this table is compiled, see page 14).

Unions and employers (pp. 16, 18)
The tables of the top trade unions and employers' associations are making their second appearance in *The Times 1000*. The Transport and General Workers Union, the biggest in the UK now has more than two million members (an increase of 140,000 since last year). It also has the largest funds. At £36m plus, they are a third more than those of the second biggest union, the Amalgamated Union of Engineering Workers. All the top ten unions, except the National Union of Mineworkers, reported an increase in membership over the year, with the National and Local Government Officers' Association overtaking the National Union of Public Employees in fourth place, and the Association of Scientific, Technical and Managerial Staffs moving into sixth place ahead of the Union of Shop Distributive and Allied Workers. The National Union of Teachers lost more members than any other union, down from 296,092 to 258,117. The employers' associations present a contrast. The largest subscription income, the criterion of rank in this table, is that of the Engineering Employers' Federation, but in terms of total funds and members, the National Farmers' Union is way out in front, with 127,622 members and almost £8m in total funds. Its nearest rival in numbers is the National Federation of Retail Newsagents, with 29,829 members but with total funds of less than £1m. The Cement Makers' Federation has the smallest number of members—six.

The financial sector
Changes in the financial sector are rarely dramatic, but in the long term there are clearly discernible alterations. Among accepting houses, for instance, several merchant banks have formerly held the top place. This time Schroders, previously number three, has overtaken Kleinwort, Benson, Lonsdale. Hill Samuel, once number one, has dropped from second to fourth place, and another former leader, Hambros, is moving up again.

Among the clearing banks Barclays stays at the top, but National Westminster has narrowed the gap between them. Midland Bank and Lloyds have changed places over the year. Lombard North Central has increased its lead over the other finance houses, whilst Mercantile Credit has moved into the number three spot, closing the gap between it and United Dominions Trust, which stays in second place. Among discount houses, Union Discount has replaced Garrard and National Discount as the leading company. The only other change of note in this section is the resurgence of First National Finance Corporation, which has moved from fourteenth to first place in Table 12, **Other financial institutions.**

Companies outside Europe
The largest United States companies are, like those in Europe, dominated by the oil industry. There are eight oil companies in the top twenty, the biggest of which is Exxon, the world's largest industrial grouping. This company, with annual sales of £29,407,676,000, dwarfs British Petroleum, which, however, is larger than any other US oil company. The roll call of the world's top twenty industrial groupings would comprise twelve US companies, two in the UK, two in the Netherlands, three in Germany and one in Italy. No Japanese company would qualify.

Margaret Allen

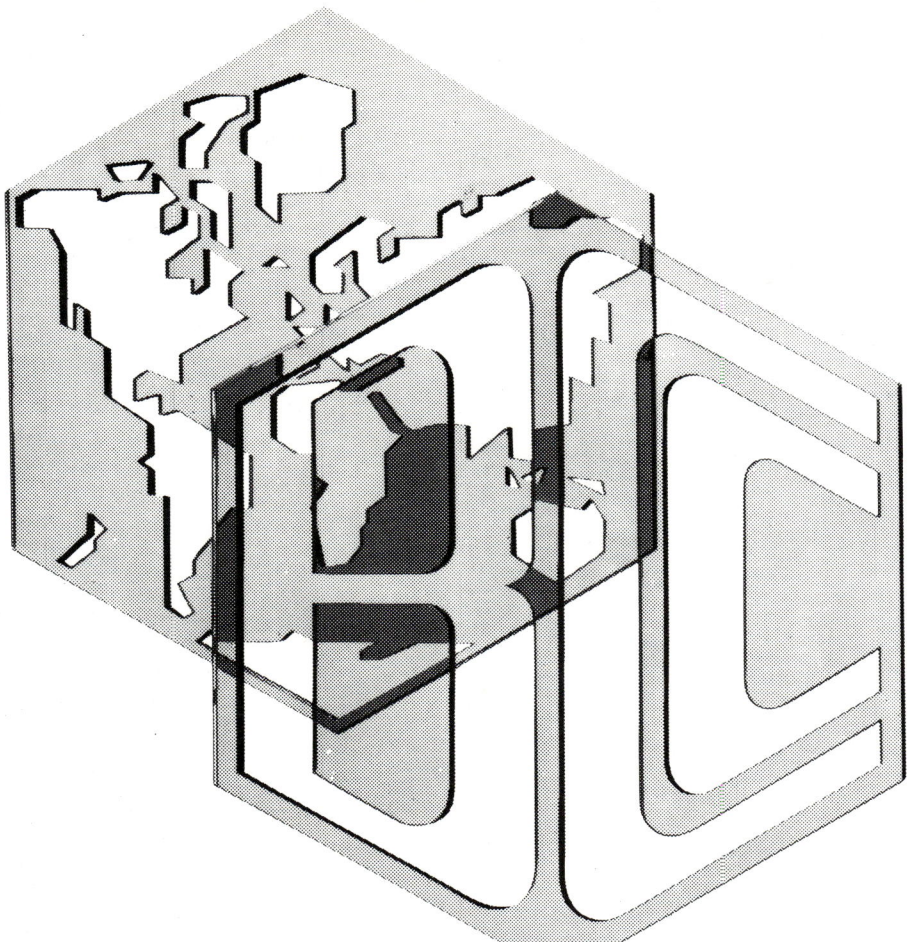

The way to look at international banking is through BCC

The Bank of Credit and Commerce International was *born* international – a fact which has certainly helped its growth. The BCC Group now has offices in 38 countries. Capital funds stand at over US $170 million and total assets exceed US $2.8 billion.

Whatever your international banking needs, a talk with your local BCC manager could be very useful. Speed, efficiency and *your* convenience are what count at BCC.

Contact us at any of our offices – there are 45 in the United Kingdom alone – or get in touch at the following address.

BANK OF CREDIT AND COMMERCE INTERNATIONAL
UNITED KINGDOM MAIN OFFICE: 100 LEADENHALL STREET, LONDON EC3A 3AD. TELEPHONE: 01-283 8566. TELEX: 881 3651.

Bangladesh, Canada, Djibouti, Egypt, France, Gabon, Germany (West), Ghana, Grand Caymen, Hong Kong, India, Indonesia, Iran, Ivory Coast, Japan, Jordan, Kenya, Korea (South), Lebanon, Liberia, Luxembourg, Mauritius, Morocco, Nigeria, Oman, Pakistan, Seychelles Islands, Sierra Leone, Sri Lanka, Sudan, Swaziland, United Arab Emirates, United Kingdom, U.S.A., Venezuela, Yemen (North).

Compilation

Extel Statistical Services are once again responsible for almost all the tabulations in *The Times 1000*. The figures are compiled on the basis used for Extel Statistical Cards. For any queries regarding figures in the tables, readers should either telephone 01-253-3400, or write to Extel at 37-45, Paul Street, London, EC2A 4PB.

We are indebted to the Nomura Research Institute of Technology and Economics, whose research facilities were used in the compilation of the table of the top fifty Japanese companies. We would also like to thank Mr A. Wagg of stockbrokers Pidgeon de Smith, whose services were invaluable in compiling the table of South African companies.

Extel and *The Times* would like to record their appreciation for the assistance given to them by the staff of the Certification Office for Trade Unions and Employers' Associations in the compilation of the tables covering trade unions and employers' associations. Two tables were not prepared by Extel. The table of the fifty top UK advertisers was prepared for us by the research department of J. Walter Thompson, the advertising agency. This analysis of advertising expenditure is based on data supplied by Media Expenditure Analysis Limited, a company which monitors all display advertisements in national and provincial newspapers and the larger-circulation general, women's and special-interest magazines. For television, details are taken from all contractors' daily transmission logs. In every case information about special positions is coded. The rate or time for each advertisement is then costed at published rate cards, allowing for published premium position rates. No allowance has been made for GHI or other special schemes, or for column or series discounts, etc. The figures do not claim to be exact estimates of companies' total advertising expenditure. Only television and press advertising are included in the figures.

The list of foreign bank branches in the UK was drawn up in the office of *The Times*, using Bank of England data. No profit figures are available publicly for these branches.

The guide can now be used to make valid comparisons of the size of companies in the leading industrialised nations, at least in terms of total sales. Only the South African table is exceptional, in that capital employed and not turnover is the criterion of size. Any attempt to carry comparisons of size beyond sales, however, would be of doubtful validity. Definitions of capital employed and profit, for example, vary from one country to another—in some countries, for instance, reported profits may be just enough to cover dividends to shareholders. This means that profit comparisons, particularly in Europe and the UK, should be avoided.

Certain companies include in their reported turnover figures relating to the turnover of associated companies.

To aid comparison with companies which do not adopt such a policy, these details have been excluded in arriving at the turnover reported in the tables.

There is the further problem, when making comparisons, of differing year ends. Most companies draw up their balance sheets on 31 December, but by no means all of them do. In Table 1 and the other tables relating to British institutions almost every company whose year ended on 31 December 1978 or 31 March 1979 is included. *No full accounts published after 30 June 1979 have been included and preliminary figures are not used.* As a further aid to readers, Table 1 shows the accounting period to which the figures relate. Due to various industrial actions, including the dispute at Companies Registration Office and the postal services, particularly in Ireland, there has been a marked decline in the speed at which information has been published; as a result, we have encountered a considerable number of problems in compiling this edition. We are confident, however, that the necessary data has been obtained to make this, as usual, a fully comprehensive edition.

Exchange rates used for conversion purposes in all the tables involving foreign companies were supplied to Extel by the Press Association as at 31 December 1978 for Europe and at 30 June 1979 for the other overseas tables. The fluctuation of exchange rates over the year would once again have led to a misrepresentation of the growth rate of foreign companies in comparison with those in the UK. To avoid this, Extel have converted 1977 figures at the same rate for sterling as that for 1978. This means that the figures given for 1977 in this edition are not the same as those in the previous edition of *The Times 1000*; calculated in this way, however, the sales and profit figures reflect real growth or decline, adjusted only by the companies' home-based inflation. The figures in the table of Irish companies are reported in Irish currency and do not reflect the break in parity between the 'punt' and sterling.

Extel has used declared turnover in grading the companies. This is usually net for French companies and gross for most others. Wherever available, consolidated accounts and, as a consequence, consolidated turnover have been used. Readers should note, however, that profit figures for European and British companies are not strictly comparable, since in a number of cases for which the consolidated turnover may be available, consolidated profits are not, and only the parent company's own profits are included.

We have kept notes down to a minimum and have included only essential definitions. Details of chairmen and managing directors are based on available information as we went to press. Every effort has been made to ensure complete accuracy, and we are grateful to the many companies in all fields who have helped us to produce information which is as up-to-date as possible.

The top 25 trade unions

Rank	Name—*General Secretary*	Year ended	Number of members	Members' contributions £000	Net income £000	Funds £000
1	Transport and General Workers' Union *M. Evans*	31.12.78	2,072,818	20,308	**700**	36,208
2	*Amalgamated Union of Engineering Workers *J. Boyd*	31.12.77	1,449,069	16,145	**2,944**	21,273
3	National Union of General and Municipal Workers *D. Basnet*	31.12.78	964,836	12,946	**1,967**	18,906
4	National and Local Government Officers' Association *G. A. Drain*	31.12.78	729,405	9,932	**6**	11,597
5	National Union of Public Employees *A. Fisher*	31.12.78	712,392	7,880	**2,258**	10,291
6	Association of Scientific, Technical and Managerial Staffs *C. Jenkins*	31.12.78	471,000	6,140	**827**	3,288
7	Union of Shop Distributive and Allied Workers *Lord Allen*	31.12.78	462,178	4,471	**461**	4,845
8	Electrical, Electronic, Telecommunication and Plumbing Union *F. J. Chapple*	31.12.78	438,269	5,412	**1,455**	7,041
9	National Union of Mineworkers *L. Daly*	31.12.77	370,194	6,204	**1,540**	17,936
10	Union of Construction, Allied Trades and Technicians *G. F. Smith*	31.12.77	305,727	3,399	**126**	2,323
11	National Union of Teachers *F. Jarvis*	31.12.78	258,117	2,693	**317**	6,597
12	Civil and Public Services Association *K. R. Thomas*	31.12.77	226,495	3,776	**851**	3,827
13	Confederation of Health Service Employees *E. A. G. Spanswick*	31.12.78	215,246	2,576	**708**	2,417
14	Society of Graphical and Allied Trades *W. H. Keys*	31.12.77	198,182	2,564	**288**	2,853
15	Union of Post Office Workers *T. Jackson*	31.12.78	197,157	4,069	**4,100**	4,535
16	National Union of Railwaymen *S. Weighell*	31.12.78	171,411	3,513	**1,123**	16,594
17	Association of Professional, Executive, Clerical and Computer Staff *R. Grantham*	31.12.78	152,534	2,054	**344**	2,295
18	Amalgamated Society of Boilermakers, Shipwrights, Blacksmiths and Structural Workers *J. Chalmers*	31.12.77	129,956	1,483	**176**	3,165
19	National Association of Schoolmasters/Union of Women Teachers *T. A. Casey*	31.12.77	127,056	1,087	**179**	1,287
20	Banking Insurance and Finance Union *L. A. Mills*	31.12.78	126,343	1,190	**112**	492
21	Post Office Engineering Union *B. Stanley*	31.12.77	122,564	2,113	**46**	2,693
22	National Union of Tailors and Garment Workers *A. R. Smith*	31.12.78	116,095	1,014	**153**	3,372
23	Iron and Steel Trades Federation *W. Sirs*	31.12.78	113,432	1,472	**473**	9,990
24	National Graphical Association *J. F. Wade*	30.9.78	109,904	2,127	**851**	8,336
25	Society of Civil and Public Servants *B. A. Gillman*	31.12.78	106,903	2,400	**350**	2,891

NOTE: * Comprising four constituent branches: Constructional (33,689 members); Engineering (1,173,000); Foundry (58,888); Technical Administrative and Supervisory (183,492).

Talk to the Prudential about pension fund investment

John Clark is the man to talk about professional fund management.

66At the end of June, 1979 Prudential Pensions, through its Group Investment Linked Pension policies, was managing assets exceeding £460 million on behalf of over 170 pension funds.

Trustees of exempt approved pension funds can choose how their contributions are split between our equity, fixed interest or property funds or leave that decision to us.

We're a wholly-owned subsidiary of the Prudential and we have the benefits of their experience and expertise developed in managing assets exceeding £6,500 million, including a property portfolio valued at over £1,700 million.

Ring 01-405 9222 ext. 6048 for all the details.

A fully descriptive booklet and our latest annual report are also available.99

Prudential Pensions Ltd.
142, Holborn Bars, London EC1N 2NH

Keith Spickett is the man to talk about insured pension plans.

66The Prudential has been a market leader in insured pensions since 1933. We manage schemes involving some 750,000 lives and 110,000 pensioners.

We have a variety of plans to offer – cash accumulation contracts for groups of 25 people or more, cash retirement schemes for any number of employees, executive pension plans which are tailor made for directors and key staff.

We can meet your investment needs and offer a most comprehensive range of services for insured plans – advisory, administrative and documentary.

Ring 01-405 9222 ext. 2206 and we'll be happy to discuss your needs, arrange meetings with you or your professional advisers, and give you any further information.99

The Prudential Assurance Company Ltd.
142, Holborn Bars, London EC1N 2NH

The top 25 employers' associations

Rank	Name—*General Secretary*	Year ended	Subscription income £000	Number of members	Net income £000	Funds £000
1	*Engineering Employers' Federation *A. F. Frodsham*	31.12.78	4,742	6,228	**379**	6,114
2	National Farmers' Union *H. M. Haynes*	31.12.78	4,706	127,622	**244**	7,774
3	National Federation of Building Trades Employers *H. L. Foster*	31.12.78	3,199	10,176	**Deficit 22**	1,644
4	General Council of British Shipping/British Shipping Federation *M. W. Gamble*	31.12.78	1,602	240	**Deficit 122**	1,110
5	**British Printing Industries Federation *E. Dixon*	31.3.78	1,145	7,214	**58**	648
6	Chemical Industries Association *A. J. Chant*	30.6.78	1,092	306	**33**	84
7	British Paper and Board Industry Federation *K. H. Proctor*	31.12.78	765	112	**12**	123
8	Federation of Civil Engineering Contractors *D. V. Gaulter*	31.12.77	682	580	**110**	201
9	Newspaper Society *C. G. Page*	31.12.78	610	293	**44**	184
10	Incorporated National Association of British and Irish Millers *E. T. J. Hurle*	31.12.77	607	43	**11**	275
11	Freight Transport Association *G. Turvey*	31.12.78	549	15,282	**138**	878
12	National Federation of Retail Newsagents *K. E. J. Peters*	31.12.77	542	29,829	**68**	715
13	Road Haulage Association *E. W. Russell*	31.12.78	521	15,286	**12**	568
14	Electrical Contractors' Association *P. A. Day*	31.12.78	466	(c)2,151	**Deficit 37**	250
15	Newspaper Publishers' Association *J. E. Le Page*	31.12.77	425	10	**17**	22
16	Cement Makers' Federation *Admiral C. K. Wheen*	31.12.77	416	6	**Nil**	68
17	Federation of Master Builders *W. S. Hilton*	31.12.78	406	20,236	**Deficit 12**	206
18	Publishers' Association *C. Bradley*	31.12.78	361	252	**7**	**Deficit 33**
19	Dairy Trade Federation *W. R. Freeman*	31.12.78	343	4,400	**Deficit 17**	4
20	Heating and Ventilating Contractors' Association *D. Edwards*	31.12.78	321	1,048	**9**	163
21	British Rubber Manufacturers' Association *R. T. Byford*	31.12.78	296	90	**(a)**	17
22	British Textile Employers' Association (Cotton, Man Made and Allied Fibres) *J. Platt*	31.3.78	248	247	**Deficit 9**	39
23	National Farmers' Union of Scotland *D. S. Johnston*	31.12.77	246	19,121	**Deficit 20**	89
24	National Association of Master Bakers, Confectioners and Caterers *M. Zimmerman*	31.12.78	205	3,729	**20**	138
25	Northern Brick Federation *J. M. Hall*	30.6.78	194	23	**(b)**	12

NOTE: * Comprising 18 separate engineering employers' associations.
** Comprising 12 constituent associations (a) £196, (b) £197, (c) 1977 figure.

Ten-year record table

Rank by turnover	Company	Item			Accounting period ended
1	BRITISH PETROLEUM CO.	Net capital employed Ratio of turnover to *net capital employed Net profit before interest and tax % to *net capital employed	£000 £000		31 Dec.
2	'SHELL' TRANSPORT & TRADING[1]	Net capital employed Ratio of turnover to *net capital employed Net profit before interest and tax % to *net capital employed	£000 £000		31 Dec.
3	BAT INDUSTRIES[3]	Net capital employed Ratio of turnover to *net capital employed Net profit before interest and tax % to *net capital employed	£000 £000		30 Sept.
4	IMPERIAL CHEMICAL INDUSTRIES	Net capital employed Ratio of turnover to *net capital employed Net profit before interest and tax % to *net capital employed	£000 £000		31 Dec.
5	UNILEVER LTD	Net capital employed Ratio of turnover to *net capital employed Net profit before interest and tax % to *net capital employed	£000 £000		31 Dec.
6	IMPERIAL GROUP	Net capital employed Ratio of turnover to *net capital employed Net profit before interest and tax % to *net capital employed	£000 £000		31 Oct.
7	BL	Net capital employed Ratio of turnover to *net capital employed Net profit before interest and tax % to *net capital employed	£000 £000		30 Sept. 1969-75 31 Dec. 1976-8
8	FORD MOTOR CO.	Net capital employed Ratio of turnover to *net capital employed Net profit before interest and tax % to *net capital employed	£000 £000		31 Dec.
9	GENERAL ELECTRIC CO.	Net capital employed Ratio of turnover to *net capital employed Net profit before interest and tax % to *net capital employed	£000 £000		31 Mar.
10	SHELL UK	Net capital employed Ratio of turnover to *net capital employed Net profit before interest and tax % to *net capital employed	£000 £000		31 Dec.
11	ESSO PETROLEUM CO.	Net capital employed Ratio of turnover to *net capital employed Net profit before interest and tax % to *net capital employed	£000 £000		31 Dec.
12	ALLIED BREWERIES	Net capital employed Ratio of turnover to *net capital employed Net profit before interest and tax % to *net capital employed	£000 £000		30 Sept. 1968-77 3 Mar. 1979
13	RIO TINTO-ZINC CORPORATION	Net capital employed Ratio of turnover to *net capital employed Net profit before interest and tax % to *net capital employed	£000 £000		31 Dec.

NOTES: *Net capital employed at beginning of year.
[1] Based on 40% of Royal Dutch Shell Group.
[2] On capital employed at end of year.
[3] Figures for years 1969-75 relate to British-American Tobacco Co.
N/A Not available

1969	1970	1971	1972	1973	1974	1975	1976	1977	1978
1,813,700	1,962,600	2,082,500	2,277,000	2,918,200	3,606,900	4,269,700	5,099,700	5,503,400	8,389,200
1·4	1·4	1·6	1·6	2·0	3·2	2·6	3·0	2·9	2·1²
384,300	466,500	738,500	776,400	1,213,300	2,405,500	1,626,400	1,959,600	2,393,800	2,695,200
24·2	25·7	37·6	37·3	53·3	82·4	45·1	45·9	46·9	32·1²
1,961,690	2,005,791	2,173,208	2,363,900	2,612,588	3,111,600	3,745,200	4,461,200	5,154,000	5,641,200
1·3	1·3	1·5	1·5	1·8	2·6	2·3	2·7	2·6	2·3
335,435	397,348	491,430	500,354	856,803	1,720,000	1,431,600	1,651,200	1,747,200	1,495,200
18·4	20·3	24·5	23·0	36·2	65·8	46·0	44·1	39·2	29·0
667,720	779,030	833,740	913,320	1,265,100	1,422,610	1,742,260	2,373,000	2,493,000	2,550,000
2·4	2·5	2·3	2·4	3·1	2·8	3·0	3·0	2·6	2·6
141,560	167,590	169,610	178,360	249,660	305,760	327,190	429,000	427,000	499,000
23·3	25·1	21·2	21·4	27·3	24·2	22·7	23·2	19·9	20·0
1,581,300	1,713,000	1,851,800	1,936,800	2,216,300	2,493,200	2,828,000	3,564,000	3,781,000	4,097,000
0.9	0.9	0.9	0.9	1·1	1·3	1·3	1·5	1·3	1·2
212,700	196,400	191,800	217,500	417,000	581,700	427,000	655,000	612,000	558,000
14·1	12·4	11·2	11·7	21·5	26·2	17·1	23·2	17·2	14·8
548,000	570,800	580,900	644,900	728,100	838,000	979,000	1,268,100	1,421,200	1,600,500
2·1	2·4	2·4	2·6	3·0	3·4	3·4	3·9	3·1	2·8
68,000	74,100	89,200	108,200	149,400	175,800	227,800	365,400	348,400	367,400
12·6	13·5	15·6	17·9	23·2	24·1	27·2	33·3	27·5	25·9
528,208	568,480	604,753	782,723	797,162	780,883	924,915	971,279	1,116,047	1,132,734
2·1	2·4	2·2	2·2	1·9	2·2	2·9	2·9	3·1	2·9
62,057	72,353	80,203	88,685	127,689	114,352	151,463	168,098	171,135	165,483
11·2	13·7	14·1	14·7	16·3	14·3	19·4	18·2	17·6	14·8
408,371	436,550	429,364	467,878	511,464	510,485	552,015	814,322	994,971	1,268,400
2·8	2·5	2·7	3·0	3·3	3·1	3·7	4·2	3·2	3·1
55,594	25,616	55,629	51,458	76,446	42,190	Loss 23,631	112,407p.a.	72,519	77,000
16·0	6·3	12·7	12·0	16·3	8·2	—	20·4p.a.	8·9	7·7
239,600	264,100	293,700	277,600	356,600	463,200	453,200	474,900	741,900	875,000
2·3	2·5	2·2	2·7	3·2	2·7	2·5	3·6	4·7	3·2
43,100	26,800	Loss 19,200	56,500	76,500	25,100	40,800	140,200	263,100	261,000
18·0	11·2	—	19·2	27·6	7·0	8·8	30·9	55·4	35·2
620,333	583,599	582,201	563,681	624,131	681,150	786,400	896,000	1,036,600	1,207,200
1·6	1·4	1·6	1·7	1·8	1·8	2·1	2·3	2·3	2·3
45,179	81,819	84,023	92,961	133,777	165,884	177,200	219,100	292,000	356,800
14·6	13·2	14·4	16·0	23·7	26·6	26·0	28·5	32·6	34·4
N/A	N/A	N/A	N/A	N/A	N/A	1,127,679	1,494,176	1,947,900	2,247,900
						N/A	1·9	1·3²	1·2
						89,581	38,997	109,500	116,500
						N/A	3·5	5·6²	6·0
346,773	404,443	445,431	478,995	530,309	621,273	930,031	1,160,778	1,416,533	1,689,463
1·7	1·8	1·7	1·6	1·7	2·7	2·6	2·1	1·9	1·6
14,809	11,846	32,287	61,614	65,384	152,100	133,890	117,171	139,317	119,661
4·5	3·4	7·9	13·6	13·7	28·7	21·6	12·6	12.0	8·4
319,332	327,984	352,235	405,943	513,184	528,199	569,900	610,600	734,200	1,085,000
1·2	1·2	1·3	1·4	1·3	1·2	1·4	1·6	1·8	2.02
37,460	41,897	50,157	63,574	74,388	69,917	75,199	77,800	95,800	152,700
12·8	13·1	15·3	18·0	18·3	13·6	14·2	13·7	15·7	14·1²
528,411	714,800	863,500	1,027,700	1,247,200	1,255,900	1,556,100	1,926,000	1,924,600	2,005,100
0·7	0·8	0·6	0·7	0·9	0·9	0·9	1·1	0·9	1·0
80,400	98,500	81,400	119,200	264,600	317,200	191,600	328,700	322,800	334,300
17·6	18·6	11·4	13·8	25·7	25·4	15·3	21·1	16·8	17·4

Rank by turnover	Company	Item		Accounting period ended
14	GRAND METROPOLITAN	Net capital employed Ratio of turnover to *net capital employed Net profit before interest and tax % to *net capital employed	£000 £000	30 Sept.
15	ROTHMANS INTERNATIONAL	Net capital employed Ratio of turnover to *net capital employed Net profit before interest and tax % to *net capital employed	£000 £000	30 June. 1969-73 31 Mar. 1974-8
16	GUEST, KEEN & NETTLEFOLDS	Net capital employed Ratio of turnover to *net capital employed Net profit before interest and tax % to *net capital employed	£000 £000	31 Dec.
17	GEORGE WESTON HOLDINGS	Net capital employed Ratio of turnover to *net capital employed Net profit before interest and tax % to *net capital employed	£000 £000	31 Mar.
18	COURTAULDS	Net capital employed Ratio of turnover to *net capital employed Net profit before interest and tax % to *net capital employed	£000 £000	31 Mar. 1970-9
19	INCHCAPE & CO.	Net capital employed Ratio of turnover to *net capital employed Net profit before interest and tax % to *net capital employed	£000 £000	31 Mar.
20	CAVENHAM	Net capital employed Ratio of turnover to *net capital employed Net profit before interest and tax % to *net capital employed	£000 £000	31 Mar.
21	REED INTERNATIONAL	Net capital employed Ratio of turnover to *net capital employed Net profit before interest and tax % to *net capital employed	£000 £000	31 Mar.
22	BOWATER CORPORATION	Net capital employed Ratio of turnover to *net capital employed Net profit before interest and tax % to *net capital employed	£000 £000	31 Dec.
23	TEXACO	Net capital employed Ratio of turnover to *net capital employed Net profit before interest and tax % to *net capital employed	£000 £000	31 Dec.
24	GALLAHER	Net capital employed Ratio of turnover to *net capital employed Net profit before interest and tax % to *net capital employed	£000 £000	31 Dec.
25	DUNLOP HOLDINGS	Net capital employed Ratio of turnover to *net capital employed Net profit before interest and tax % to *net capital employed	£000	31 Dec.
26	MARKS & SPENCER	Net capital employed Ratio of turnover to *net capital employed Net profit before interest and tax % to *net capital employed	£000 £000	31 Mar. 1969-78

NOTES: * Net capital employed at beginning of year.
      ² On capital employed at end of year.
      N/A Not available.

1969	1970	1971	1972	1973	1974	1975	1976	1977	1978
76,285	137,598	211,477	554,289	666,505	737,054	880,562	888,747	922,539	993,160
1·0	1·7²	1·5²	1·1	1·6	1·4	1·6	1·7	1·8	2·0
6,089	18,985	28,066	61,277	86,588	82,670	98,375	113,106	133,527	154,511
13·7	14·8²	13·3²	13·9²	15·6	12·4	13·3	12·8	15·0	16·7
53,251	61,260	63,162	65,746	226,233	263,877	297,548	330,660	405,715	493,941
2·8	2·7	2·6	2·6	4·2²	4·4	3·9	4·1	4·5	4·4
9,569	9,519	11,902	12,317	50,883	53,183 p.a.	44,760	62,593	93,157	107,730
20·3	17·9	19·4	19·5	22·5²	23·5 p.a.	17·0	21·0	28·2	26·6
320,940	322,900	395,610	443,720	522,050	626,070	818,520	1,020,430	1,068,000	1,128,600
1·6	1·5	1·7	1·6	1·8	2·2	1·9	1·8	1·6	1·6
42,822	49,140	56,420	57,530	88,390	128,920	105,000	138,460	118,800	133,300
13·5	15·3	17·5	14·5	19·9	24·7	16·8	16·9	11·6	12·5
N/A	N/A	N/A	N/A	229,670	278,245	306,777	373,697	433,741	500,443
				4·1	3·8	3·9	4·3	4·0	3·9
				41,314	47,164	57,808	76,550	91,266	88,242
				23·2	20·5	20·8	25·0	24·4	20·3
510,475	556,122	563,985	640,655	758,027	841,100	909,200	942,300	943,200	881,200
1·4	1·3	1·2	1·4	1·5	1·5	1·4	1·7	1·7	1·8
67,046	59,816	61,809	85,603	140,107	148,100	75,200	116,800	86,500	95,300
14·7	11·7	11·1	15·2	21·9	19·5	8·9	12·8	9·2	10·1
53,608	60,982	75,777	85,342	118,201	191,361	238,472	323,530	433,360	462,568
2·6	2·4	2·7	2·9	4·0	4·5	3·8	3·8	3·9	3·8
6,540	7,516	10,074	13,647	20,506	39,074	41,739	55,887	94,116	82,755
15·0	14·0	16·5	18·0	24·1	33·1	21·8	23·4	29·1	19·1
4,293	5,564	9,982	135,905	167,699	291,021	316,312	341,239	378,530	363,094
6·4	2·3	3·5²	0·9²	3·5	4·4	4·8	5·2	5·0	4·4
302	953	2,465	6,860	25,544	39,329	46,654	53,313	58,723	48,284
7·1	22·2	24·7²	5·0²	18·8	23·5	16·0	16·9	17·2	12·8
235,658	258,741	344,700	337,400	409,300	478,600	519,300	623,100	790,800	723,800
1·3	1·3	1·9	1·9	1·8	1·8	2·0	2·0	2·4	2·1
23,866	28,330	34,300	43,400	56,100	84,200	107,300	65,200	114,200	121,600
10·8	12·0	10·0²	12·6	16·6	20·6	22·4	12·6	18·3	15·4
296,732	293,583	267,452	391,309	490,365	530,839	609,800	728,500	728,200	756,900
1·0	1·0	0·9	1·5²	2·6	2·4	2·1	2·5	2·4	2·1
27,359	25,026	16,970	37,241	67,629	89,309	84,900	113,000	120,100	121,300
10·1	8·5	5·8	9·5	17·3	18·2	15·0	18·5	16·5	16·7
130,841	147,618	178,490	200,477	234,892	313,368	300,055	466,884	379,603	N/A
N/A	1·9	2·0	1·6	2·4	3·9	3·1	4·8	3·3	
Loss 2,854	4,566	2,327	8,791	Loss 4,003	Loss 4,277	2,909	Loss 41,935	40,630	
—	3·5	1·6	4·9	—	0·9	—	—	8·7	
125,141	121,641	127,041	140,798	169,962	184,733	207,225	230,043	319,577	285,585
3·7	3·5	3·7	4·1	3·9	4·3	5·0	5·5	6·1	4·8
19,564	20,487	23,627	29,471	38,003	39,657	44,586	47,123	40,087	56,385
15·9	16·4	19·4	23·2	27·0	23·3	24·1	22·7	17·4	17·6
307,284	325,844	453,960	445,395	517,700	595,943	628,500	774,100	789,000	847,000
1·8	1·8	1·8	1·4	1·6	1·7	1·7	2·1	1·8	1·9
36,116	38,369	50,932	53,386	54,633	66,135	75,000	100,900	84,000	74,000
13·4	12·5	15·6	11·8	12·0	12·8	12·6	16·1	10·9	9·4
169,502	174,061	183,193	210,217	235,817	407,034	446,724	479,839	562,026	611,735
2·2	2·3	2·5	2·9	2·7	3·1	2·2	2·5	2·6	2·6
46,419	53,293	56,944	73,214	80,003	85,078	88,937	114,491	129,539	176,233
29·5	31·4	32·7	40·0	38·1	36·1	21·9	25·6	27·0	31·4

Rank by turnover	Company	Item		Accounting period ended
27	S. & W. BERISFORD	Net capital employed Ratio of turnover to *net capital employed Net profit before interest and tax % to *net capital employed	£000 £000	30 Sept.
28	C. T. BOWRING & CO.	Net capital employed Ratio of turnover to *net capital employed Net profit before interest and tax % to *net capital employed	£000 £000	31 Dec.
29	RANKS HOVIS MCDOUGALL	Net capital employed Ratio of turnover to *net capital employed Net profit before interest and tax % to *net capital employed	£000 £000	31 Aug.
30	LONRHO	Net capital employed Ratio of turnover to *net capital employed Net profit before interest and tax % to *net capital employed	£000 £000	30 Sept.
31	BOC INTERNATIONAL	Net capital employed Ratio of turnover to *net capital employed Net profit before interest and tax % to *net capital employed	£000 £000	30 Sept.
32	P. & O. STEAM NAVIGATION CO.	Net capital employed Ratio of turnover to *net capital employed Net profit before interest and tax % to *net capital employed	£000 £000	30 Sept. 1969-74 31 Dec. 1975-8
33	GREAT UNIVERSAL STORES	Net capital employed Ratio of turnover to *net capital employed Net profit before interest and tax % to *net capital employed	£000 £000	31 Mar.
34	TATE & LYLE	Net capital employed Ratio of turnover to *net capital employed Net profit before interest and tax % to *net capital employed	£000 £000	30 Sept.
35	BURMAH OIL CO.	Net capital employed Ratio of turnover to *net capital employed Net profit before interest and tax % to *net capital employed	£000 £000	31 Dec.
36	TUBE INVESTMENTS[5]	Net capital employed Ratio of turnover to *net capital employed Net profit before interest and tax % to *net capital employed	£000 £000	31 Dec.
37	SEARS HOLDINGS	Net capital employed Ratio of turnover to *net capital employed Net profit before interest and tax % to *net capital employed	£000 £000	31 Jan. 1970-9
38	CZARNIKOW GROUP[4]	Net capital employed Ratio of turnover to *net capital employed Net profit before interest and tax % to *net capital employed	£000 £000	30 Sept.
39	RANK XEROX	Net capital employed Ratio of turnover to *net capital employed Net profit before interest and tax % to *net capital employed	£000 £000	31 Oct.

NOTES:　* Net capital employed at beginning of year.
　　　　[2] On capital employed at end of year.
　　　　[4] Figures for years 1969-74 relate to C. Czarnikow.
　　　　[5] Aluminium interests not consolidated 1971-7.
　　　　N/A Not available.

1969	1970	1971	1972	1973	1974	1975	1976	1977	1978
12,342	14,250	20,502	27,243	32,239	28,211	37,145	78,851	122,499	173,443
10·1	10·5	10·6	6·6	12·6²	16·5	21·2	20·7	16·0	11·0
2,537	2,747	3,081	3,431	7,694	12,380	12,308	14,994	27,361	34,296
23·8	22.3	21·6	16·7	23·9²	38·4	43·6	40·4	34·7	19·9
54,896	64,026	89,452	104,077	123,143	144,810	151,299	175,311	213,909	272,294
5·1²	6·2	6·0	4·9	4·9	4·0	5·9	6·2	6·2	6·0
13,331	17,577	21,992	26,609	36,392	36,309	34,105	44,081	47,438	57,912
24·3²	32.0	34·3	29·7	35·0	29·5	29·7	29·1	27·1	27·1
164,025	171,508	177,799	183,413	213,132	243,414	266,897	290,920	359,465	443,715
2·6	2·3	2·4	2·5	2·8	3·3	3·3	3·5	3·8	3·4
20,418	20,947	22,951	28,943	33,931	33,171	42,432	51,508	51,127	47,630
14·8	12.8	13·4	16·3	18·5	15·6	17·4	19·3	17·6	13·3
124,759	139,879	143,520	156,120	183,690	211,520	355,530	519,120	626,580	717,130
1·2²	1·5	1·4	1·5	1·6	1·8	1·5²	2·8	2·3	1·9
16,549	17,680	18,870	22,520	33,860	51,950	74,870	107,900	101,310	108,630
13·3²	14.2	13·5	15·7	21·7	28·3	21·1²	30·3	19·5	17·3
181,795	201,117	221,395	236,168	289,192	369,802	436,583	531,323	626,800	1,115,700
1·0	1·1	1·2	1·1	1·4	1·4	1·3	1·4	1·3	1·1²
19,317	23,946	28,025	30,899	38,889	53,152	69,283	94,270	105,200	100,300
12·5	13.2	13·9	14·0	16·5	18·7	18·7	21·6	19·8	9·0²
273,250	305,066	330,567	336,356	556,473	750,267	819,469	827,961	812,462	824,086
0·7	0·7	0·8	0·8	0·7	0·7	0·8	0·9	1·2	1·4
15,056	16,070	9,978	19,554	42,682	70,290	38,583 p.a.	59,358	64,983	51,878
5·9	5.9	3·3	5·9	12·7	12·6	5·1 p.a.	7·2	7·8	6·4
218,257	235,761	254,410	277,694	341,101	382,060	426,342	472,721	543,822	567,071
1·9	1·9	1·9	2·0	2·2	1·9	1·9	2·0	2·1	2·1
49,451	52,667	54,729	62,660	80,208	85,964	92,541	101,835	116,223	132,000
25·2	24.1	23·2	24·6	28·9	25·2	24·2	23·9	24·6	24·3
166,385	172,980	174,564	185,066	181,210	197,210	264,693	283,809	407,881	368,400
1·6	1·6	2·0	2·4	2·5	3·8	6·4	5·0	4·4	2·8
11,954	15,157	16,348	21,125	22,709	46,760	55,536	58,212	57,070	43,400
8·2	9.1	9·5	12·1	12·3	25·8	28·2	22·0	20·1	10·6
766,182	713,621	784,303	905,637	981,738	964,100	1,001,916	653,000	638,807	654,808
0·8	0·4	0·5	0·6	0·7	1·0	1·1	1·0	1·5	1·8
45,396	49,914	50,156	54,097	75,469	55,350	29,793	17,472	24,445	45,352
15·0	6.5	7·0	6·9	8·3	5·6	3·1	1·7	3·7	7·1
246,829	273,211	216,682	241,255	270,079	300,736	354,850	389,890	460,100	560,900
1·4	1·4	1·4²	1·5	1·7	1·9	2·1	2·0	2·0	2·4
22,353 p.a.	28,728	24,865	28,057	41,234	51,820	55,489	63,933	68,500	93,500
10·9 p.a.	11.6	11·5²	12·9	17·1	19·2	18·5	18·0	17·6	20·3
218,205	207,636	219,766	332,899	352,925	397,190	426,236	457,842	592,857	632,657
1·3	1·4	1·6	2·2	1·6	1·7	1·8	1·9	2·1	1·9
28,291	33,339	38,271	53,160	55,057	43,555	56,111	55,550	74,612	101,198
12·8	15.3	18·4	24·2	16·5	12·3	14·1	13·0	16·3	17·1
6,911	8,041	9,425	10,772	11,444	17,087	13,809	17,578	20,898	26,421
37·9	51·8	53·8	64·2	50·5	64·9	86·2²	60·4²	63·5	52·7
888	886	942	1,425	1,062	3,449	6,713	3,648	5,514	6,158
12·9	9.9	11·7	15·1	9·8	30·1	48·6²	20·8²	31·4	29·5
N/A	122,475	198,231	186,875	269,426	461,427	562,024	598,548	731,100	798,900
	2·2	1·7	1·4	2·0	1·8	1·3	1·4	1·6	1·5
	69,675 p.a.	89,345	111,722	152,667	179,742	192,741	215,755	290,900	261,000
	81·2 p.a.	73·0	66·9	81·7	66·7	41·8	38·4	48·6	35·7

Rank by turnover	Company	Item		Accounting period ended
40	THORN ELECTRICAL INDUSTRIES	Net capital employed Ratio of turnover to *net capital employed Net profit before interest and tax % to *net capital employed	£000 £000	31 Mar.
41	BOOTS CO.	Net capital employed Ratio of turnover to *net capital employed Net profit before interest and tax % to *net capital employed	£000 £000	31 Mar. 1970-9
42	THOMAS TILLING	Net capital employed Ratio of turnover to *net capital employed Net profit before interest and tax % to *net capital employed	£000 £000	31 Dec.
43	BASS	Net capital employed Ratio of turnover to *net capital employed Net profit before interest and tax % to *net capital employed	£000 £000	30 Sept.
44	CADBURY SCHWEPPES	Net capital employed Ratio of turnover to *net capital employed Net profit before interest and tax % to *net capital employed	£000 £000	31 Dec.
45	HAWKER SIDDELEY GROUP	Net capital employed Ratio of turnover to *net capital employed Net profit before interest and tax % to *net capital employed	£000 £000	31 Dec.
46	BICC	Net capital employed Ratio of turnover to *net capital employed Net profit before interest and tax % to *net capital employed	£000 £000	31 Dec.
47	J. SAINSBURY	Net capital employed Ratio of turnover to *net capital employed Net profit before interest and tax % to *net capital employed	£000 £000	18 Mar. 1970-9
48	UNIGATE	Net capital employed Ratio of turnover to *net capital employed Net profit before interest and tax % to *net capital employed	£000 £000	31 Mar.
49	LUCAS INDUSTRIES	Net capital employed Ratio of turnover to *net capital employed Net profit before interest and tax % to *net capital employed	£000 £000	31 July
50	AMALGAMATED METAL CORPORATION	Net capital employed Ratio of turnover to *net capital employed Net profit before interest and tax % to *net capital employed	£000 £000	31 Dec.

NOTES: * Net capital employed at beginning of year.
ˢ On capital employed at end of year.
N/A Not available.

1969	1970	1971	1972	1973	1974	1975	1976	1977	1978
145,820	169,397	203,138	234,877	253,628	318,730	388,904	411,279	469,810	515,600
1·8[2]	2·0	2·0	2·0	2·2	2·5	2·3	2·2	2·5	2·3
33,363	34,811	41,415	53,265	73,853	80,831	76,869	83,296	112,952	118,400
22·9[2]	23·9	24·4	26·2	31·4	31·9	24·1	21·4	27·5	25·2
110,397	123,205	129,368	154,414	184,653	232,535	280,000	337,900	414,400	501,000
2·1	2·3	2·5	2·8	2·7	2·7	2·6	2·6	2·6	2·5
21,114	25,905	35,256	57,716	64,792	66,820	82,202	101,100	109,300	116,600
19·5	23·5	28·6	44·6	42·0	36·2	35·4	36·1	32·3	28·1
99,519	109,026	120,086	145,668	191,374	224,489	235,400	266,700	343,800	430,300
2·4	2·5	2·9	3·3	3·5	2·9	2·8	2·9	3·0	3·0
12,939	15,975	22,179	29,413	40,433	40,586	44,700	52,400	65,500	79,500
16·7	16·1	20·3	24·5	27·8	21·2	19·9	22·3	24·6	23·1
332,377	337,008	353,130	382,700	518,600	545,200	571,700	625,400	662,200	715,900
1·0	1·0	1·1	1·2	1·3	1·0	1·2	1·4	1·4	1·5
32,549	38,728	46,051	56,500	66,200	61,700	69,500	77,900	100,100	109,100
10·0	11·7	13·7	16·0	17·3	11·9	12·7	13·6	16·0	16·5
188,716	181,438	177,376	199,708	262,812	292,100	357,800	398,800	420,300	429,700
1·5	1·4	1·6	2·0	2·2	2·1	2·2	2·2	2·2	2·4
21,646	21,456	24,884	31,715	38,426	36,841	49,100	57,800	62,300	60,800
12·1	11·4	13·7	17·9	19·2	14·0	16·8	16·2	15·6	14·5
238,548	243,299	223,470	254,383	276,455	331,602	408,515	408,924	469,570	588,900
1·9	1·9	1·9	2·1	2·3	2·3	2·5	2·4	1·9	2·1
20,410	21,137	28,172	37,824	51,886	59,855	74,083	99,727	107,209	120,800
9·7	8·9	11·6	16·9	21·1	21·7	22·3	24·4	22·3	25·7
212,801	225,595	224,402	249,293	313,206	356,687	347,894	371,748	383,369	363,044
2·2	2·2	2·0	2·1	2·5	2·5	2·1	2·6	2·7	2·6
26,162	31,677	35,584	38,918	51,672	52,336	43,633	52,569	57,667	68,492
13·9	14·9	15·8	17·3	20·7	16·7	12·2	15·1	15·5	17·9
46,460	51,750	62,017	133,545	142,896	167,819	182,188	187,601	209,266	241,363
4·7	4·8	5·1	4·8	2·7	3·1	3·2	3·6	4·2	4·7
5,466	6,802	10,585	11,948	14,207	16,128	17,205	28,583	28,096	33,176
13·6	14·6	20·5	19·3	10·6	11·3	10·3	15·7	15·0	15·9
91,466	94,217	99,440	103,564	130,010	141,044	162,592	164,599	200,124	212,886
4·3	3·4	3·6	4·0	3·9	3·6	4·2	4·7	5·2	4·9
10,736	11,043	12,009	14,718	16,031	19,996	25,779	28,598	30,727	38,400
15·2	12·1	12·7	14·8	15·5	15·4	18·3	17·6	18·7	19·2
116,017	134,022	179,323	217,984	242,028	266,000	293,085	384,808	473,180	533,410
2·4	2·4	2·4	1·9	1·8	1·9	2·1	2·5	2·3	2·1
20,186	16,093	22,067	27,762	32,566	25,758	42,856	65,967	90,790	83,730
18·9	13·9	16·5	15·5	14·9	10·6	16·1	22·5	23·6	17·7
25,317	20,650	20,223	23,787	28,660	31,451	48,930	61,064	56,772	60,684
13·3	11·9	11·8	9·6	13·9	23·8	15·3[2]	21·5	17·3	17·1
3,167	2,248	137	1,327	4,999	13,079	9,628	12,464	9,662	11,992
15·7	8·9	0·7	6·6	21·0	45·6	30·6[2]	25·5	15·8	21·1

The 50 leading UK advertisers*

Rank	Company	1978 Total £000	1978 TV £000	1978 Press £000	1977 Total £000	1977 TV £000	1977 Press £000	Rank last year
1	Unilever	32,036	26,589	5,447	29,259	23,678	5,581	1
2	H.M. Government	21,535	8,350	13,185	13,310	5,117	8,193	5
3	Cadbury Schweppes	18,985	17,361	1,624	16,697	15,531	1,166	3
4	Mars	17,101	16,916	185	14,159	13,987	172	4
5	Imperial Group	16,089	8,355	7,735	21,021	8,056	12,065	2
6	Beecham Group	12,721	10,510	2,211	12,801	10,397	2,404	6
7	Rowntree Mackintosh	12,124	11,263	861	9,520	8,800	720	9
8	Co-operative Wholesale Society	11,198	3,609	7,589	10,629	3,883	6,746	7
9	British Leyland	9,413	3,960	5,453	7,934	3,819	4,115	12
10	Boots	9,245	2,230	7,015	7,586	2,265	5,624	15
11	British Gas	8,612	5,089	3,523	7,126	3,987	3,139	18
12	Electricity Council	8,441	3,978	4,463	7,596	4,549	3,047	14
13	Proctor & Gamble	8,255	8,124	131	8,485	8,235	250	10
14	Nestlé	7,548	5,035	2,513	7,320	5,056	2,264	17
15	Bass Charrington	7,546	4,996	2,550	5,485	3,905	1,580	26
16	Reed International	7,525	5,252	2,273	9,878	6,000	3,878	8
17	Grand Metropolitan	6,985	4,782	2,203	4,885	3,411	1,474	31
18	Gallaher	6,880	2,106	4,774	8,108	2,230	5,878	11
19	Brooke Bond Liebig	6,874	5,834	1,040	5,668	4,698	976	24
20	Reckitt & Colman	6,722	4,901	1,821	7,359	5,711	1,648	16
21	United Biscuits	6,656	6,227	429	5,598	4,394	1,204	25
22	Rothmans International	6,568	428	6,140	6,380	—	6,380	20
23	Allied Breweries	6,543	3,387	3,156	7,876	5,861	2,015	13
24	Guinness	6,336	5,895	471	5,964	5,508	456	22
25	Tesco	6,271	2,673	3,598	6,556	3,140	3,416	19
26	Thorn Electrical Industries	6,034	1,485	4,549	4,544	1,242	3,302	32
27	Imperial Chemical Industries	5,999	3,682	2,317	5,402	3,419	1,983	27
28	National Post Office	5,958	3,968	1,990	4,313	2,891	1,432	35
29	Midland Bank	5,902	2,887	3,515	4,525	1,996	2,529	33
30	Ranks Hovis McDougall	5,594	4,082	1,512	5,839	4,730	1,109	23
31	Philips Electronic	5,512	3,723	1,789	4,983	2,468	2,515	29
32	Allied Retailers	5,439	3,816	1,623	4,661	3,567	1,094	31
33	British Rail	5,409	2,268	3,141	3,757	1,160	2,597	43
34	Woolworth, F.W.	5,369	2,613	2,756	4,508	1,971	2,537	34
35	Chrysler United Kingdom	5,264	2,935	2,329	2,710	736	1,974	—
36	Debenhams	4,974	1,296	3,678	3,878	638	3,240	40
37	BAT Industries	4,887	3,270	1,617	6,279	4,969	1,310	21
38	Scottish & Newcastle Breweries	4,859	4,475	384	3,955	3,627	328	39
39	Fiat	4,696	1,956	2,740	3,611	814	2,797	45
40	Kellogg Co. of Great Britain	4,642	3,795	847	3,431	3,044	387	46
41	Whitbread & Co.	4,565	3,128	1,437	3,336	2,224	1,112	47
42	General Foods	4,535	4,306	229	3,108	2,879	229	50
43	Gillette	4,365	3,414	951	4,091	3,743	348	38
44	Barclays Bank	4,348	377	3,971	4,151	143	4,008	37
45	Sears Holdings	4,346	569	3,777	3,835	365	3,470	42
46	Colgate Holdings (UK)	4,307	3,885	422	3,674	3,597	77	44
47	Wittington Investments	4,262	2,197	2,065	3,249	1,462	1,787	48
48	Lonrho	4,254	770	3,484	2,179	47	2,132	—
49	Lyons, J.	4,167	3,716	451	3,852	2,964	888	41
50	General Motors	4,144	835	3,309	1,637	135	1,502	—

NOTES: *See page 14 for further details.

The method includes only display advertisements; classified, financial, trade and technical are broadly omitted. Further not *all* the press is covered, nor are local advertisers. The method of costing, on gross card rates, will usually overestimate the actual charge to the advertiser. Production costs are not included. The definition of a holding company is generally taken to be that used in *Who Owns Whom*, but there are some exceptions such as H.M. Government, which does not appear there. Sources: *MEAL A1 Reports* and *Who Owns Whom* 1978/79.

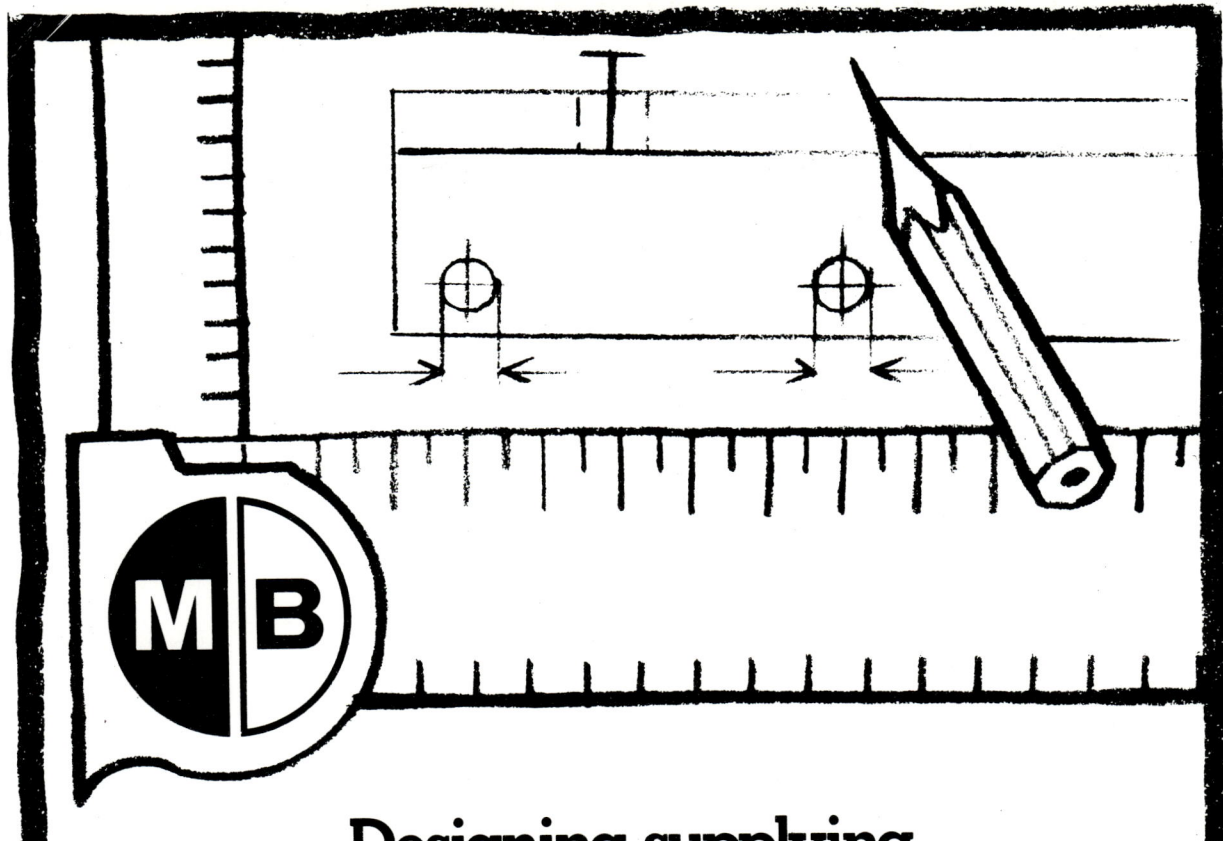

Designing, supplying and servicing the most efficient packaging equipment for customers; it's Metal Box's business.

As the people who know more about packaging in a wide range of materials than anyone else in Europe, we're often asked for help on anything from better filling equipment to more efficient factory layout.

We provide it, too.

Our customers range from the giant multinational food companies, to the State packing industries of Eastern Europe.

And our products range from precision tools to computer programmes for improving filling line design to obtain maximum throughput.

It's a service that goes far beyond providing better packaging; but it's all in a day's work for Metal Box.

PLUM (Production Line Uprating Method): a Metal Box simulation system for achieving more efficient packaging lines.

Metal Box
A good business to be in

Queens House, Forbury Road, Reading RG1 3JH. Telephone: 0734 581177. Telex: 847437.

Rank by turn-over	COMPANY	Main activity	Chairman and Managing Directors (in italics) §‖	Accounting period ended
1 (1)	British Petroleum Co.	Oil industry	Sir David Steel (J.M.D.) (see page 70)	31–12–78
2 (2)	'Shell' Transport & Trading[12]	Oil industry	C. C. P. Pocock (J.M.D.), *P. B. Baxendell*	31–12–78
3 (3)	BAT Industries	Tobacco, retailing, paper & cosmetics	P. Macadam	30– 9–78
4 (4)	Imperial Chemical Industries	Chemicals, fibres, paints, etc.	Sir Maurice Hodgson	31–12–78
5 (5)	Unilever Ltd.	Food products, detergents, etc.	Sir David Orr	31–12–78
6 (6)	Imperial Group	Tobacco, food, drink and packaging	Sir John Pile	31–10–78
7 (7)	BL	Motor vehicle manufacturers	Sir Michael Edwardes	31–12–78
8 (8)	Ford Motor Co.	Motor vehicle manufacturers	Sir Terence Beckett (M.D.)	31–12–78
9 (10)	General Electric Co.	Electrical engineers	Lord Nelson of Stafford, *Sir Arnold Weinstock*	31– 3–78
10 (N/A)	Shell UK	Oil industry	P. B. Baxendell	31–12–78
11 (9)	Esso Petroleum Co.	Oil industry	A. W. Pearce, A. W. Forster, W. D. Stevens	31–12–78
12 (30)	Allied Breweries[37]	Brewers, vintners, hoteliers, etc.	K. S. Showering	3– 3–79
13 (11)	Rio Tinto-Zinc Corporation	Mining & industrial – metals & fuel	Sir Mark Turner	31–12–78
14 (14)	Grand Metropolitan	Hotel props., milk prds. brewers, etc.	Maxwell Joseph, *S. G. Grinstead, E. H. Sharp*	30– 9–78
15 (18)	Rothmans International	Tobacco manufacturers	Sir David Nicolson	31– 3–78
16 (15)	Guest, Keen & Nettlefolds	Steel & eng. products, fastenings, etc.	Sir Barrie Heath, *G. T. Holdsworth*	31–12–78
17 (17)	George Weston Holdings	Food manufacturers & distributors	W. G. Weston	1– 4–78
18 (16)	Courtaulds	Man-made fibres, textiles, chemicals	Sir Arthur Knight	31– 3–79
19 (24)	Inchcape & Co.	International merchants	Earl of Inchcape (see page 70)	31– 3–78
20 (13)	Cavenham	Food, drink, tobacco, etc., products	Sir James Goldsmith, *J. Greenhalgh*	1– 4–78
21 (19)	Reed International	Paper, packaging, printing & publishing	Sir Alexander Jarratt	31– 3–79
22 (12)	Bowater Corporation	Paper manufacturers, intl. trading	Lord Erroll of Hale, *C. F. Popham*	31–12–78
23 (20)	Texaco	Oil industry	*T. E. Cottrell*	31–12–77
24 (21)	Gallaher	Tobacco, cigarette, cigar & snuff man.	A. W. H. Stewart-Moore	31–12–78
25 (22)	Dunlop Holdings	Rubber goods & sports requisites, etc.	Sir Campbell Fraser (M.D.)	31–12–78
26 (26)	Marks & Spencer	General store proprietors	Sir Marcus Sieff (J.M.D.) (see page 70)	31– 3–79
27 (23)	S. & W. Berisford	Sugar importers & mchts, etc.	E. S. Margulies (M.D.)	30– 9–78
28 (31)	C. T. Bowring & Co.	Insurance brokers, finance, eng., etc.	P. Bowring, *G. A. Cooke*	31–12–78
29 (29)	Ranks Hovis McDougall	Food manufacturers and distributors	J. Rank, *P. W. J. Reynolds*	2– 9–78
30 (27)	Lonrho	Mining, agric., textiles, constr., etc.	Lord Duncan Sandys, *R. W. Rowland*	30– 9–78
31 (62)	BOC International	Manfrs. of gases & associated eqpmt.	Sir Leslie Smith, *R. V. Giordano*	30– 9–78
32 (37)	P. & O. Steam Navigation Co.	Shipowners	Earl of Inchcape (see page 70)	31–12–78
33 (38)	Great Universal Stores	Stores & mail order	Sir Isaac Wolfson (J.M.D.), *Sir Leonard Wolfson*	31–3–78
34 (25)	Tate & Lyle	Sugar refiners, etc.	Earl Jellicoe	30– 9–78
35 (35)	Burmah Oil Co.	Oil industry	Sir Alastair Down, *S. J. Wilson*	31–12–78
36 (52)	Tube Investments	General engineers	Sir Brian Kellett (J.M.D.) (see page 70)	31–12–78
37 (36)	Sears Holdings	Footwear, stores, engineering, etc.	L. Sainer	31– 1–79
38 (28)	Czarnikow Group	Commodity brokers, etc.	R. E. Liddiard	30– 9–78
39 (55)	Rank Xerox	Xerographic equipment, etc.	J. M. Thomas, *W. F. Glavin*	31–10–78
40 (33)	Thorn Electrical Industries	Electrical & electronic engineers	Sir Richard G. Cave, *P. Laister*	31– 3–78
41 (44)	Boots Co.	Manfg., wholesale & retail chemists	Sir Gordon Hobday, *D. E. M. Appleby*	31– 3–79
42 (49)	Thomas Tilling	Industrial holding co.	Sir Robert Taylor, *P. M. Meaney*	31–12–78
43 (42)	Bass	Brewers	D. Palmar (C.E.)	30– 9–78
44 (45)	Cadbury Schweppes	Confectionery, soft drinks, food, etc.	Sir Adrian Cadbury, *B. E. S. Collins*	30–12–78
45 (41)	Hawker Siddeley Group	Mech. & electrical eng. & metals	Sir Arnold Hall (M.D.)	31–12–78
46 (34)	BICC	Cable makers, elec. engineers & contrs.	C. H. Broughton Pipkin	31–12–78
47 (51)	J. Sainsbury	Retail distribution of food	J. D. Sainsbury	3– 3–79
48 (46)	Unigate	Dairymen & food manufacturers, etc.	J. Clement	25– 3–78
49 (43)	Lucas Industries	Vehicle & aircraft accessory manfrs.	Sir Bernard Scott, *R. G. C. Messervy*	31– 7–78
50 (32)	Amalgamated Metal Corpn.	Metal & ores	Sir John Saunders	31–12–78

NOTES: *Total tangible assets less current liabilities (other than bank loans and overdrafts and future tax). †As percentage of capital employed at beginning of the year. ‡As at 13 July 1979. §Appendix on page 70 gives list of Managing Directors whose names cannot be fitted into the main text. ‖M.D. = Managing Director; J.M.D. = Joint Managing Director: A.C. = Acting Chairman. C.E. = Chief Executive. ¶As percentage of capital employed at end of the year. N/A Not available. [1]UK only. [4]Including added value and sales taxes in overseas territories but excluding UK VAT. [5]Including excise duties but excluding VAT. [6]Including excise duties and VAT. [10]Including duties and sales taxes. [11]Including £634,887,000 premium income earned overseas. [12]Based on 40% of Royal Dutch/Shell Group. [13]Including sales taxes, excise duties and similar levies. [37]Profit, turnover and export figures taken from pro-forma annualised figures.

TURNOVER Total £000	Export £000	*CAPITAL EMPLOYED £000	Rank Latest year	Rank Previous year	Latest year £000	Rank	Previous year £000	% to turnover Latest year	†% to capital employed Latest year	Previous year	**No. of employees	‡Equity market cap. £M.
17,559,800	1,259,000	8,389,200	1	1	2,695,200	1	2,393,800	15.3	¶32·1	46·9	108,700	4,783·2
11,684,800[13]	—	5,641,200	2	2	1,495,200	2	1,747,200	12·8	29·0	39·2	—	2,000·9
6,512,000[4]	175,000	2,550,000	4	4	499,000	4	472,000	7·7	20·0	19·9	153,000	941·2
4,533,000	856,000	4,097,000	3	3	558,000	3	612,000	12·3	14·8	17·2	151,000	1,872·9
4,004,600	468,042	1,600,500	8	6	367,400	5	348,800	9·2	25·9	27.5	89,277[1]	951·9
3,240,400	61,000	1,132,734	11	8	165,483	12	171,135	5·1	14·8	17.6	101,200	635·7
3,072,700	910,000	1,268,400	9	11	77,000	44	72,519	2·5	7·7	8.9	191,853	237·3
2,363,000	775,000	875,000	17	18	261,000	8	263,100	11·0	35·2	55.4	78,000	USA
2,342,700	665,000	1,207,200	10	10	356,800	6	292,000	15·2	34·4	32·6	191,000	1,921·2
2,330,600[5]	338,000	2,247,900	5	N/A	116,500	26	109,500	5·0	6·0	¶ 5·6	19,817[1]	HOL
2,275,106[6]	206,800	1,689,463	7	7	119,661	23	139,317	5·3	8·4	12.0	8,864[1]	USA
2,137,600	41,200	1,085,000	14	19	152,700	15	95,800	7·1	¶14·1	15·7	83,360	563·9
1,953,900	95,200	2,005,100	6	5	334,300	7	322,800	17·1	17·4	16·8	50,644	673·3
1,850,285	65,479	993,160	15	13	154,511	14	133,527	8·4	16·7	15.0	100,415[1]	715·0
1,800,234	168,470	493,941	44	48	107,730	30	93,157	6·0	26·6	28·2	7,236[1]	86·4
1,754,700	193,100	1,128,600	12	9	133,300	18	118,800	7·6	12·5	11·6	104,412	423·7
1,687,585	35,102	500,443	43	41	88,242	38	91,266	5·2	20·3	24.4	71,166[1]	UQ
1,661,600	425,000	881,200	16	12	95,300	35	86,500	5·7	10·1	9·2	103,003[1]	232·3
1,661,574	109,000	462,568	46	42	82,755	40	94,116	5·0	19·1	29.1	7,590[1]	209·6
1,657,960	8,344	363,094	63	53	48,284	77	58,723	2·9	12·8	17·2	55,300	FR
1,610,900	87,200	632,000	27	15	120,500	22	121,600	7·5	16·6	15·4	68,000	173·2
1,564,000	31,200	756,900	22	17	121,300	20	120,100	7·8	16·7	16·5	36,500	242·6
1,538,000[5]	112,000	379,603	59	35	40,630	86	Loss41,935	2·6	8·7	—	4,358[1]	USA
1,523,325	27,082	285,585	79	64	56,385	61	40,087	3·7	17·6	17·4	29,419	USA
1,475,000	152,000	847,000	18	16	74,000	46	84,000	5·0	9·4	10·9	100,000	86·4
1,472,954	44,024	611,735	29	27	176,233	10	129,539	12·0	31·4	27·0	43,968[1]	1,455·6
1,341,500	17,858	173,443	123	150	34,296	101	27,361	1·8	19·9	34·7	3,350	300·2
1,281,114	639,939[11]	272,294	84	88	57,912	57	47,438	4·5	27·1	27·1	9,600	108·5
1,228,000	13,576	443,715	48	63	47,630	78	51,127	3·9	13·3	17·6	58,700	175·3
1,213,930	30,300	717,130	23	24	108,630	29	101,310	8·9	17·3	19·5	128,000	132·3
1,196,100	66,500	1,115,700	13	22	100,300	33	105,200	8·4	¶ 9·0	19·8	55,500	237·6
1,168,896	—	824,086	19	14	51,878	69	64,983	4·4	6·4	7·8	15,350[1]	141·3
1,154,441	31,514	567,071	32	29	132,000	19	116,223	11·4	24·3	24·6	36,267[1]	895·2
1,146,800	67,100	368,400	62	47	43,400	82	57,070	3·8	10·6	20·1	18,908	74·2
1,122,321[10]	72,092	654,808	25	23	45,352	79	24,445	4·0	7·1	3·7	32,200	210·2
1,106,000	230,000	560,900	34	37	93,500	37	68,500	8·5	20·3	17·6	60,300[1]	202.4
1,103,484	47,000	632,657	26	25	101,198	32	74,612	9·2	17·1	16·3	59,000[1]	448·5
1,102,030	5,792	26,421	493	525	6,158	396	5,514	0·6	29·5	31·4	693[1]	UQ
1,092,300	136,200	798,900	21	26	261,000	9	290,900	23·9	35·7	48·6	32,358	USA
1,091,900	123,900	515,600	38	34	118,400	24	112,952	10·8	25·2	27·5	83,283	562·5
1,053,000	48,000	501,000	42	45	116,600	25	109,300	11·1	28·1	32·3	73,878	705·2
1,026,400	44,300	430,300	50	58	79,500	41	65,500	7·7	23·1	24·6	42,400	339·9
1,014,400	11.000	715,900	24	21	109,100	28	100,100	10·8	16·5	16·0	61,193[1]	604·2
1,012,700	49,100	429,700	51	43	60,800	55	62,300	6·0	14·5	15·6	46,730	209·2
1,007,000	361,000	588,900	31	39	120,800	21	107,209	12·0	25·7	22·3	53,100	374·4
991,100	195,600	363,044	64	52	68,492	49	57,667	6·9	17·9	15·5	51,659	184·4
988,870	0	241,363	95	93	33,176	106	28,096	3·4	15·9	15·0	34,838	272·2
973,843	11,200	212,886	107	97	38,400	94	30,727	3·9	19·2	18·7	38,000[1]	165·9
971,170	154,640	533,410	36	33	83,730	39	90,790	8·6	17·7	23·6	85,600	223·3
971,000	27,000	60,684	282	266	11,992	244	9,662	1·2	21·1	15·8	1,300[1]	19·8

The following letters in the Market Capitalisation column denote unquoted companies and country of control: FR = France. HOL = Holland. UQ = Unquoted.
USA = United States of America.

Rank by turn-over	COMPANY	Main activity	Chairman and Managing Directors (in italics) §‖	Accounting period ended
51 (39)	Consolidated Gold Fields	Mining finance, industry, commerce	Lord Erroll of Hale	30– 6–78
52 (61)	Tesco Stores (Holdings)	Multiple retailing	L. Porter, *I. C. MacLaurin*	25– 2–78
53 (40)	Tozer, Kemsley & Millbourn	Internl finance & investment	K. A. C. Thorogood	31–12–78
54 (48)	Distillers Co.	Whisky distillers	J. R. Cater	31– 3–78
55 (47)	EMI	Music, electronics, leisure, TV, etc.	Sir John Read, Lord Delfont (C.E.) (*see p. 70*)	30– 6–78
56 (58)	Beecham Group	Pharmaceuticals, toiletries, drinks, etc.	G. J. Wilkins	31– 3–78
57 (75)	Trafalgar House	Contracting, civil eng., shipping, etc.	N. Broackes, *E. W. Parker*	30– 9–78
58 (57)	F. W. Woolworth & Co.[7]	General retail merchants	*S. J. Owen* (J.M.D.), *G. Rodgers*	31– 1–79
59 (50)	Metal Box	Packaging containers & closures	D. I. Allport, *R. J. W. Frost*	31– 3–78
60 (64)	Western United Inv. Co.	Foodstuffs & by-products	*None*	31–12–76
61 (71)	Vauxhall Motors	Motor vehicle manufacturers	F. Beickler (M.D.)	31–12–78
62 (63)	Littlewoods Organisation	Mail order trading & retail stores	P. Moores, *P. D. Carter*	31–12–78
63 (56)	Dalgety	International merchants	D. L. Donne, *G. T. Pryce*	30– 6–78
64 (65)	Babcock & Wilcox	Engineers & contractors	Sir John King, *T. Carlile*	31–12–78
65 (54)	Brooke Bond Liebig	Tea, coffee, meat & other food prods.	Sir Humphrey Prideaux	30– 6–78
66 (67)	Tarmac	Roadstone & civil eng.	E. W. Wright, *E. J. Pountain*	31–12–78
67 (73)	Spillers	Millers, bakers, food manufacturers	W. M. Vernon	3– 1–79
68 (70)	Philips Electronic & Assoc.	Electric & electronic products	G. Jeelof (M.D.)	31–12–78
69 (72)	United Biscuits (Holdings)	Manfrs. of biscuits, cakes, crisps, etc.	Sir Hector Laing	30–12–78
70 (59)	Gill & Duffus Group	Commodity brokers, mchts. & processrs	T. P. H. Aitken, *C. G. Palmer*	31–12–78
71 (60)	Rolls-Royce	Aero engines	Sir Kenneth Keith	31–12–77
72 (68)	Coats Patons	Thread, yarns, fashion & clothing	W. R. Henry	31–12–78
73 (66)	Mobil Oil Co.	Oil industry	G. W. Pusack, *Sir Nevil J. W. Macready*	31–12–78
74 (—)	George Wimpey[32]	Bldg, civil, mech. & elec. eng. contrs.	R. B. Smith (*see page 70*)	31–12–78
75 (78)	Whitbread & Co.	Brewers	C. H. Tidbury	3– 3–79
76 (86)	Arthur Guinness Son & Co.	Brewers	Earl of Iveagh, *A. J. R. Purssell*	30– 9–78
77 (81)	Ready Mixed Concrete	Building materials suppliers, etc.	J. Camden (M.D.)	31–12–78
78 (85)	British Electric Traction	Industrial holding co.	Sir John Spencer Wills, *H. S. L. Dundas*	31– 3–78
79 (82)	Trusthouse Forte	Hotels, catering and leisure group	Lord Thorneycroft	31–10–78
80 (79)	Plessey Co.	Electric & electronic products	Sir John Clark	31– 3–78
81 (80)	Reckitt & Colman	Food & h/hold products, pharms, etc.	J. A. S. Cleminson	30–12–78
82 (90)	Hanson Trust	Agriproducts, industrial services	Sir James Hanson	30– 9–78
83 (91)	Ultramar Co.	Petroleum exploration & development	C. L. Nelson (M.D.)	31–12–78
84 (84)	Booker McConnell	International food, eng. & tdg co.	M. H. Caine	31–12–78
85 (89)	British Aircraft Corpn (Hds.)	Aircraft manufacturers	Lord Beswick	31–12–77
86 (77)	IBM United Kingdom Holdings	Information handling eqpt. mfrs.	Earl of Cromer, *E. R. Nixon*	31–12–77
87 (N/A)	Thomson British Holdings	Oil, travel, printing & publishing	Lord Thomson of Fleet, *G. C. Brunton*	31–12–78
88 (99)	Conoco	Petroleum products	R. A. Fowler	31–12–78
89 (87)	House of Fraser	Departmental stores	Sir Hugh Fraser, *W. G. Crossan*	27– 1–79
90 (92)	Rowntree Mackintosh	Confectionery & grocery products	Sir Donald Barron	30–12–78
91 (76)	Harrisons & Crosfield	Eastern mchts., exporters & importers	T. Prentice	31–12–78
92 (88)	Glaxo Holdings	Pharmaceutical preparations, etc.	A. E. Bide	30– 6–78
93 (108)	Turner & Newall	Asbestos, plastics, insulation, etc.	P. W. C. Griffith, *C. W. Newton*	31–12–78
94 (83)	Massey-Ferguson Holdings	Manfrs. of agricultural machinery	H. A. R. Powell, *M. G. Bird*	31–10–78
95 (104)	Associated Dairies[34]	Dairymen, supermarkets, etc.	A. N. Stockdale, *E. G. Bousfield*	29– 4–78
96 (94)	IMI	Metals, fabricated products, etc.	Sir Michael J. S. Clapham, *E. Swainson*	31–12–78
97 (127)	Nafta (GB)	Traders in petroleum products	*V. A. Artunian*	31–12–77
98 (110)	Thomas Borthwick & Sons	International meat traders	W. A. Bullen, *D. F. Burditt*	30– 9–78
99 (106)	ICL	Data processing systems	T. C. Hudson, *C. M. Wilson*	30– 9–78
100 (95)	Standard Telephones & Cables	Telecommunications & electronics	Lord Caccia, *K. G. Corfield*	31–12–78

NOTES: *Total tangible assets less current liabilities (other than bank loans and overdrafts and future tax).   †As percentage of capital employed at beginning of the year.   ‡As at 13 July 1979.   §Appendix on page 70 gives list of Managing Directors whose names cannot be fitted into the main text.   ‖M.D. = Managing Director; J.M.D. = Joint Managing Director; A.C. = Acting Chairman; C.E. = Chief Executive.   N/A Not available.   [1]UK only.   [3]Gross sale value of all equipment exported (only rental or net selling price included in turnover).   [6]Including excise duties and VAT.   [7]Turnover, exports and employees relate to group. Other figures relate to parent co. only.   [8]Not calculated.   [17]Contract value of work executed.   [18]Contract work overseas.   [32]All figures and rankings relate to Wimpey Construction UK Ltd.   [34]Now a sub. co. of Associated Dairies Group Ltd.

TURNOVER Total £000	Export £000	*CAPITAL EMPLOYED £000	Rank Latest year	Rank Previous year	Latest year £000	Rank	Previous year £000	% to turnover Latest year	†% to capital employed Latest year	†% to capital employed Previous year	**No. of employees	‡Equity market cap £M.
953,200	16,000	508,100	41	40	99,400	34	73,800	10·4	22·5	16·6	97,500	316·0
952,994	48	143,358	150	144	28,677	119	30,424	3·0	22·7	28·2	38,008	243·1
900,000	65,000	96,369	200	198	19,160	171	17,413	2·1	18·2	16·2	4,724	27.4
876,100	299,600	819,400	20	20	175,300	11	144,801	20·0	24·0	22·8	19,440[1]	789·9
872,555	94,424	343,187	66	68	40,372	87	77,611	4·6	14·2	35·7	49,700	113·4
866,100	82,500	431,800	49	54	158,300	13	138,400	18·3	43·0	50·1	32,600	857·9
825,003	4,396	353,945	65	55	77,520	43	58,237	9·4	21·5	21·0	25,698[1]	160·3
823,392	4,838	615,645	28	65	57,826	58	51,973	7·0	18·8	18·6	61,200[1]	283·5
807,459	59,300	386,171	58	51	65,681	53	66,547	8·1	19·3	23·6	33,916[1]	193·7
805,800	19,220	6,618	899	888	116	966	344	—[8]	1·9	4·3	16,691[1]	UQ
804,880	229,000	168,548	127	125	13,002	235	5,273	1·6	8·7	3·8	33,344	USA
799,310	0	391,103	56	60	57,509	60	53,167	7·2	17·2	20·0	29,698	UQ
787,100	36,700	317,100	71	72	36,900	95	30,000	4·7	12·7	12·8	15,448	139·5
777,707	152,731	238,178	96	92	43,897	81	35,997	5·6	20·9	15·9	36,315	171·1
756,202	23,841	310,620	72	59	51,199	71	59,591	6·8	15·2	26·0	9,459[1]	110·6
752,031	6,557	165,800	132	115	31,781	108	29,556	4·2	19·6	18·7	32,000	98·0
729,000	11,400	174,954	120	108	21,619	155	15,107	3·0	14·9	8·9	18,356[1]	55·9
718,000	166,971	487,644	45	38	28,711	118	39,770	4·0	6·0	8·4	40,908[1]	HOL
710,400	21,300	236,170	98	90	48,663	76	44,052	6·9	22·0	28·38	41,000	217·5
706,000	13,782	118,546	169	190	27,258	129	22,471	3·9	30·6	36·4	596[1]	91·9
703,900	285,000	404,800	53	49	21,700	154	Loss 9,300	3·1	5·6	—	61,786	UQ
678,829	62,744	425,252	52	50	78,264	42	90,448	11·5	19·7	24·9	66,000	163·2
671,633[6]	79,900	269,248	87	85	5,907	409	31,972	0·9	2·6	15·8	2,389[1]	USA
663,000[17]	343,000[18]	399,927	54	—	66,899	51	61,834	10·1	19·2	20·9	26,000[1]	186·9
659,886	12,625	554,087	35	32	68,070	50	55,782	10·3	13·4	11·4	39,786	291·0
642,700	57,800	270,500	85	79	53,100	67	47,892	8·3	21·9	22·7	20,916	166·2
632,190	742	220,840	104	126	40,040	90	32,970	6·3	27·8	22·7	8,998[1]	105·9
631,154	38,900	457,426	47	44	76,985	45	66,547	12·2	18·4	18·2	54,000	166·2
613,800	1,500	513,400	40	46	73,100	48	56,100	11·9	17·7	15·7	72,000	296·0
611,100	120,461	328,453	69	61	55,752	63	50,514	9·1	16·7	15·7	58,692	248.3
606,640	38,440	254,390	91	83	66,280	52	62,220	10·9	29,4	29·8	34,800	252·8
604,600	6,900	149,500	145	136	34,000	103	31,000	5·6	25·1	23·4	25,000	105·2
595,133	—	250,935	92	89	50,126	74	35,806	8·4	23·4	16·0	202[1]	135·4
587,700	64,200	122,058	164	167	26,286	136	23,893	4·5	26·2	26·6	17,986	101·2
578,921	410,587	124,645	161	149	53,657	66	43,533	9·3	43·8	41·3	33,018	UQ
578,842	263,730	292,999	76	66	110,268	27	86,962	19·0	45·5	41·6	13,814	USA
576,400	62,100	332,400	67	N/A	146,600	16	107,200	25·4	49·6	¶36·3	20,812[1]	CAN
574,000	153,200	214,600	106	87	34,900	98	23,459	6·1	16·4	10·6	2,244	USA
568,635	15,671	294,359	75	70	45,309	80	40,373	8·0	16·8	17·3	30,107[1]	216·3
562,705	61,307	292,062	78	91	52,081	68	47,246	9·3	24·7	31·0	31,400	175·0
546,000	28,000	187,476	116	178	54,330	65	24,814	10·0	¶29·0	28·7	5,009[1]	311·0
543,546	123,000	387,342	57	56	94,760	36	95,113	17·4	26·4	31·0	30,901	376·2
540,681	109,400	369,710	61	62	51,041	72	54,626	9·4	15·3	20·3	40,187	135·8
538,211	363,800	182,380	118	100	30,667	112	53,514	5·7	15·6	35·1	21,172	CAN
536,000	86	73,452	245	281	25,551	139	23,950	4·8	48·3	67·5	15,833[1]	—[34]
524,006	102,200	265,154	88	77	40,307	88	41,096	7·7	16·4	17·9	27,278[1]	106·3
519,131	—	111,803	176	163	2,207	726	4,543	0·4	2·1	3·9	—	USSR
512,160	3,401	115,112	170	223	13,524	226	10,545	2·6	19·1	14·2	4,919[1]	33·9
509,400	92,400[3]	294,400	74	73	51,500	70	40,125	10·1	19·7	18·8	33,978	152·8
508,719	113,018	255,070	90	75	39,529	91	45,604	7·8	15·9	21·2	36,199[1]	182·0

The following letters in the Market Capitalisation column denote unquoted companies and country of control: CAN = Canada. HOL = Holland. UQ = Unquoted.
USA = United States of America. USSR = Union of Soviet Socialist Republics.

Rank by turn-over	COMPANY	Main activity	Chairman and Managing Directors (in italics) §‖	Accounting period ended
101 (107)	John Lewis Partnership	Department stores & food retailing	P. T. Lewis	27– 1–79
102 (100)	Fitch Lovell	Food mfrs., wholesalers & retailers	M. G. T. Webster	29– 4–78
103 (101)	Debenhams	Department stores, supermarkets, etc.	Sir Anthony Burney	27– 1–79
104 (102)	Rank Organisation	Films, entertainment, xerography	H. Smith, *R. W. Evans*	31–10–78
105 (97)	Ocean Transport & Trading	Shipping, distribution, etc.	Sir Lindsay Alexander	31–12–78
106 (112)	W. H. Smith & Son (Holdings)	Newspaper distributors, booksellers	P. W. Bennett, *S. Hornby*	3– 2–79
107 (113)	Pilkington Bros.	Glass manufacturing & processing	Sir Alastair Pilkington	31– 3–78
108 (114)	Ladbroke Group	Bookmaking, hotels, leisure, property	C. Stein (M.D.)	2– 1–79
109 (98)	Chrysler United Kingdom	Motor vehicle manufacturers	G. Turnbull, *G. A. Lacy*	31–12–77
110 (115)	Northern Engineering Indsts.	Electrical & mechanical eqpt. mfrs.	Sir James Woodeson, *D. McDonald*	31–12–78
111 (93)	Delta Metal Co.	Metals, alloys, engineers, etc.	Viscount Caldecote, *T. R. M. Kinsey, G. H. Wilson*	30–12–78
112 (124)	Guinness Peat Group	Manufacturers, gen. mchts. & brokers	E. Dell	30– 4–78
113 (—)	John Laing[15]	Construction engineers	Sir Maurice Laing	31–12–78
114 (131)	Bunge & Co.	Grain, cotton & commodity merchants	W. Hugaerts, *R. G. Pendered*	31–12–77
115 (119)	Blue Circle Industries	Cement and allied products	Sir Rowland Wright, *J. D. Milne*	31–12–78
116 (120)	Johnson, Matthey & Co.	Gold, silver & platinum refiners, etc.	Sir Peter Matthews, *Dr. B. F. Willetts*	31– 3–78
117 (105)	Wheatsheaf Distbn. & Trdng.[19]	Wholesale & retail distribution	V. G. Williams	25– 2–78
118 (117)	FMC	Meat & by-products	D. H. Darbishire, *G. H. B. Cattell*	29– 4–78
119 (125)	Total Oil Great Britain	Marketing of petroleum products	T. E. Hutton	31–12–77
120 (116)	Dickinson Robinson Group	Paper, packaging materials, printers	J. S. Camm (M.D.)	31–12–78
121 (96)	Wood Hall Trust	Civil & gen. eng., pastoral tdg., etc.	M. Richards, *A. I. Annand*	30– 6–78
122 (123)	Tootal	Thread & textile manufacturers	R. F. Audsley	31– 1–79
123 (137)	S. Pearson & Son	Newspapers, publishing, indl., etc.	Lord Gibson	31–12–78
124 (141)	Lex Service Group	Car dealers, hoteliers, etc.	T. E. Chinn (M.D.)	31–12–78
125 (130)	Michelin Tyre Co.	Tyre manufacturers	M. J. De Logeres, *G. Gazareth*	31–12–78
126 (136)	UDS Group	Retail stores and mail order	B. Lyons, *S. Lyons*	27– 1–79
127 (—)	Costain Group[30]	Construction and development	J. P. Sowden	31–12–78
128 (109)	Vickers	Engineering, office eqpt., etc.	Lord Robens of Woldingham, *Sir Peter Matthews*	31–12–78
129 (74)	Lonconex	Metal and ore merchants	A. Golodetz, *M. Shaw*	30– 9–78
130 (126)	Scottish & Newcastle Brews.	Brewers	P. E. G. Balfour	30– 4–78
131 (160)	BTR	General rubber manufacturers	Sir David Nicholson, *O. Green*	30–12–78
132 (132)	Wellcome Foundation	Pharmaceuticals, chemicals, etc.	A. J. Shepperd	26– 8–78
133 (142)	Davy Corporation	Industrial plant manufacturers	Sir John Buckley, *R. J. Withers*	31– 3–78
134 (121)	Stenhouse Holdings	Insurance bkg., gen. engineers, etc.	J. G. Stenhouse	30– 9–78
135 (118)	Anglo Chemical & Ore Co.	Metal dealers	*None*	31–12–78
136 (122)	Taylor Woodrow	Builders & civil eng. contractors	R. G. Puttick (*see page 70*)	31–12–78
137 (139)	Hoechst UK	Chemical, pharms., dyestuffs, paints	N. M. Mischler, *D. von Winterfeldt*	31–12–78
138 (144)	Food Manufacturers (GB Co.)[9]	Food manufacturers	R. C. Edwards	31–12–77
139 (128)	Powell Duffryn	Ship. eng., fuel dis., timber, indl. serv.	C. S. Aston, *W. J. Franklin*	31– 3–78
140 (134)	Albright & Wilson[28]	Manfrs. of chemical & allied prods.	G. H. Meason, *D. W. Livingstone*	25–12–78
141 (145)	Petrofina (UK)	Petroleum products	Baron E. De Selys Longchamps, *H. D. Newlyn*	31–12–77
142 (138)	Louis Dreyfus & Co.	Merchants and shippers	J. Louis-Dreyfus	31–12–78
143 (150)	Fisons	Chemical fertilizers, etc.	Sir George Burton	31–12–78
144 (143)	Linfood Holdings	Wholesale, retail, cash & carry distn.	Lord Kissin, *D. G. T. Linell*	29– 4–78
145 (146)	Associated Engineering	Precision component manfrs. & distbs.	J. N. Ferguson, *J. G. Collyear*	30– 9–78
146 (140)	Carrington Viyella	Textile manufacturers	L. Regan	31–12–78
147 (147)	Glynwed	Eng. & building products, steel	L. Fletcher	30–12–78
148 (230)	Mardon Packaging Intl.	Packaging manufacturers & printers	J. F. D. Cornish (M.D.)	30– 9–78
149 (178)	Coral Leisure Group	Turf accountants, etc.	N. Coral, *J. M. Hoare*	28–12–78
150 (156)	British Home Stores	Retail stores	Sir Jack Callard, *C. W. Paterson*	31– 3–79

NOTES: *Total tangible assets less current liabilities (other than bank loans and overdrafts and future tax). †As percentage of capital employed at beginning of the year. ‡As at 13 July 1979. §Appendix on page 70 gives list of Managing Directors whose names cannot be fitted into the main text. ‖M.D. = Managing Director; J.M.D. = Joint Managing Director; A.C. = Acting Chairman. C.E. = Chief Executive. ¶As percentage of capital employed at end of the year. N/A Not available. [1]UK only. [6]Including excise duties and VAT. [9]Co. published accounts on current cost accounting basis (ED 18) [15]Comparable figures for previous year not available. [19]Now a sub co. of Linfood Holdings Ltd. [28]Now a sub. co. of Tenneco International Holdings Ltd. [30]All figures and rankings relate to Richard Costain Ltd.

TURNOVER Total £000	Export £000	*CAPITAL EMPLOYED £000	Rank Latest year	Rank Previous year	Latest year £000	Rank	Previous year £000	% to turnover Latest year	†% to capital employed Latest year	†% to capital employed Previous year	**No. of employees	‡Equity market cap £M.
505,440	7,188	170,308	126	121	43,391	83	32,362	8·6	28·4	23·6	26,300	UQ
501,284	10,864	69,340	256	264	9,505	300	11,258	1·9	16·6	19·8	17,043[1]	37·7
496,140	4,800	326,566	70	84	28,091	123	24,434	5·7	12·5	11·2	27,538[1]	110·9
485,096	49,019	592,890	30	28	143,934	17	148,504	29·7	25·7	26·5	34,242	422·9
485,067	3,300	396,578	55	36	30,210	115	51,694	6·2	7·4	13·3	15,671	110·9
474,131	1,522	93,976	202	195	21,300	158	21,274	4·5	24·6	29·4	21,298	148·8
469,500	60,000	561,200	33	30	101,400	31	89,369	21·6	19·4	21·8	32,600	385·7
469,088	0	160,873	139	168	42,773	84	25,276	9·1	41·6	32·1	15,589	103·8
457,983	175,607	125,630	160	145	Loss 8,231	998	Loss 31,902	—	—	—	22,800	FR
451,000	115,000	170,742	125	120	34,816	99	28,753	7·7	22·7	¶18·7	35,989	98·0
448,700	68,600	244,000	94	78	38,740	93	36,910	8·6	15·8	15·3	29,150	102·7
444,728	18,880	112,394	175	184	17,782	179	16,011	4·0	17·9	29·0	2,272[1]	62·1
443,500	920	88,662	212	—	16,518	194	17,288	3·7	¶18·6	¶28·6	18,600[1]	29·6
437,000	4,289	55,261	300	314	7,446	346	8,782	1·7	16·8	26·6	887[1]	NA
436,700	69,600	533,200	37	31	73,900	47	67,200	16·9	14·4	13·6	12,097[1]	210·7
427,012	115,751	174,087	122	119	23,794	148	25,643	5·6	15·4	20·0	5,769[1]	119·3
426,009	0	30,380	442	412	3,345	592	6,179	0·8	14·6	35·0	6,532	—[19]
422,509	9,513	45,237	343	318	2,772	655	5,413	0·7	6·3	13·5	7,900[1]	8·0
417,900[6]	20,000	131,964	158	133	3,728	537	1,243	0·9	2·7	1·1	1,223	FR
401,744	38,255	167,474	129	114	28,333	121	26,636	7·1	17·5	16·6	25,521	85·4
401,518	19,453	82,312	223	197	11,350	256	10,935	2·8	14·7	16·2	2,335[1]	21·6
401,384	53,704	214,803	105	103	29,869	117	28,048	7·4	16·6	16·8	29,500	69·1
401,309	76,713	300,257	73	69	59,717	56	51,501	14·9	22·0	20·4	32,984	179·7
398,541	708	121,042	166	180	23,137	149	18,816	5·8	26·2	25·2	8,925[1]	57·3
398,418	85,017	273,291	82	80	27,298	128	34,351	6·9	11·4	16·3	18,728[1]	FR
395,259	43,700	370,015	60	86	35,547	96	26,125	9·0	16·0	12·2	27,780	181·2
395,000	4,000	121,544	165	—	49,024	75	38,066	12·4	47·0	42·5	5,872[1]	97·3
391,355	62,900	263,722	89	67	24,670	144	36,500	6·3	8·3	12·6	26,548	71·1
391,280	72,000	5,129	933	937	729	911	1,487	0·2	10·2	38·6	—	USA
389,549	7,698	292,760	77	71	38,778	92	39,060	10·0	14·4	14·7	26,740[1]	190·1
385,768	39,500	208,647	108	155	50,871	73	33,192	93·2	40·7	31·5	24,000	323·3
381,678	87,223	272,808	83	74	57,809	59	55,536	15·1	22·2	25·6	7,134[1]	UQ
371,321	73,000	104,663	187	192	26,849	131	19,934	7·2	30·4	40·3	14,900	86·8
371,000	2,058	27,500	475	490	11,554	252	11,520	3·1	51·3	59·0	4,268[1]	27·7
367,898	—	48,099	324	479	6,775	372	5,947	1·8	23·2	25·3	—	USA
367,000	26,000	232,993	100	96	27,961	125	26,105	7·6	13·9	13·5	9,976[1]	105·6
351,749	13,808	142,027	151	156	20,255	166	17,276	5·8	17·0	14·6	6,437[1]	G
348,966	33,772	105,868	185	201	9,814	290	8,646	2·8	11·6	16·4	8,822[1]	USA
343,630	34,105	110,117	181	160	15,702	203	13,876	4·6	17·1	17·1	12,045	51·1
342,058	88,600	198,066	111	95	30,397	114	40,102	8·9	15·1	22·1	10,000	—[28]
341,348	28,836	110,921	179	164	6,239	390	7,036	1·8	6·2	11·0	1,927	B
332,196	11,715	92,456	205	194	2,275	716	3,451	0·7	2·6	4·7	272[1]	FR
328,660	53,693	226,739	102	99	28,287	122	25,213	8·6	14·4	14·8	12,791	96·6
327,405	285	24,873	510	478	5,644	420	6,333	1·7	24·0	¶26·9	8,327[1]	51·1
324,000	54,100	201,800	109	117	35,100	97	37,209	10·8	22·1	29·8	29,476	74·5
322,706	41,015	174,736	121	107	20,403	164	22,557	6·3	11·8	13·9	27,188[1]	50·8
316,437	12,000	105,188	186	166	19,978	167	16,559	6·3	19·1	17·2	17,502	67·2
311,149	8,698	118,621	168	217	26,484	135	23,006	8·5	26·4	30·9	11,940	UQ
309,000	0	98,225	195	300	26,549	134	20,431	8·6	¶27·0	¶43·7	13,827[1]	95·3
307,324	4,194	114,658	172	177	34,235	102	27,407	11·1	35·3	28·8	25,669	250·4

The following letters in the Market Capitalisation column denote unquoted companies and country of control: B = Belgium.   FR = France.   G = Germany.
NA = Netherlands Antilles.   UQ = Unquoted.   USA = United States of America.

Rank by turn-over	COMPANY	Main activity	Chairman and Managing Directors (in italics) §‖	Accounting period ended
151 (155)	Chloride Group	Battery, etc., manufacturers	Sir Alastair Pilkington	31– 3–78
152 (151)	British Sugar Corpn.	Sugar products	Sir Gerald Thorley (*see page 70*)	24– 9–78
153 (163)	Northern Foods	Dairymen, food manufacturers, brewers	N. Horsley	30– 9–78
154 (157)	Ciba-Geigy (UK)	Manufacture & sale of chemicals	A. A. S. Rae, *H. R. Wust, K. W. Humphreys*	25–12–77
155 (133)	INCO Europe	Nickel refiners	A. T. Shadforth, *R. B. Nicholson*	31–12–78
156 (173)	Overseas Containers	Container operators	Sir Ronald Swayne	3–12–77
157 (180)	John Brown & Co.	Engineering, machine tools, etc.	J. Mayhew-Sanders	31– 3–78
158 (170)	Consolidated Petroleum	Oil industry	N/A	31–12–77
159 (496)	Coalite Group	Smokeless fuel, coal oil, coal petrol	Viscount Ward of Witley, *C. E. Needham*	31– 3–79
160 (159)	BPB Industries	Gypsum, bldg. materials, paper & eng.	F. G. Flood, *A. G. Turner*	31– 3–78
161 (148)	Blackwood Hodge	Earthmoving eqpmt., sales & service	W. A. Shapland, *C. L. Ferguson*	31–12–78
162 (211)	Wilkinson Match	Matches, personal products, etc.	D. Randolph, *C. Lewington*	31– 3–79
163 (161)	Redland	Construction materials	C. R. Corness	25– 3–78
164 (152)	Alcan Aluminium (UK)	Aluminium & associated products	D. A. Pinn (M.D.)	31–12–78
165 (185)	Cocoa Merchants	General produce merchants	Sir John Rodgers *A. H. D. Weldon, I. Jay*	30– 9–78
166 (177)	Tradax, England	Grain & commodity merchants	D. A. Nelson-Smith	31– 5–78
167 (162)	Heron Corpn.	Property inv. & trdg., garage opertrs.	H. Ronson	31– 3–78
168 (299)	Foster Wheeler	Petroleum & chemical engineers	H. Dudek (M.D.)	31–12–78
169 (154)	Amoco (UK)	Marketing of petroleum products	J. A. Parker	31–12–77
170 (188)	BSG International	Vehicle distbn. servicing, leasing, etc.	H. G. Cressman, *T. C. Cannon*	31–12–78
171 (175)	British & Commonwealth Shpg.	Ship and aircraft operators, etc.	Sir W. Nicholas Cayzer	31–12–78
172 (167)	Smiths Industries	Vehicle, aviation & marine eqpmt. etc.	E. R. Sisson, *F. R. Hurn*	5– 8–78
173 (158)	Guthrie Corporation	Plantations, carpets & floorcoverings	M. J. Gent (J.M.D.), *I. L. Coates*	31–12–78
174 (164)	Gestetner Holdings	Duplicating machines, etc., manfrs.	D. Gestetner, J. Gestetner	4–11–78
175 (166)	Kodak	Photographic goods manufacturers	F. J. Moorfoot (M.D.), *R. Milner*	29–10–78
176 (174)	Marley	Manfrs. of building trade products	O. A. Aisher	31–10–78
177 (184)	Granada Group	Entertainments	A. Bernstein	30– 9–78
178 (207)	Nestlé Company	Food manufacturers & distributors	W. A. Manahan, *R. A. Wilson*	31–12–77
179 (210)	C. & J. Clark	Footwear	J. D. Clark (M.D.)	30–12–78
180 (153)	Mitchell Cotts Group	Eng., transport, commodity trdg., etc.	P. P. Dunkley, *K. N. Jenkins, J. R. C. Wren*	30– 6–78
181 (236)	Continental (London)	Commodity dealers	P. J. Lowe (M.D.)	31–12–77
182 (182)	APV Holdings	Process engineers & plant manfrs.	H. P. N. Benson, *K. A. G. Miller*	31–12–78
183 (169)	Montague L. Meyer	Timber merchants	J. M. Meyer	31– 3–78
184 (129)	Tampimex Oil	Oil traders	J. B. Eldridge, *C. Oatley*	31–12–77
185 (171)	Hepworth Ceramic Holdings	Manfrs. vitrified clay pipes, etc.	P. Goodall	31–12–78
186 (203)	UBM Group	Builders merchants, etc.	M. G. Phillips (M.D.)	28– 2–79
187 (179)	AAH	Fuel distbn., builders supplies, etc.	W. M. Pybus	31– 3–78
188 (181)	Nurdin & Peacock	Cash & carry wholesalers	W. M. Peacock, *G. A. King, T. V. Grimwood*	30–12–78
189 (195)	Simon Engineering	Engineers & plant contractors	H. C. Harrison	31–12–78
190 (183)	H. J. Heinz Company	Food manufacturers	H. J. Heinz II, *C. F. Lowe*	29– 4–78
191 (190)	English China Clays	China clay manufacturers	Lord Aberconway	30– 9–78
192 (165)	Croda International	Chemical processors	Sir Frederick Wood (*see page 70*)	31–12–78
193 (225)	Fairclough Construction Grp	Civil eng. & building contractors	O. Davies	31–12–78
194 (212)	Caterpillar Tractor Co.	Manfrs. of earthmoving equipment	M. W. Dargel (M.D.)	30– 9–77
195 (275)	Derby & Co.	Metal & mineral merchants	E. Fraenkel	31–12–77
196 (193)	Johnson & Firth Brown	Specialist engineers	J. M. Clay	30– 6–78
197 (172)	Thos. W. Ward	Heavy engineering, etc.	J. P. Frost (M.D.)	30– 9–78
198 (176)	Steetley Company	Minerals, chems., high temp. ceramics	T. G. Boardman	31–12–78
199 (213)	Racal Electronics	Radio communication, electronic eqpt.	E. T. Harrison (M.D.)	31– 3–79
200 (168)	Gerald Metals	Metal merchants	G. L. Lennard, *R. Kestenbaum*	30– 4–78

NOTES : * Total tangible assets less current liabilities (other than bank loans and overdrafts and future tax).   † As percentage of capital employed at beginning of the year.   ‡ As at 13 July 1979.   § Appendix on page 70 gives list of Managing Directors whose names cannot be fitted into the main text.   ‖ M.D. = Managing Director; J.M.D. = Joint Managing Director; A.C. = Acting Chairman; C.E. = Chief Executive.   ¶ As percentage of capital employed at end of the year.   N/A Not available.   ¹ UK only.   δ Including excise duties but excluding VAT.

| TURNOVER | | *CAPITAL EMPLOYED | | | NET PROFIT BEFORE INTEREST AND TAX | | | | | | **No. of employees | ‡Equity market cap £M. |
Total £000	Export £000	£000	Rank Latest year	Rank Previous year	Latest year £000	Rank	Previous year £000	% to turnover Latest year	†% to capital employed Latest year	Previous year		
306,229	31,444	198,036	112	110	31,140	111	31,794	10·2	18·7	26·1	21,727	120·2
304,223	282	164,548	133	139	30,047	116	24,246	9·9	22·5	27·1	7,300	93·0
302,637	2,776	73,496	243	224	24,367	146	19,830	8·1	34·8	35·6	15,377[1]	144·8
302,632	116,380	221,310	103	98	25,141	141	17,443	8·3	12·6	9·6	10,933[1]	SWZ
292,642	139,893	164,113	134	105	12,745	238	18,138	4·4	7·8	10·3	7,241[1]	CAN
289,149	—	234,863	99	123	56,102	62	48,932	19·4	37·3	40·8	3,069[1]	UQ
283,814	97,141	77,672	229	222	24,482	145	13,476	8·6	34·3	18·3	14,719[1]	96·2
281,661	0	52,204	308	286	18,933	172	21,606	6·7	37·6	36·8	—	UQ
278,053	12,150	63,524	270	364	18,623	177	17,514	6·7	31·2	¶29·3	7,371	66·3
274,628	12,572	160,740	140	127	33,303	105	32,968	12·1	23·1	27·0	11,500	130·6
273,430	15,600	151,025	144	141	27,721	126	26,267	10·1	21·1	20·1	6,000	38·9
271,686	25,162	172,388	124	158	25,689	138	18,366	9·5	21·3	15·5	17,035	45·3
270,560	6,660	176,210	119	122	42,500	85	37,010	15·7	28·0	29·4	6,874[1]	183·5
269,710	56,700	196,910	113	102	18,780	175	32,323	7·0	10·5	18·1	9,015[1]	56·4
267,310	0	17,385	639	896	11,802	249	1,679	4·4	201·3	81·3	—	LU
265,968	39,198	34,976	404	851	4,096	504	2,248	1·5	53·8	16·0	395	PAN
265,522	1,143	166,531	130	124	16,453	195	15,807	6·2	11·0	11·7	4,744	UQ
264,388	107,857	16,583	658	832	10,499	275	5,496	4·0	92·3	49·3	3,343[1]	USA
262,653[5]	38,590	107,659	182	162	Loss 2,980	991	Loss 1,322	—	—	—	1,345	USA
256,100	7,111	58,845	290	297	11,932	247	11,222	4·7	25·1	26·0	6,048[1]	23·7
256,100	20,692	280,168	80	81	33,969	104	35,873	13·3	13·4	15·0	7,521[1]	115·0
254,750	43,000	133,139	157	152	24,693	143	23,087	9·7	20·5	22·8	20,349	98·7
253,976	14,480	247,638	93	106	26,652	133	25,558	10·5	15·2	13·7	30,000	163·7
253,012	48,458	182,990	117	113	31,525	109	33,844	12·5	19·4	20·8	4,184[1]	64·8
252,457	94,342	149,072	146	147	34,506	100	35,504	13·7	28·0	31·6	10,942[1]	USA
250,931	16,276	143,932	149	140	22,138	151	18,374	8·8	16·7	17·9	7,927[1]	82·6
250,159	4,847	168,438	128	118	40,158	89	31,293	16·1	25·4	19·0	10,389	205·4
249,042	32,661	163,165	135	142	2,506	685	11,973	1·0	1·9	10·7	8,062[1]	SWZ
249,041	10,725	97,937	197	206	21,485	157	14,117	8·6	26·2	24·5	12,825[1]	UQ
248,173	2,431	80,090	226	214	13,683	225	15,566	5·5	17·9	22·2	9,829	18·0
247,867	1,093	21,244	568	631	343	946	Loss 1,293	0·1	2·3	—	270	USA
247,800	30,300	100,207	193	186	20,665	162	18,922	8·3	22·7	22·1	7,763[1]	58·1
247,000	5,123	110,396	180	165	17,234	183	19,585	7·0	16·4	26·0	7,942	54·0
246,988	1,529	5,308	931	891	Loss 1,129	986	1,458	—	—	31·6	—	USA
246,901	32,831	146,842	148	143	32,298	107	28,973	13·1	24·8	31·3	10,900[1]	134·7
246,713	8,269	58,892	289	287	8,731	312	5,700	3·5	17·4	11·8	8,191	29·2
246,061	7,676	25,250	506	480	7,328	350	6,775	3·0	31·4	34·7	4,719[1]	15·7
237,811	0	19,492	598	609	5,387	436	4,858	2·3	32·7	37·3	1,956	33·1
235,601	79,753	75,949	236	235	18,146	178	15,437	7·7	28·2	28·6	9,117	72·1
234,948	5,922	114,633	173	181	17,347	182	17,315	7·4	18·3	20·3	10,115	USA
234,244	93,447	232,785	101	101	25,851	137	30,222	11·0	13·9	19·5	11,703[1]	133·9
234,130	38,400	111,676	178	182	16,604	192	15,332	7·1	17·6	18·8	6,392[1]	55·7
232,909	3,168	39,522	373	444	9,731	292	7,155	4·2	36·7	32·5	9,518[1]	29·6
232,587	139,012	73,508	242	256	31,456	110	22,857	13·5	53·5	52·7	5,114[1]	USA
230,591	—	48,179	323	403	6,619	378	8,217	2·9	20·7	46·2	554[1]	USA
229,722	41,007	134,319	156	157	16,875	188	16,323	7·3	14·2	17·5	13,904[1]	56·4
226,930	13,035	97,794	198	173	14,574	219	11,282	6·4	14·9	11·9	7,964[1]	38·0
226,824	24,564	154,044	141	129	24,713	142	27,354	10·9	17·4	21·5	6,009	80·0
225,270	107,353	166,383	131	138	62,372	54	54,200	27·7	46·8	53·0	6,069[1]	506·5
219,626	484	22,729	540	870	1,177	856	2,586	0·5	17·5	76·1	—	USA

The following letters in the Market Capitalisation column denote unquoted companies and country of control: CAN = Canada.　　LU = Luxembourg.　　PAN = Panama. SWZ = Switzerland.　　UQ = Unquoted.　　USA = United States of America.

Rank by turn-over	COMPANY	Main activity	Chairman and Managing Directors (in italics) §‖	Accounting period ended
201 (202)	Transport Development Group	Road transport, warehousing, etc.	J. B. Duncan, *J. D. Lockhart*	31–12–78
202 (196)	William Press & Son	Civil & mech. engineering contrs.	W. A. Hawken, *R. A. Daniels*	31–12–78
203 (201)	Kenning Motor Group	Motor distributors	G. Kenning (J.M.D.), *D. B. Kenning*	30– 9–78
204 (199)	Berec Group	Battery manfrs. and engineers	C. G. Stapleton	3– 3–79
205 (261)	Paterson, Zochonis & Co.	West African merchants	J. B. Zochonis, *B. Spoudeas*	31– 5–78
206 (204)	Hoover	Household appliance manufacturers	M. Rawson, *G. L. Lloyd*	31–12–78
207 (191)	Monsanto	Chemical & plastic products	E. Sharp	31–12–78
208 (205)	Mallinson-Denny	Timber merchants & manufacturers	Sir Frederick Catherwood, *R. T. S. MacPherson*	31–12–78
209 (189)	Bunzl Pulp & Paper	Paper & paper products	G. G. Bunzl, *E. G. Beaumont, F. R. Davenport*	31–12–78
210 (209)	Safeway Food Stores	Food retailing	T. E. Spratt (M.D.)	30– 9–78
211 (198)	Birmid Qualcast	Mfrs. of foundry products, etc.	J. F. Insch, *B. K. Fitton*	28–10–78
212 (192)	Danish Bacon Co.	Sale & distbn. of groceries & provs.	E. Trautmann (M.D.), *K. Bonefeld*	30–12–78
213 (241)	Chubb & Son	Security systems, etc.	Lord Hayter, *W. E. Randall*	31– 3–78
214 (246)	Norcros	Industrial investments	J. V. Sheffield, *W. K. Roberts*	31– 3–79
215 (278)	Wadham Stringer	Motor vehicle distributors, etc.	F. C. Stringer, *M. J. Stringer*	31–12–78
216 (200)	Associated Biscuit Manfrs.	Biscuit manufacturers, etc.	G. W. N. Palmer	31–12–78
217 (218)	Foseco Minsep	Special products for industry	D. V. Atterton, *A. G. T. Chubb*	31–12–78
218 (226)	John Menzies (Holdings)	Newsagents, booksellers, stationers	J. M. Menzies, *D. G. MacDonald*	3– 2–79
219 (194)	Lead Industries Group	Metal refining & smelting, paints, etc.	I. G. Butler (J.M.D.) *(see page 70)*	31–12–78
220 (221)	Cawoods Holdings	Fuel distribution, etc.	E. Binks (M.D.)	31– 3–78
221 (222)	General Motors	Vehicle comps. & domestic appl. mnfrs.	R. A. White	31–12–78
222 (216)	Henry W. Peabody Grain	Grain shippers	J. B. Faller (C.E)	30– 9–78
223 (253)	Kwik Save Discount Group	Supermarket operators	I. F. D. Hill, *I. M. Howe, M. J. R. Weeks*	2– 9–78
224 (217)	Stone-Platt Industries	Textile machy., marine eng., pumps, etc.	Sir Francis Hawkings, *E. G. Smalley*	31–12–78
225 (234)	Currys	Retlrs. of electrical appliances, etc.	D. Curry, *M. Curry, T. R. Curry*	24– 1–79
226 (239)	Henlys	Motor car dealers	G. R. Chandler (M.D.)	30– 9–78
227 (262)	Pauls & Whites	Maltsters & manfrs. of animal foods	M. G. Falcon, *J. R. Clayton*	31– 3–79
228 (256)	Haden Carrier	Bldg. services & metal finishing eng.	P. G. Simonis, *D. J. Hyam*	31–12–78
229 (235)	Procter & Gamble	Detergents and allied products	W. R. Gurganus, *A. D. Garrett*	30– 6–78
230 (277)	Dowty Group	Engineering	Sir Robert Hunt	31– 3–78
231 (206)	Goodyear Tyre & Rubber (GB)	Tyres and rubber products	W. Hansen (M.D.)	31–12–77
232 (227)	Marchwiel	Building, civil engineering, etc.	A. J. McAlpine	31–10–78
233 (243)	Phillips-Imperial Petroleum	Oil refiners	C. M. Kittrell	31–12–77
234 (214)	Decca	Records, TV, radio, radar, electronics	Sir Edward Lewis	31– 3–78
235 (250)	Freemans (London S.W.9)	Mail order business	A. Rampton, *R. H. C. Aldred*	27– 1–79
236 (229)	Geest Holdings	Shipping, importing, etc., of produce	L. van Geest	31–12–77
237 (270)	Dutton-Forshaw Group	Vehicle distrs. & automobile eng.	R. F. Hockin, *C. R. Gray*	31–12–78
238 (238)	Weir Group	Engineers	Viscount Weir, *J. J. B. Young*	29–12–78
239 (254)	Dixons Photographic	Retailers of photographic eqpt., etc.	S. Kalms (M.D.)	29– 4–78
240 (281)	Palmer and Harvey	Wholesale tobacconists & confectnrs.	Sir Donald Gosling, *J. H. Chedzoy*	31– 3–77
241 (197)	Duport	Steel foundry, eng., domestic eqpmt.	E. C. Sayers, *J. H. Russell*	31– 1–79
242 (248)	Cape Industries	Bldg., friction & insulation matls., etc.	L. G. S. Sackville, *G. A. Higham*	31–12–78
243 (240)	Automotive Products	Vehicle & aircraft eqpmt. manfrs.	J. T. Panks, *G. D. Pears*	29–12–78
244 (237)	Chevron Oil (U.K.)	Petroleum distributors	J. R. Smits, *P. M. J. Wilson*	31–12–77
245 (208)	Furness, Withy & Co.	Shipowners, etc.	B. P. Shaw	31–12–78
246 (244)	News International	Printing, publishing, paper, etc.	K. R. Murdoch, *H. C. Hardy*	31–12–78
247 (245)	Cable and Wireless	International telecommunications	Lord Glenamara, *P. A. McCunn*	31– 3–78
248 (223)	Bridon	Wire, wire rope, fibre & plastic products	J. Laird, *J. W. Naylor*	31–12–78
249 (259)	Du Pont (UK)	Chemical manufacturers	R. W. Grimble, *J. L. Foght*	20–12–77
250 (233)	Smith & Nephew Assoc. Cos.	Surgical, medical & sanitary prods.	K. R. Kemp	30–12–78

NOTES: *Total tangible assets less current liabilities (other than bank loans and overdrafts and future tax). †As percentage of capital employed at beginning of the year. ‡As at 13 July 1979. §Appendix on page 70 gives list of Managing Directors whose names cannot be fitted into the main text. ‖M.D. = Managing Director; J.M.D. = Joint Managing Director; A.C. = Acting Chairman; C.E. = Chief Executive. ¶As percentage of capital employed at end of the year. N/A Not available. ¹UK only. ¹⁶Virtually all revenue earned abroad.

TURNOVER Total £000	Export £000	*CAPITAL EMPLOYED £000	Rank Latest year	Previous year	NET PROFIT BEFORE INTEREST AND TAX Latest year £000	Rank	Previous year £000	% to turnover Latest year	†% to capital employed Latest year	Previous year	**No. of employees	‡Equity market cap. £M.
219,448	2,378	141,568	152	161	22,822	150	19,873	10·4	21·0	20·7	13,200	86·4
218,000	10,600	42,686	355	350	13,037	234	10,270	6·0	34·2	34·0	12,700[1]	28·1
215,059	3,846	61,693	279	261	9,308	304	8,194	4·3	16·2	17·2	7,115	22·1
214,852	53,255	151,261	142	130	22,125	152	27,125	10·3	15·6	21·6	17,173	69·0
213,528	49,975	84,055	219	265	22,029	153	20,045	10·3	38·6	25·7	2,732[1]	23·7
212,064	40,820	105,918	184	174	6,466	383	12,290	3·0	6·6	13·2	15,705	33·7
211,743	66,976	269,610	86	82	10,776	271	11,113	5·1	4·7	6·8	5,100[1]	USA
207,936	12,839	84,561	218	227	14,367	222	13,097	6·9	20·8	21·3	4,814	34·5
206,250	14,721	92,772	204	185	15,531	207	15,142	7·5	16·8	17·1	7,081	26·2
204,590	—	30,232	446	514	7,627	341	6,879	3·7	35·5	26·0	6,879	USA
204,249	20,701	84,762	217	204	8,856	309	12,682	4·3	10·7	17·2	15,236[1]	33·0
203,025	0	22,072	554	558	1,675	786	2,324	0·8	8·6	13·1	2,967	1·9
199,254	28,900	99,794	194	202	16,090	200	15,975	8·1	19·2	23·3	17,859	77·2
198,860	28,879	93,804	203	213	20,453	163	17,949	10·3	23·6	23·3	10,448[1]	73·5
198,668	818	32,850	421	413	5,851	412	4,394	2·9	19·5	21·4	4,965	11·3
198,508	14,231	79,573	227	234	11,301	258	12,832	5·7	17·4	21·0	22,428	50·6
197,878	10,681	83,385	220	216	19,245	170	16,319	9·7	26·1	23·5	8,509	75·0
197,674	501	26,668	489	593	6,302	389	5,191	3·2	36·0	36·0	6,661	35·3
195,268	28,700	161,728	137	128	20,782	161	23,124	10·6	14·5	20·0	5,503[1]	63·4
194,400	7,191	26,704	488	491	7,884	332	7,142	4·1	35·0	36·8	2,127	51·1
194,375	44,500	62,080	276	251	10,492	278	12,006	5·4	17·6	23·6	8,489	USA
193,582	3,151	10,737	792	872	466	940	1,704p.a.	0·2	7·0	25·2p.a.	—	SWZ
192,890	0	28,757	459	586	9,735	291	8,775	5·0	54·7	73·0	2,804	79·2
192,778	82,300	95,654	201	191	12,504	239	17,256	6·5	14·1	20·0	12,956	32·3
191,714	—	50,125	313	298	11,372	254	9,572	5·9	24·1	23·8	6,712	44·2
191,100	—	41,180	366	374	6,627	377	5,244	3·5	19·1	16·6	3,963[1]	15·1
188,798	10,887	61,312	280	285	8,980	307	7,031	4·8	17·8	17·5	2,228[1]	37·6
188,712	366	22,704	541	551	3,664	546	2,294	1·9	18·5	10·2	6,718	8·3
188,664	36,900	38,769	379	354	11,454	253	9,156	6·1	30·5	27·5	3,460	USA
188,441	50,894	102,160	190	200	26,822	132	19,785	14·2	31·7	30·1	16,050	199·5
187,571	31,932	98,156	196	171	4,520	475	5,412	2·4	5·4	7·7	11,432[1]	USA
187,544	297	63,320	271	262	13,981	223	13,717	7·5	24·3	27·9	9,066	32·4
187,037	43,552	24,275	518	424	684	913	3,505	0·4	2·3	14·3	—	UQ
186,300	59,400	113,196	174	170	15,355	211	19,303	8·2	15·0	21·1	11,826	59·0
186,016	3,493	70,561	254	268	17,384	181	13,735	9·3	31·0	30·8	5,068	110·2
185,086	1,890	30,257	445	388	3,077	619	2,174	1·7	9·2	7·7	5,235[1]	UQ
183,593	1,348	38,730	380	390	6,419	384	5,060	3·5	19·3	19·1	3,950	11·9
183,532	93,435	76,292	234	237	11,346	257	12,408	6·2	17·7	20·9	9,500	21·2
183,396	1,811	61,970	277	302	10,615	274	10,979	5·8	23·0	31·8	4,843[1]	51·4
181,855	—	11,617	778	771	2,899	643	3,177	1·6	29·1	59·4	2,643	UQ
181,325	17,219	86,676	214	189	8,093	327	9,916	4·5	9·0	12·7	8,190[1]	31·5
180,278	15,745	92,040	206	203	15,306	212	13,715	8·5	18·4	18·2	8,622[1]	47·5
179,426	41,093	97,306	199	209	16,864	189	15,351	9·4	21·0	21·0	12,410	47·8
179,056	—	54,552	301	277	642	919	Loss 990	0·4	1·2	—	—	USA
178,800	1,690	236,748	97	94	18,920	173	23,572	10·6	9·1	13·1	5,810[1]	73·7
177,849	2,144	91,522	208	215	27,192	130	20,762	15·3	35·9	29·7	9,046	61·6
177,301[16]	—	194,022	115	109	54,346	64	58,986	30·7	32·3	42·4	10,645	UQ
176,890	45,565	139,255	153	134	20,283	165	15,725	11·5	15·3	13·0	7,189[1]	68·5
176,887	55,781	83,122	221	212	9,625	297	8,222	5·4	12·4	13·9	2,812[1]	USA
176,300	31,223	104,193	188	172	24,175	147	21,321	13·7	24·6	24·6	14,009	112·6

The following letters in the Market Capitalisation column denote unquoted companies and country of contol: SWZ = Switzerland.   UQ = Unquoted.
USA = United States of America.

Rank by turn-over	COMPANY	Main activity	Chairman and Managing Directors (in italics) §‖	Accounting period ended
251 (251)	Grattan Warehouses	Mail order business	J. M. Pickard, *M. M. Place*	31– 1–79
252 (219)	Matthew Hall & Co.	Industrial engineers, etc.	Sir Rupert Spier, *A. H. J. Hoskins*	31–12–78
253 (215)	600 Group	Machine tool mfrs., engineers, etc.	Sir Jack Wellings, *K. H. Williams*	31– 3–78
254 (249)	British Printing Corpn.	Printers, publishers, bookbinders, etc.	P. Robinson (M.D.)	30–12–78
255 (265)	Charterhouse Group	Indl. investment & merchant banking	G. N. Mobbs, *G. C. Rowett*	31–12–78
256 (264)	Esso Chemical	Production & sale of chemicals	D. Smith (M.D.)	31–12–78
257 (309)	Datsun UK	Vehicle importers & distributors	O. Botnar (M.D.)	31–12–77
258 (228)	J. Bibby & Sons	Feeds, seeds, foods, farm prods., paper	L. C. Young, *A. G. Thompson, J. P. Wood*	30–12–78
259 (273)	Westland Aircraft	Helicopter manufacturers, etc.	Lord Aldington	30– 9–78
260 (284)	Tenneco International Hlgs.	Agricultural eqpt. mfrs., chemicals, etc.	*R. A. Robinson*	31–12–77
261 (232)	Ellerman Lines	Shipowners, brewers, insurance	D. F. Martin-Jenkins, *P. Laister*	31–12–77
262 (252)	French Kier Holdings	Bldg. & civil engineering contrs.	J. C. S. Mott	31–12–78
263 (263)	Anchor Foods	Dairy produce distributors	A. L. Friis, *S. T. Murphy*	31– 3–78
264 (267)	BSR	Manfrs. of record changers, etc.	J. N. Ferguson (M.D.)	6– 1–79
265 (260)	Cope Allman International	Packaging, leisure, eng., fashions	L. J. Manson	1– 7–78
266 (287)	Ferranti	Electrical & electronic engineers	S. Z. De Ferranti, *J. D. Alun-Jones*	31– 3–78
267 (285)	Associated Newspapers Group	Newspaper proprietors, etc.	Lord Rothermere, *R. M. P. Shields*	31– 3–78
268 (255)	McKechnie Bros.	Non-ferrous metals & chemicals, eng.	C. C. Taylor	31– 7–78
269 (283)	Imperial Continental Gas As.	Fuel and power industries	F. E. Zollinger, *P. V. C. Colebrook, T. M. O'Rorke*	31– 3–78
270 (186)	London and Northern Group	Contracting, quarrying, bldg., prods., etc.	J. H. M. MacKenzie, *J. Barker*	31–12–78
271 (357)	Arthur Bell & Sons	Scotch whisky distillers & blenders	R. C. Miquel (M.D.)	30– 6–78
272 (291)	Rolls-Royce Motors Hldgs.	Transport engineers	I. J. Fraser, *D. A. S. Plastow*	31–12–78
273 (282)	European Ferries	Sea transport, harbour services	K. D. Wickenden, *K. Siddle*	31–12–78
274 (292)	Laird Group	Metal ind., transport eng., etc.	Sir Ian Morrow	31–12–78
275 (286)	United Glass	Manfrs. of glass & plastic containers	J. M. Connell, *V. C. Hender*	2–12–78
276 (149)	Gulf Oil (Great Britain)	Distbn. of petroleum products	*W. H. Hamilton*	31–12–77
277 (276)	Intl. Harvester Co. of GB	Agricultural & construction eqpmt.	G. C. D'Arcy Biss, *L. A. Abbott*	31–10–78
278 (231)	United City Merchants	Intl. merchants, leather mfrs.	E. C. Sosnow	30– 6–78
279 (280)	Compair	Air compressors, pneumatic tools, etc.	Sir William Mather	1–10–78
280 (290)	Acrow	Engineering	W. A. De Vigier	31– 3–78
281 (257)	Newarthill	Construction, property and investmt.	T. R. Grieve	31–10–78
282 (258)	Caledonian Airways	Air transportation	A. Thomson	31–10–77
283 (388)	Ceres (UK)	Grain dealers & merchants	A. J. Sear	31–12–78
284 (301)	Low & Bonar Group	Packaging, eng., textiles, flooring	A. J. M. Miller, *B. G. Gilbert*	30–11–78
285 (353)	Sperry Rand	Engineering, business machines, etc.	Sir Alan Dawtry	31– 3–78
286 (339)	Tricentrol	Oil & gas expln., motor trade, etc.	J. G. S. Longcroft	31–12–78
287 (288)	John Mowlem & Co.	Bldg., civil eng., prop. devmt. & invmt.	Sir Edgar Beck	31–12–78
288 (272)	Burton Group	Retailers, men's outerwear manfrs.	L. O. Rice, *C. Spencer*	26– 8–78
289 (296)	Renault	Motor vehicle distributors	C. J. Weets, *A. de Costecaude de Saint-Victor*	31–12–77
290 (305)	LCP Holdings	Industrial holding co.	D. M. Rhead	31– 3–78
291 (271)	Moore Business Forms	Business systems, eng., packaging, etc.	J-P. R. M. Evans, *W. M. Nichols*	31–12–76
292 (—)	Hunting Petroleum Services	Oil and gas interests	L. C. Hunting	31–12–78
293 (274)	Tioxide Group	Titanium oxide & titanium compounds	J. K. Pitts	31–12–78
294 (269)	International Timber Corpn.	Timber	R. E. Groves	1– 4–78
295 (295)	Makro Self Service Whslrs.	Cash & carry merchants	P. Fentener van Vlissingen, *R. P. Hoegen*	31–12–77
296 (332)	Dobson Park Industries	Mining & specialised engineers	C. F. Ward	30– 9–78
297 (335)	Wolseley-Hughes	Merchanting, eng., agric. & gardng. eqpt.	J. Lancaster (M.D.)	31– 7–78
298 (289)	USMC International	Machry. for leather & plastics indry.	R. J. Hodge, *L. E. Dowley*	31–12–78
299 (310)	Mothercare	Maternity & children's wear, etc.	S. K. Zilkha (M.D.)	30– 3–79
300 (313)	Greenall, Whitley & Co.	Brewers, bottlers & distillers	C. J. B. Hatton, *J. D. Pritchard-Barrett*	29– 9–78

NOTES: *Total tangible assets less current liabilities (other than bank loans and overdrafts and future tax). †As percentage of capital employed at beginning of the year. ‡As at 13 July 1979. §Appendix on page 70 gives list of Managing Directors whose names cannot be fitted into the main text. ‖M.D. = Managing Director; J.M.D. = Joint Managing Director; A.C. = Acting Chairman; C.E. = Chief Executive. ¶As percentage of capital employed at end of the year. N/A Not available. ¹UK only. ⁵Including excise duties but excluding VAT. ⁶Including excise duties and VAT.

TURNOVER		*CAPITAL EMPLOYED			NET PROFIT BEFORE INTEREST AND TAX						**No. of employees	‡Equity market cap. £M.
Total £000	Export £000	£000	Rank Latest year	Previous year	Latest year £000	Rank	Previous year £000	% to turnover Latest year	†% to capital employed Latest year	Previous year		
175,602	3,377	66,675	263	279	11,298	259	12,258	6·4	21·1	24·3	5,232	50·6
175,414	15,751	20,429	580	604	7,174	356	6,203	4·1	42·9	49·8	6,901[1]	34·2
175,220	47,467	89,802	209	199	13,330	230	13,168	7·6	15·7	17·8	7,600	36·0
174,084	18,200	77,057	231	225	10,840	267	9,281	6·2	15·5	13·2	11,963	16·6
172,314p.a.	16,275p.a.	101,989	191	187	14,920p.a.	216	13,676	8·7	16·3p.a.	15·7	9,664	58·3
170,484[6]	58,200	44,394	348	328	13,389	228	13,261	7·9	31·6	33·2	883[1]	USA
169,714	1,709	23,532	528	628	10,309	279	5,809	6·1	67·4	55·8	459	CI
166,996	2,164	45,881	337	343	9,320	303	7,656	5·6	23·8	19·4	3,528	33·4
166,577	54,718	72,481	249	183	Loss 770	981	6,490	—	—	7·5	12,169[1]	32·6
164,655	80,000	73,676	241	231	15,639	205	11,475	9·5	22·9	25·4	7,654[1]	USA
163,971	0	136,393	155	135	11,162	262	14,220	6·8	9·2	15·8	5,861[1]	UQ
163,200	4,500	33,331	414	421	8,026	329	6,961	4·9	27·1	22·5	4,756[1]	15·7
160,043	—	10,312	812	781	1,064	872	977	0·7	11·1	14·0	215	NZ
159,763	75,500	111,678	177	175	15,980	202	20,737	10·0	16·4	25·5	16,079[1]	40·1
158,905	23,092	66,484	264	255	10,805	270	11,490	6·8	18·6	22·3	9,976	28·1
156,861	32,115	73,476	244	242	11,034	265	8,391	7·0	17·9	15·8	17,360	84·3
156,799	4,917	65,679	267	258	15,502	208	12,060	9·9	26·6	23·6	13,328	63·8
155,700	12,000	88,996	211	207	17,125	184	17,532	11·0	21·1	29·3	8,600	40·1
154,539	1,760	196,222	114	104	28,048	124	23,903	18·1	15·6	14·5	4,230	223·6
153,880	16,141	63,531	269	257	15,197	215	9,906	9·9	24·2	16·9	5,345[1]	22·7
152,731	14,654	63,235	272	271	15,408	209	10,352p.a.	10·1	24·4	18·6p.a.	1,886[1]	81·1
152,182	60,266	74,–59	239	283	16,541	193	12,768	10·9	32·2	28·0	10,000	46·0
151,978	0	148,873	147	131	30,554	113	26,722	20·1	21·7	21·6	6,023	147·8
150,979	25,923	67,133	261	248	12,433	241	10,796	8·2	20·7	16·8	8,255[1]	40·9
149,683	9,909	85,585	215	228	16,087	201	13,102	10·7	23·4	22·3	10,613	GB/US
149,612[5]	63,084	331,272	68	132	Loss 1,190	987	11,849	—	—	9·3	1,126[1]	USA
149,269	90,041	77,358	230	249	10,270	280	17,998	6·9	17·1	36·5	6,594	USA
148,449	18,673	14,189	710	656	4,582	471	4,804	3·1	32·3	42·8	612[1]	9·8
147,346	38,920	78,842	228	230	14,379	221	15,346	9·8	21·0	27·6	5,133[1]	34·6
147,223	87,099	73,784	240	263	15,624	206	13,411	10·6	27·2	29·4	7,392[1]	37·7
147,000	162	62,520	274	232	9,690	294	12,229	6·6	14·5	21·6	5,033[1]	16·8
146,616p.a.	—	39,806	372	340	7,870p.a.	333	8,473	5·4	18·5p.a.	22·8	4,866[1]	UQ
143,116	7,000	4,184	949	904	1,140	859	451	0·8	20·5	¶12·8	—	HOL
142,624	20,510	65,726	266	238	10,204	281	7,985	7·2	16·3	16·4	5,430[1]	20·1
141,538	43,309	92,004	207	254	12,155	242	7,326	8·6	15·3	12·0	7,031	USA
141,524	543	120,846	167	299	11,952	245	5,854	8·4	11·8	7·8	2,539	111·9
141,145	—	28,217	467	466	6,095	397	6,268	4·3	24·6	33·0	6,166[1]	15·0
141,070	1,802	161,964	136	112	9,853	288	1,358	7·0	6·0	0·8	12,393[1]	97·8
139,589	—	27,932	471	524	3,406	579	1,090	2·4	16·3	10·1	971	FR
139,444	1,244	48,434	321	361	5,919	408	5,215	4·2	16·4	20·7	3,429	42·1
139,403	6,245	82,946	222	205	11,039	264	9,537	7·9	14·3	12·3	9,231	CAN
139,386	3,646	13,128	738	—	2,427	697	2,339	1·7	¶18·5	¶17·8	268	12·8
136,781	26,300	131,302	159	148	8,766	311	13,930	6·4	7·2	13·1	2,612[1]	UQ
134,656	2,236	70,584	253	219	7,676	340	10,172	5·7	10·4	16·2	3,726	33·0
134,415	—	7,920	874	805	1,655	787	2,488	1·2	19·0	61·1	2,056	HOL
132,012	24,350	55,330	299	324	13,741	224	11,096	10·4	32·0	32·1	6,154[1]	75·6
131,808	10,895	44,850	345	345	9,594	298	6,656	7·3	24·9	24·0	3,864	34·6
131,551	40,162	62,324	275	245	15,298	213	13,973	11·6	25·3	23·0	8,081	USA
130,677	12,106	45,259	342	370	16,153	197	13,965	12·4	45·5	49·3	5,772	111·2
130,634	1,042	122,544	163	193	13,174	233	11,209	10·1	14·9	14·5	11,582	90·2

The following letters in the Market Capitalisation column denote unquoted companies and country of control: CAN = Canada.   CI = Channel Islands.   FR = France.
GB/US = Great Britain/United States of America.   HOL = Holland.   NZ = New Zealand.   UQ = Unquoted.   USA = United States of America.

Rank by turn-over	COMPANY	Main activity	Chairman and Managing Directors (in italics) §‖	Accounting period ended
301 (303)	Bishop's Stores	Wholesale & retail grocers	J. H. Bradfield	3– 3–79
302 (347)	Appleyard Group of Cos.	Distrs. & retlrs. of vehicles, etc.	I. Appleyard, *J. Limb*	31–12–78
303 (306)	Nottingham Manufacturing Co.	Knitwear, hosiery & carpet manfrs.	H. A. S. Djanogly, *J. E. Parsons*	31–12–78
304 (321)	Christian Salvesen	Housebuilding, cold storage, fish, etc.	L. M. Harper Gow, *G. H. Elliot*	30– 9–78
305 (376)	Comet Radiovision Services	Retailers of electrical goods, etc.	M. J. Hollingbery	2– 9–78
306 (328)	Barratt Developments	Builders, estate developers	L. A. Barratt (M.D.)	30– 6–78
307 (319)	Staveley Industries	Machine tools, foundries, elect., chem.	Sir Harry Moore, *A. Frankel*	1– 4–78
308 (268)	Borregaard Industries	Pulp, paper, textiles, etc.	A. Sanengen	31–12–77
309 (338)	Electrolux	Domestic appliances	Sir Alex Page, *J. B. Redman*	31–12–78
310 (365)	Fiat Motor Co. (UK)	Fiat car distributors	E. Spinelli	31–12–77
311 (324)	Securicor Group	Industrial security	P. A. C. Smith	29– 9–78
312 (298)	Hargreaves Group	Fuel, trnpt., quarrying, contrg., etc.	D. A. E. R. Peake, *R. B. Strachan*	31– 3–79
313 (330)	Trebor Group	Confectionery manufacturers, etc.	J. G. Marks, *I. R. Marks*	30–12–78
314 (316)	BBA Group	Manfrs. of insulating & friction mat.	D. M. Pearson, *C. M. Fenton*	31–12–78
315 (323)	Sime Darby London	Commodity traders, engineers, etc.	L. R. Patterson (M.D.)	30– 6–78
316 (392)	Industrial Specialty (I & S)	Metal merchants	G. S. Panchaud, *L. T. J. Rolls*	31– 3–78
317 (311)	Avon Rubber Co.	Tyre manufacturers, etc.	Lord Farnham, *P. M. Fisher*	30– 9–78
318 (220)	De La Rue Co.	Security printers, plastics, graphics	Sir Arthur Norman	31– 3–79
319 (410)	Norwest Holst	Civil eng. & building contractors	S. E. Baucher, *P. Orchard*	31– 3–79
320 (293)	Illingworth, Morris & Co.	Manfrs. of wool & cotton textiles	I. C. Hill (*see page 70*)	31– 3–78
321 (331)	May & Baker	Chemicals & pharmaceuticals	G. G. A. Pirrone, *N. Chancellor*	31–12–77
322 (294)	Seagram Distillers	Prodn. of whisky & gin, blending, etc.	I. Tennant	31– 7–77
323 (325)	Davies & Newman Holdings	Shipbrokers & agent & airline oprts.	F. E. F. Newman (M.D.)	31–12–78
324 (317)	William Baird & Co.	Textiles, industrials, investments	S. A. Field	31–12–78
325 (370)	Burroughs Machines	Computational equipment	R. W. Akers	30–11–78
326 (327)	3M United Kingdom	Coated materials & related products	M. J. Monteiro, *D. R. Osmon*	31–10–78
327 (304)	Carpets International	Manfr. & sale of floorcoverings	J. M. Carpenter	30–12–78
328 (N/A)	Wormald Intnl. Hldgs. (UK)	Fire protection & detection equipt.	J. W. Utz	30– 6–78
329 (375)	CPC (United Kingdom)	Food, glucose syrups, starches, etc.	W. G. Redley, *P. M. Ware*	30– 9–78
330 (329)	General Foods	Manfrs. & dealers in food products	J. C. Tappan, *D. F. Hurwitt*	1– 4–78
331 (360)	Kaye Organisation	Materials handling equipment	Sir Emmanuel Kaye	30– 4–78
332 (348)	Assoc. Communications Corp.	Television contrs., theatres, etc.	Lord Grade	26– 3–78
333 (297)	Renold	Power transmission prods., machinery	L. J. Tolley, *E. Garlick*	2– 4–78
334 (366)	Wm. Morrison Supermarkets	Supermarket proprietors	K. D. Morrison (M.D.)	3– 2–79
335 (302)	Rubery, Owen Holdings	Manufacturers & merchants	A. D. Owen (M.D.)	30– 9–77
336 (447)	Honda (UK)	Vehicle importers	K. Amemiya (M.D.)	31–12–77
337 (405)	John Howard and Co.	Civil engineering contrs., etc.	Sir John Howard	31–12–77
338 (343)	London Brick Co.	Brick manufacturers, etc.	J. Rowe (J.M.D.) (*see page 70*)	31– 7–28
339 (322)	Laporte Industries (Hldgs.)	Chemical manufacturers	R. M. Ringwald (M.D.)	31–12–78
340 (341)	Empire Stores (Bradford)	Mail order house	J. Gratwick, *R. Scott*	27– 1–79
341 (350)	Rockware Group	Glass & plastic container manfrs.	J. H. Craigie, *D. Bailey*	31–12–78
342 (337)	James Budgett & Son	Sugar, dried fruits, canned goods, etc.	R. A. Budgett	27– 1–78
343 (326)	Averys	Weighing, testing & measuring equipt.	R. C. Hale (M.D.)	31–12–78
344 (334)	Magnet & Southerns	Timber imptrs., joinery etc. products	S. Oxford (*see page 70*)	31– 3–78
345 (356)	Molins	Tobacco, paper & packaging mchy. mfrs.	Sir Harry Moore, *J. A. Mills*	31–12–78
346 (314)	S. Hoffnung & Co.	Gen. merchants, retail & manfg.	H. R. Bourne	31– 3–78
347 (390)	Dow Chemical Co.	Chemicals & plastics	C. H. Boyd, *E. H. Huggins*	31–12–77
348 (352)	Hunting Assoc. Industries	Aviation support, eng., tech. survey etc.	L. C. Hunting	31–12–78
349 (626)	Peugeot Automobiles UK	Motor vehicle distributors	P. Peugeot, *H. Hassid*	31–12–78
350 (342)	Swift & Co.	Food distributors & manufacturers	B. M. Jeffery (M.D.)	22–10–77

NOTES: *Total tangible assets less current liabilities (other than bank loans and overdrafts and future tax).   †As percentage of capital employed at beginning of the year.   ‡As at 13 July 1979.   §Appendix on page 70 gives list of Managing Directors whose names cannot be fitted into the main text.   ‖M.D. = Managing Director; J.M.D. = Joint Managing Director; A.C. = Acting Chairman; C.E. = Chief Executive.   ¶As percentage of capital employed at end of the year.   N/A Not available.   ¹UK only.

TURNOVER Total £000	Export £000	*CAPITAL EMPLOYED £000	Rank Latest year	Rank Previous year	NET PROFIT BEFORE INTEREST AND TAX Latest year £000	Rank	Previous year £000	% to turnover Latest year	†% to capital employed Latest year	Previous year	No. of **employees	‡Equity market cap. £M.
128,901	0	15,964	674	643	1,740	777	1,008	1·3	11·9	8·1	3,970	7.7
128,254	119	21,056	570	605	2,847	651	2,093	2·2	17·1	15·5	2,888	6·9
126,729	10,820	67,037	262	259	16,151	198	14,383	12·7	27·7	30·1	14,006	70·1
124,210	12,046	88,175	213	196	11,927	248	10,201	9·6	13·9	12·5	6,785[1]	UQ
123,937	671	16,865	649	743	6,417	385	3,870	5·2	58·9	62·9	2,305	42·8
122,210	0	76,408	232	236	13,305	231	10,502	10·9	20·7	17·9	4,106	40·3
121,994p.a.	15,043p.a.	47,850	328	347	10,767p.a.	272	7,601	8·8	28·2p.a.	22·7	7,699[1]	40·7
121,925	—	74,982	237	210	Loss 3,941	995	Loss 1,103	—	—	—	—	NOR
121,625	18,800	59,955	285	301	12,096	243	9,614	9·9	21·4	20·6	9,403[1]	SW
121,396	1,685	15,708	680	383	5,273	444	3,069	4·3	15·7	14·1	627[1]	IT
121,080	—	30,185	447	497	5,716	416	5,248	4·7	25·7	28·6	33,923	18·9
121,015	9,570	26,979	482	474	4,194	496	3,882	3·5	17·5	18·3	2,708	16·5
120,892	4,836	28,455	461	471	4,086	507	4,942	3·4	16·8	22·0	3,615[1]	UQ
120,495	12,612	53,968	303	294	9,268	305	8,370	7·7	19·3	18·5	7,252	26·1
120,432	7,177	21,379	566	496	2,547	679	3,841	2·1	11·4	28·1	3,492[1]	MAL
120,274	38,986	20,314	583	849	1,895	762	2,440	1·6	14·3	31·6	278	SWZ
119,867	31,506	35,452	400	393	5,688	418	6,838	4·7	17·2	23·2	7,517[1]	9·3
119,816	82,237	114,666	171	240	27,564	127	29,110	23·0	30·1	46·9	9,349	186·5
119,726	0	21,484	561	695	5,471	432	5,527	4·6	33·1	44·1	5,556[1]	10·9
119,710	47,298	55,965	296	243	7,593	343	7,694	6·3	12·4	14·1	9,598	10·0
118,993	38,230	59,254	288	291	11,603	251	11,983	9·8	23·7	29·1	4,588[1]	FR
118,028	63,300	161,435	138	116	20,863	160	5,199	17·7	13·5	4·0	2,219[1]	CAN
117,505	25,896	17,571	635	716	2,470	692	1,262	2·1	20·9	11·6	3,407[1]	6·1
116,491	8,102	48,530	320	356	11,240	261	9,193	9·6	30·4	32·1	12,325	27·7
116,475	44,449	72,867	248	211	16,739	190	15,104	14·4	21·0	19·1	5,144	USA
116,242	18,268	55,468	298	288	20,984	159	14,492	18·1	42·2	29·1	3,800	USA
115,460	13,200	60,650	283	250	7,010	363	3,930	6·1	11·8	6·8	7,131	12·6
114,903	17,078	65,745	265	N/A	4,396	484	6,304p.a.	3·8	6·7	¶ 9·7p.a.	6,406[1]	AUS
114,704	6,046	48,464	319	372	7,284	353	3,717	6·4	17·6	23·8	3,229	USA
114,315	5,356	33,781	411	426	2,089	740	65	1·8	7·2	0·3	2,277	USA
113,961	26,050	47,644	329	378	11,751	250	8,026	10·3	34·1	28·9	5,339[1]	UQ
113,588	—	100,458	192	239	15,382	210	13,867	13·5	24·7	21·6	4,678[1]	72·2
113,498	26,992	122,695	162	154	13,230	232	17,097	11·7	11·0	15·9	13,238	37·3
113,213	0	15,851	678	765	3,800	529	3,290	3·4	34·9	33·7	3,501	34·6
112,316	12,410	47,947	327	269	3,998	513	3,730	3·6	7·2	7·0	7,269[1]	UQ
111,838	—	33,887	410	810	1,751	774	5,687	1·6	12·8	66·7	200[1]	JAP
111,772	104,137	20,505	576	427	3,832	524	2,786	3·4	13·2	10·5	2,384[1]	UQ
111,300	4,031	64,304	268	272	16,216	196	13,189	14·6	29·6	26·4	9,488	37·5
110,885	35,867	104,046	189	179	14,676	218	12,582	13·2	15·2	14·3	4,677[1]	56·5
109,232	1,343	35,353	402	381	8,511	319	7,414	7·8	25·0	28·0	3,610	47·6
108,419	7,545	61,747	278	270	8,118	326	8,975	7·5	14·8	19·4	7,048	22·0
107,496	—	3,004	967	972	198	963	556	0·2	8·8	35·8	226[1]	UQ
106,911	16,036	73,176	247	244	18,645	176	15,550	17·4	30·6	28·4	12,400	94·1
105,630	1,170	67,370	260	253	14,522	220	15,127	13·7	24·5	29·9	4,099[1]	80·3
105,540	57,900	76,290	235	221	13,510	227	10,350	12·8	18·4	13·9	7,630	40·2
105,319	4,523	35,825	395	367	4,191	497	5,719	4·0	11·7	16·9	2,464	10·2
103,587	15,218	31,397	429	418	2,969	629	3,748	2·9	9·9	21·8	536[1]	USA
103,089	22,143	28,113	468	454	6,711	374	5,583	6·5	26·2	26·5	4,307[1]	35·6
102,758	2,710	18,520	617	939	6,508	381	4,009	6·3	79·3	104.3	189	FR
102,431	1,766	8,698	849	850	1,742	776	2,286	1·7	22·8	32·4	1,498	USA

The following letters in the Market Capitalisation column denote unquoted companies and country of control: AUS = Australia.   CAN = Canada.   FR = France. IT = Italy.   JAP = Japan.   MAL = Malaysia.   NOR = Norway.   SW = Sweden.   SWZ = Switzerland.   UQ = Unquoted.   USA = United States of America.

Rank by turn-over	COMPANY	Main activity	Chairman and Managing Directors (in italics) §‖	Accounting period ended
351 (372)	Honeywell	Computers, indl. & medical instruments	L. R. Price	31–12–77
352 (355)	Electronic Rentals Group	Retail, rental of TV & elect. goods	M. A. Fry	31– 3–78
353 (345)	Wilmot-Breeden (Holdings)	Mfrs. of eng. products	D. L. Breeden (J.M.D.), *M. L. Breeden*	31–12–78
354 (349)	Morgan Crucible Co.	Materials & components for industry	I. Weston Smith, *J. C. R. Gilbert*	31–12–78
355 (416)	Sterling-Winthrop Group	Chemicals, pharmaceuticals, etc.	E. E. Barber	31–10–77
356 (608)	Bos Kalis Westminster	Dredging contractors	J. Kraaijeveld van Hemert (C.E.)	31–12–77
357 (354)	Rugby Portland Cement Co.	Cement manufacturers	Lord Boyd-Carpenter, *M. Jenkins*	31–12–78
358 (412)	Borg-Warner	Engineering & chemicals	R. D. Bass (*see page 70*)	31–12–78
359 (344)	Sangers Group	Wholesale chemists	H. T. Nicholson, *J. Nichols*	28– 2–79
360 (373)	Owen Owen	Departmental stores	J. A. H. Norman (M.D.)	27– 1–79
361 (371)	Hartwells Group	Vehicle distributors, etc.	F. S. Huggins	28– 2–79
362 (430)	Vernons Organisation	Pools promoters, financiers, etc.	V. Sangster, *G. R. Kennerly*	31– 7–77
363 (312)	J. H. Rayner & Co.	Commodity merchants	N/A	30– 9–77
364 (346)	Steel Brothers Holdings	Construction, foodstuffs, mfg., etc.	J. H. Gaunt	31–12–78
365 (413)	Bayer UK	Marketing of products of Bayer AG	Lord William Bentinck. *J. V. Webb*	31–12–77
366 (336)	Twil	Wire manufacturers	A. S. Watts, *J. Fouldes*	31– 7–77
367 (377)	Dawson International	Cashmere, camelhair & wool manfrs.	A. Smith	31– 3–79
368 (315)	Higgs & Hill	Bldg. & civil engineering contrs.	E. W. Phillips, *B. J. Hill*	31–12–78
369 (308)	Williams Hudson Group	Transport, fuel distbn, shipping, etc.	D. J. Rowland (M.D.)	31– 3–78
370 (367)	Bestobell	Fluids engineering, insulation, etc.	A. B. Marshall, *D. Spencer*	31–12–78
371 (382)	Kraft Foods	Food manufacturers	J. F. Scull (M.D.)	31–12–77
372 (419)	Coutinho Caro & Co.	Steel, chemicals & plant suppliers	H. A. Oppenheimer, *H. Edmonds*, *R. D. Oppenheimer*	31–12–78
373 (379)	London Merchant Securities	Investment holding co.	Lord Rayne	31– 3–78
374 (362)	Adams Foods	Mktg., distbn., packg., of food products	A. Boardman, *W. P. O'Grady*	31–12–77
375 (404)	Crown House	Glass manfrs. elec. & mech. engineers	P. Edge-Partington	31– 3–78
376 (391)	SGB Group	Building equipment & services	N. L. Clifford-Jones (J.M.D.), *C. Beck*	30– 9–78
377 (408)	Initial Services	Linen supply, cleaning, light eng. etc.	A. F. R. Carling, *G. R. A. Metcalfe*, *E. F. Weston*	31–03–78
378 (396)	William Jackson & Son	Bakers, confectioners, meat products	P. B. Oughtred (J.M.D.), *B. N. Oughtred*	6– 5–78
379 (398)	Serck	Control equip., heat transfer, valves	R. G. Martin	30– 9–78
380 (358)	LRC International	General rubber products	Sir Edward Howard, *M. M. Sellers*	31– 3–78
381 (361)	Dunbee-Combex-Marx	Manfrs. of toys, plastics, toiletries	Lord Westwood, *R. J. Beecham, B. S. Feldman*	31–12–77
382 (407)	Geo. Bassett Holdings	Confectionery mfg. & distbn.	W. R. Mills, *C. J. Ede*	31– 3–78
383 (389)	Kellogg Co. of Gt. Britain	Cereal food manufacturers	G. D. Robinson (M.D.)	31–12–77
384 (393)	Bejam Group	Rtlrs. of frozen food & deep freezers	J. D. Apthorp, *L. Don*	1– 7–78
385 (351)	Pirelli General Cable Works	Electrical wire & cable manfrs.	Lord Thorneycroft, *A. C. Essex*	31–12–78
386 (417)	Macarthy's Pharmaceuticals	Wholesale & retail chemists, etc.	A. R. Ritchie, *A. L. Slow*	30– 4–78
387 (363)	Union Carbide UK	Metals, chemicals, eng., carbon prods.	P. F. Hilton, *J. T. Harvey*	31–12–78
388 (438)	Capper-Neill	Process plant & pipework for indsty.	W. P. Capper (M.D.)	31– 3–79
389 (418)	Ingersoll-Rand Holdings	Engineers	F. I. H. Wood	31–12–78
390 (397)	Bath & Portland Group	Minerals, agric., bldg., civil eng.	Sir Kenneth Selby, *J. A. G. Clarke*, *G. R. A. Metcalfe*	31–10–78
391 (463)	Lesney Products & Co.	Toys, hobby prods., comm. diecastings	P. M. Tapscott, *L. C. Smith*	28– 1–79
392 (N/A)	Bowater-Scott Corpn.	Paper products	W. S. Wesson (M.D.)	31–12–77
393 (359)	Fyffes Group	Fruit importers	S. Milstein, *A. J. Ellis*	31–12–77
394 (394)	Lindustries	Engineering, polymer and textiles	P. A. Rippon (M.D.)	1– 4–78
395 (369)	Ransome Hoffman Pollard	Ball & roller bearings mfrs. etc.	M. Harrison, *P. Holmes*	29– 9–78
396 (378)	Coates Bros. & Co.	Print. inks & indl. surface coatings	Sir Richard Meyjes	31–12–78
397 (444)	Harold Perry Motors	Ford main dealers	J. F. MacGregor (M.D.)	31–12–78
398 (402)	Britannia Lead Co.	Lead and silver refiners	R. H. Y. Mills, *K. R. Barrett*	30– 6–78
399 (435)	Cummins Engine Co.	Diesel engine & component manfrs.	T. A. Lyon	31–12–77
400 (406)	Readicut International	Rug making kits, carpets, textiles	P. J. F. Croset, *G. M. L. Hirst, J. P. M. Denny*	31– 3–79

NOTES: *Total tangible assets less current liabilities (other than bank loans and overdrafts and future tax). †As percentage of capital employed at beginning of the year. ‡As at 13 July 1979. §Appendix on page 70 gives list of Managing Directors whose names cannot be fitted into the main text. ‖M.D. = Managing Director; J.M.D. = Join Managing Director; A.C. = Acting Chairman; C.E. = Chief Executive. ¶As percentage of capital employed at end of the year. N/A Not available. ¹UK only.

| TURNOVER | | *CAPITAL EMPLOYED | | | NET PROFIT BEFORE INTEREST AND TAX | | | | | | **No. of employees | ‡Equity market cap. £M. |
Total £000	Export £000	£000	Rank Latest year	Rank Previous year	Latest year £000	Rank	Previous year £000	% to turnover Latest year	†% to capital employed Latest year	†% to capital employed Previous year		
101,216	25,100	57,284	294	325	16,675	191	11,202	16·5	38·9	25·2	5,134[1]	USA
100,948	2,491	80,922	224	220	16,984	187	14,804	16·8	21·0	20·6	6,859	158·8
100,225	7,035	45,653	341	335	6,938	364	6,857	6·9	16·9	18·1	6,447	USA
100,019	26,991	74,333	238	226	14,745	217	14,456	14·7	21·1	22·9	6,890	50·1
99,346	22,000	52,639	306	310	12,925	236	7,190	13·0	28·4	18·1	3,987[1]	USA
99,158	1,507	80,640	225	317	1,958	752	2,325	2·0	2·5	3·8	2,279	HOL
98,600	701	107,083	183	188	15,657	204	15,116	15·9	17·3	17·0	3,194[1]	63·3
98,330	50,733	71,461	251	267	2,860	650	1,287	2·9	5·0	2·3	3,791	USA
98,184	0	12,495	758	721	2,466	693	2,092	2·5	21·1	21·7	2,373	10·0
98,138	1,687	30,922	434	439	3,703	542	3,009	3·8	13·7	11·6	4,770[1]	10·5
98,113	23	20,826	573	627	2,722	662	2,445	2·8	17·7	18·2	1,872	6.8
97,665	2,328	25,485	504	518	6,866	366	4,552	7·0	31·0	21·4	2,684[1]	CI
97,618	—	10,511	804	754	Loss 812	982	Loss 1,430p.a.	—	—	—	—	LU
96,882	846	46,948	333	296	8,269	321	8,816	8·5	17·3	18·9	790[1]	19·3
96,824	802	15,943	675	616	3,463	567	3,432	3·6	21·6	30·0	705[1]	G
96,752	12,293	44,219	349	315	6,705	375	6,561	6·9	16·6	¶16·2	5,886[1]	UQ
96,174	40,300	52,050	309	341	17,002	186	16,268	17·7	42·9	62·7	5,531[1]	53·4
96,000	—	17,586	634	636	2,078	743	3,125	2·2	14·0	21·3	2,272[1]	5·1
95,593	1,258	40,785	368	334	3,851	523	6,566	4·0	9·3	9·8	1,959[1]	LU
95,496	8,110	39,451	375	377	5,849	413	6,190	6·1	17·0	20·7	5,737	27·0
95,261	5,736	30,835	436	397	1,766	771	1,833	1·9	5·4	6·4	3,882	USA
95,254	16,040	16,382	662	619	3,400	580	2,450	3·6	22·7	15·3	280[1]	UQ
95,194	9,206	137,600	154	137	15,212	214	13,177	16·0	11·3	9·4	3,826	122·2
95,078p.a.	2,735p.a.	21,256	567	812	552p.a.	933	1,670	0·6	3·7p.a.	32·8	2,104	I
93,942	9,230	17,122	644	638	3,707	540	2,872	3·9	25·0	21·6	6,375	15·9
93,805	7,232	59,867	287	303	12,479	240	9,976	13·3	27·0	24·5	5,853[1]	55·2
93,358	1,409	54,012	302	311	11,272	260	7,956	12·1	25·0	23·8	18,756[1]	61·8
93,338	0	12,272	764	715	1,599	799	1,974	1·7	13·5	20·2	5,011	UQ
93,326	20,800	41,651	362	355	6,203	391	10,117	6·6	16·6	30·3	5,825	24·5
93,240	17,942	57,567	293	295	8,184	325	10,023	8·8	17·1	21·7	8,077	25·0
92,780	6,634	45,670	340	362	9,822	289	8,481	10·6	27·2	¶23·5	4,054[1]	12·6
92,545	8,126	23,056	537	664	3,394	585	3,359	3·7	24·7	30·0	5,600[1]	12·9
91,508	6,457	57,218	295	375	10,832	268	9,923	11·8	31·2	35·9	2,867[1]	USA
90,975	48	15,702	681	697	4,513	476	4,955	5·0	36·2	49·5	2,100	35·3
90,969	19,481	58,565	292	307	8,556	316	8,662	9·4	18·7	19·2	4,331[1]	IT
90,396	1,575	16,971	647	686	3,449	571	3,049	3·8	26·1	29·4	2,870	14·5
90,342	14,894	41,924	357	306	8,059	328	7,489	8·9	17·6	17·7	2,124[1]	USA
89,897	31,341	29,174	453	512	6,175	394	5,519	6·9	28·6	42·3	4,449	19·9
89,507	46,437	71,632	250	252	3,400	581	5,759	3·8	5·7	10·2	4,636[1]	USA
89,014	3,794	29,155	454	422	7,995	330	7,661	9·0	27·0	29·8	3,304[1]	6·8
88,964	36,000	69,137	257	322	7,042	361	8,669	7·9	16·3	23·2	7,490[1]	13·9
88,823	3,057	39,110	377	N/A	9,350	301	6,058	10·5	26·2	17·1	3,396	GB/US
88,487	23	24,241	519	425	2,345	704	Loss 183	2·7	8·0	—	1,871[1]	USA
88,403	14,698	45,835	338	321	7,313	252	7,104	8·3	16·9	18·3	7,462	25·1
88,388	18,745	59,923	286	246	4,671	468	6,344	5·3	7·7	14·4	9,588	17·7
87,713	13,781	49,749	315	312	10,648	273	9,883	12·1	23·6	22·7	3,190	30·8
87,589	215	17,430	638	672	4,399	481	3,292	5·0	32·9	30·5	1,156	11·4
87,390	22,543	41,207	365	483	1,380	835	1,113	1·6	6·2	3·9	508	AUS
87,311	54,155	46,508	336	392	5,349	439	8,473	6·1	16·1	36·1	3,760	USA
86,951	23,951	48,018	325	351	9,992	286	8,308	11·5	26·3	24·8	5,062[1]	36·2

The following letters in the Market Capitalisation column denote unquoted companies and country of control: AUS = Australia. CI = Channel Islands. G = Germany. GB/US = Great Britain/United States of America. HOL = Holland. I = Ireland. IT = Italy. LU = Luxembourg. UQ = Unquoted. USA = United States of America.

Rank by turn-over	COMPANY	Main activity	Chairman and Managing Directors (in italics) §‖	Accounting period ended
401 (387)	Pegler-Hattersley	Manfrs. of taps & valves, etc.	J. M. Harrison, *A. L. Louden*	1– 4–78
402 (383)	Baker Perkins Holdings	Machinery manufacturers	I. H. G. Gilbert, *J. F. M. Braithwaite*	31– 3–78
403 (381)	Alexander Howden Group	Insurance brokers, shipping agents	K. V. Grob	31–12–78
404 (616)	E. G. Cornelius & Co.	Commodity merchants	W. R. Pick, *W. E. Brown*	30– 6–77
405 (368)	Howden Group	Engineers, gas & air handling plant	Sir Norman Elliott, *J. D. H. Hume*	30– 4–78
406 (424)	Interntl. Synthetic Rubber	Synthetic rubber manfrs., etc.	D. A. Bennett	31–12–77
407 (384)	Harp Lager	Manfr. & sale of lagers	C. E. Guinness (M.D.)	30– 9–78
408 (456)	Hewden-Stuart Plant	Plant hirers and sellers	F. Jamieson	28– 1–79
409 (420)	Wedgwood	Fine bone china & earthenware, etc.	Sir Arthur Bryan (J.M.D.), *P. Williams*	31– 3–79
410 (449)	Volvo Trucks Great Britain	Commercial vehicle dealers	L. Malmros, *S. A. Olson*	31–12–78
411 (411)	Andrew Weir & Co.	Shipping, insurance, etc.	Lord Inverforth	31–12–78
412 (443)	Armstrong Equipment	Vehicle suspension units, etc.	J. H. Hooper (M.D.)	2– 7–78
413 (401)	Portals Holdings	Papermaking, water treatment, & eng.	J. J. L. G. Sheffield, *J. W. Mather*	31–12–78
414 (374)	Fredk. H. Burgess	Agricultural engineers	H. F. Burgess, *A. F. Burgess*	31–12–78
415 (395)	Vantona Group	Household textiles, etc.	J. D. Spooner	1–12–78
416 (448)	J. E. Sanger	Meat traders	J. E. Sanger	30– 6–78
417 (458)	Corrie MacColl and Son	Commodity dealers	D. F. MacColl	30–11–77
418 (427)	Spar Food Holdings	Food marketing	G. M. Mellis, *A. R. Jones*	29– 4–78
419 (440)	Brown Boveri Kent (Holdings)	Industrial instrument makers, etc.	J. G. Vaughan	31–12–78
420 (549)	Whessoe	Engineers, etc.	Lord Erroll of Hale	30– 9–78
421 (441)	Shepherd Building Group	Building and ancillary activities	Sir Peter Shepherd	30– 6–78
422 (439)	Hillards	Supermarket operators	G. N. Hunter, *P. A. H. Hartley*	29– 4–78
423 (421)	J. H. Fenner & Co. (Holdings)	Power transmission engineers	J. Palmer	2– 9–78
424 (426)	Robertson Foods	Food industry	R. C. Robertson, *G. Cunliffe*	31– 3–79
425 (364)	Turner Curzon³¹	Forest products, engineering, etc.	C. J. Sim, *P. J. B. Dixon*	31– 3–78
426 (588)	Lummus Co.	Refinery engineers	G. R. Lawrence	31–12–77
427 (697)	Moutafian Commodities	Commodity merchants & brokers	A. N. Moutafian (M.D.)	31–12–78
428 (415)	Howard Machinery	Farm machinery manufacturers	P. Coleclough	31–10–78
429 (467)	Ibstock Johnsen	Brick manfrs. & wood pulp agents	P. C. Hyde-Thomson	31–12–78
430 (428)	Black & Decker	Power tool manufacturers	J. C. Brooman	24– 9–78
431 (610)	Holco Trading Co.	Produce merchants	W. A. Davies, *I. E. J. Foster, C. C. B. Morris*	31–12–77
432 (431)	Henry Boot & Sons	Construction engineers, etc.	E. H. Boot (J.M.D.), *D. H. Boot*	31–12–78
433 (436)	Hall Engineering (Holdings)	General engineering	R. N. C. Hall (M.D.)	31–12–78
434 (333)	Associated Fisheries	Trawling, eng., food, cold storage, etc.	H. K. Fitzgerald	30– 9–78
435 (446)	Vaux Breweries	Brewers	P. D. Nicholson (M.D.)	30– 9–78
436 (544)	Frank Fehr & Co.	Produce merchants & brokers	B. H. F. Fehr (M.D.)	31–12–77
437 (409)	NCR	Data processing eqpmt. acctg. machns.	C. E. Reynolds, *R. M. Fleet*	30–11–78
438 (452)	Martin the Newsagent	Newsagents, tobacconists, etc.	J. B. H. Martin (M.D.)	1–10–78
439 (474)	Edward Billington & Son	Food merchants, etc.	J. Billington	30– 4–77
440 (531)	Laker Airways (Internl.)	Air tour operators, hoteliers, etc.	Sir Freddie Laker (M.D.)	31– 3–78
441 (380)	Morris & David Jones	Distributors & food processors	J. D. Fletcher (C.E.)	31–12–77
442 (483)	Godfrey Davis	Car hire specialists, Ford main dlrs.	C. A. Redfern (M.D.)	31– 3–78
443 (465)	Raybeck	Retailers of ladies' & men's wear	B. Raven, *A. Simons, H. Davies*	29– 4–78
444 (340)	Entores	Metal merchants	R. Marbot (M.D.)	31–12–77
445 (432)	Inveresk Group	Paper manufacturers	T. S. Corrigan (M.D.)	31–12–78
446 (471)	Singer Co. (UK)	Sewing machines, h/hold elec. eqpmt.	J. M. Wotherspoon	31–12–77
447 (529)	Merck Sharp & Dohme (Hldgs.)	Manufacturing chemists	B. J. Crowley	31–12–77
448 (526)	James Finlay & Co.	International traders & financiers	Sir Colin Campbell	31–12–77
449 (414)	Agricultural Holdings Co.	Electronics, seeds & commodities, etc.	G. Balint (M.D.)	3– 6–78
450 (457)	Unicorn Industries	Grinding wheels & abrasives	B. G. Ball-Greene	10–12–78

NOTES: *Total tangible assets less current liabilities (other than bank loans and overdrafts and future tax).   †As percentage of capital employed at beginning of the year.   ‡As at 13 July 1979.   §Appendix on page 70 gives list of Managing Directors whose names cannot be fitted into the main text.   ‖M.D. = Managing Director; J.M.D. = Joint Managing Director; A.C. = Acting Chairman; C.E. = Chief Executive.   ¶As percentage of capital employed at end of the year.   N/A Not available.¹   UK only.
²¹57% of turnover sold overseas.   ³¹Now a sub. co. of S. & W. Berisford Ltd.

TURNOVER Total £000	Export £000	*CAPITAL EMPLOYED £000	Rank Latest year	Rank Previous year	Latest year £000	Rank	Previous year £000	% to turnover Latest year	†% to capital employed Latest year	Previous year	**No. of employees	‡Equity market cap. £M.
86,825	22,800	76,366	233	229	12,879	237	18,763	14·8	18·8	35·1	7,188	39·6
86,500	30,552	48,008	326	316	9,710	293	9,123	11·2	22·0	23·5	6,504	39·2
86,482	—	85,327	216	276	19,712	169	21,940	22·8	36·4	54·0	2,870[1]	73·5
85,297	40,790	2,708	972	988	629	920	531	0·7	30·5	31·6	—	UQ
85,205	9,929	33,975	408	333	6,202	392	6,346	7·3	14·9	16·1	4,491	19·2
84,755	26,270	41,665	361	376	Loss 826	983	4,849	—	—	22·1	988[1]	UQ
84,749	111	40,028	370	358	7,707	337	7,850	9·1	20·8	28·3	433[1]	UQ
84,409	438	51,814	310	331	8,327	320	5,812	9·9	19·9	18·7	3,729	38·1
84,202[21]	—	60,302	284	289	10,162	282	9,228	12·1	20·6	23·2	9,688[1]	32·5
84,040	4,780	28,044	470	503	6,772	373	5,527	8·1	30·7	28·4	472	SW
83,890	—	199,202	110	111	3,199	611	10,876	3·8	1·9	7·4	3,580	UQ
83,655	6,988	49,692	316	342	9,688	295	7,384	11·6	24·7	25·1	4,571[1]	29·4
82,944	27,913	47,200	331	353	9,969	287	9,145	12·0	26·6	27·0	4,353	44·3
82,736	5,407	33,615	413	410	5,073	454	4,686	6·1	16·6	26·7	2,647[1]	UQ
82,429	10,673	40,904	367	371	7,711	336	7,655	9·4	21·7	24·6	9,996[1]	24·4
82,265p.a.	1,938p.a.	10,426	809	759	150p.a.	965	1,725	0·2	1·4p.a.	31·1	551[1]	3·1
82,243	—	4,613	945	950	1,535	811	1,290	1·9	39·8	58·5	—	HOL
81,200	—	34	1000	1000	10	973	13	0·0	29·4	38·2	—	UQ
81,117	25,000	47,351	330	337	8,609	315	7,604	10·6	21·5	20·8	6,203	24·4
81,085	10,469	23,687	526	493	3,504	562	4,060	4·3	15·6	20·5	4,284	12·0
80,600	7,641	19,759	590	624	4,343	489	4,854	5·4	27·8	41·4	4,932	UQ
80,569	0	10,262	815	839	2,569	675	2,559	3·2	32·6	44·1	2,954	20·2
80,531	11,924	46,969	332	336	10,083	285	9,560	12·5	24·6	25·4	7,906	33·4
80,140	5,494	24,500	515	453	3,264	604	3,777	4·1	12·7	19·9	3,060[1]	17·0
79,109	306	8,256	868	797	974	883	1,643	1·2	11·8	19·2	711	—[31]
79,008	7,630	6,017	915	978	3,901	520	2,287	4·9	194·9	192·8	1,276	USA
78,894	—	6,610	900	977	2,418	698	2,180	3·1	49·8	107·9	—	UQ
78,460	14,607	34,108	407	363	4,143	499	3,496	5·3	11·5	9·5	3,090	8·6
78,275	—	39,140	376	472	5,984	405	4,835	7·6	24·9	24·1	2,488	14·9
78,238	34,183	38,017	384	394	9,322	302	8,833	11·9	28·2	25·1	3,370[1]	USA
78,133	—	2,399	976	973	603	924	500	0·8	27·7	28·2	—	HOL
77,957	1,538	16,321	664	562	Loss 3,647	993	2,181	—	—	11·3	4,237	4·8
77,618	3,782	31,926	426	417	6,062	400	5,494	7·8	20·3	19·3	2,647[1]	16·0
76,964	6,000	29,793	450	387	Loss 2,247	990	5,634	—	—	16·7	4,807	7·9
76,950	12	53,580	304	293	8,660	313	7,049p.a.	11·3	17·9	15·7p.a.	7,148	50·6
76,917	34,625	3,610	955	960	929	886	632	1·2	25·7	25·8	—	UQ
76,649	22,600	51,796	311	304	11,133	263	4,689	14·5	24·2	¶10·2	4,200[1]	USA
76,516	0	9,796	828	800	3,263	605	3,033	4·3	36·7	50·5	11,200	16·8
76,281	3,288	3,705	953	941	583	928	492	0·8	15·6	17·4	460[1]	UQ
75,985	—	42,915	353	458	4,100	503	3,077	5·4	16·1	11·0	1,406	UQ
75,959	82	16,204	665	647	2,868	649	1,052	3·8	19·8	10·4	1,898[1]	USA
75,910	128	25,743	498	548	4,871	463	3,901	6·4	24·4	17·9	2,326	14·4
75,496	5,365	21,168	569	601	6,411	386	4,665	8·5	37·8	34·0	4,043	42·1
75,405	4,565	10,583	798	809	595	927	1,391	0·8	6·9	28·9	—	FR
75,372	5,600	35,751	397	447	2,036	746	3,168	2·7	7·7	13·7	3,268[1]	7·7
74,721	46,259	30,341	443	380	Loss 946	984	3,295	—	—	8·6	8,009	USA
74,586	26,553	73,347	246	274	18,899	174	10,341	25·3	34·8	27·6	1,189[1]	USA
74,407	1,117	71,234	252	280	17,077	185	12,595	23·0	32·1	¶23·7	1,121[1]	36·3
74,273	10,336	24,828	512	573	3,867	521	4,322	5·2	20·7	31·9	1,164[1]	UQ
73,467	15,739	49,900	314	323	8,647	314	7,753	11·8	20·1	18·6	4,502	30·7

The following letters in the Market Capitalisation column denote unquoted companies and country of control: FR = France. HOL = Holland. SW = Sweden. UQ = Unquoted. USA = United States of America.

Rank by turn-over	COMPANY	Main activity	Chairman and Managing Directors (in italics) § ‖	Accounting period ended
451 (535)	Travis & Arnold	Builders' merchants & timber imptrs.	E. R. Travis, *E. R. A. Travis, C. G. Porter*	31-12-78
452 (454)	Giltspur	Industrial services group	M. Joseph, *T. E. D. Harker*	31- 3-78
453 (572)	Dexion-Comino International	Storage & materials hndlg. eqpmt.	S. Hinchliff (M.D.)	29-10-78
454 (495)	Whitworths Holdings	Food products	W. A. George (J.M.D.), *H. Reynolds*	31- 3-77
455 (423)	Bakelite Xylonite	Chemical & plastics mfrs.	A. McIntosh, *P. H. M. Sharrock*	31-12-77
456 (403)	Green Shield Trading Stamp	Trading stamp dealers	G. R. F. Tompkins (M.D.)	5-11-77
457 (399)	Smurfit	Mfr. & sale of paper prodts., printing	F. S. Hayes	31- 1-78
458 (400)	Oriel Foods	Distbn. & processing of foodstuffs	J. D. Fletcher (C.E.)	31-12-77
459 (481)	Kimberly-Clark	Cellulose wadding products	R. C. Ernest, *D. G. Croxon*	31-12-77
460 (442)	Hickson & Welch (Holdings)	Manfrs. of chemical products, etc.	T. Harrington, *J. D. Horner*	30- 9-78
461 (386)	John Swire & Sons	Shipowners, etc.	J. A. Swire	31-12-77
462 (503)	Combined English Stores Grp.	Multiple specialist retailing group	M. Gordon (J.M.D.), *E. J. De Winter*	27- 1-79
463 (486)	Brown Brothers Corpn.	Motor accessories, etc. distbn. & manf.	E. G. Spearing	30- 6-78
464 (596)	Newman Industries	Electrical, foundries & gen. eng., etc.	A. F. Bartlett	31-12-78
465 (433)	C. Walker & Sons	Steel stockholders	F. Walker, *J. Riley*	31- 5-77
466 (497)	Govan Shipbuilders	Shipbuilders	A. Gilchrist (M.D.)	31- 3-78
467 (451)	A. Monk & Co.	Civil eng. & building contractors, etc.	W. S. Whittingham (M.D.)	28- 2-78
468 (459)	Central & Sheerwood	Fin. service, eng., printing, publishing	F. A. Singer	31-12-78
469 (385)	Alcoa of Great Britain	Smelters & fabricators of aluminium	D. R. Norland	31-12-78
470 (470)	Ward White Group	Footwear manfrs, elect. & mech. engrs.	G. E. McWatters, *P. Birch*	31-12-78
471 (491)	Scottish & Universal Invs.	Printing & publishing, whisky, etc.	R. W. Rowland	1- 4-78
472 (522)	B. Elliott & Co.	Machine tool manufacturers	F. M. Russell, *M. J. Beer*	31- 3-78
473 (479)	Brockhouse	Eng., transport, bldg. & mtrls. handling	R. J. H. Parkes (M.D.)	30- 9-78
474 (445)	Badger	Managers, consultants, etc.	R. E. Siegfried, *M. J. Gordon*	30-11-77
475 (473)	Westinghouse Brake & Signal[36]	Electrical & mechanical engineers	L. E. Thompson, *D. Pollock*	30- 9-78
476 (425)	Firestone Tyre & Rubber Co.	Tyre manufacturers	G. W. Webber (M.D.)	31-10-78
477 (548)	Foster Bros. Clothing Co.	Clothiers, tailors & outfitters	H. G. High, *B. G. Davison*	28- 2-79
478 (628)	Reuters	International news organisation	Sir Denis Hamilton, *G. Long*	31-12-78
479 (488)	Ductile Steels	Steel production	R. Sidaway, *C. J. Baker*	1- 7-78
480 (468)	Stewart Wrightson Holdings	Insurance & ship brokers, etc.	E. J. G. Henry	31-12-78
481 (453)	John Folkes Hefo	Eng., merchanting, housing	J. W. Hearnshaw	31-12-78
482 (494)	United Baltic Corpn.	Shipowners & merchants	Lord Inverforth	31-12-77
483 (—)	Elf Aquitaine UK (Holdings)	Gas & condensate prod. oil & gas exp.	J. Pavard, *C. Menetrier*	31-12-78
484 (778)	Aurora Holdings	General & precision engineers	R. Atkinson, *A. A. Watt*	31-12-78
485 (455)	Grampian Holdings	Construction, trnspt., plant hire, eng.	D. C. Greig	31-12-78
486 (476)	Tennants Consolidated	Chemical manufacturers	K. A. Alexander	31-12-77
487 (519)	BASF United Kingdom	Chemical products, etc.	F. Schuster, *W. Maack*	31-12-77
488 (530)	Millford Grain	Grain merchants	C. J. Priday	31- 3-78
489 (562)	Crane Fruehauf	Commercial vehicle body manfrs.	W. E. Grace, *G. F. Malley*	31-12-77
490 (434)	Robert M. Douglas Holdings	Civil eng. & building contractors	J. R. T. Douglas (M.D.)	31- 3-78
491 (517)	Daily Telegraph	Newspaper proprietors	Lord Hartwell, *H. M. Stephen*	31- 3-78
492 (527)	Allied Retailers[34]	Retailers of carpets & furniture	H. Plotnek	1- 4-78
493 (499)	George Wills & Sons (Hldgs)	Importers & exporters	J. Reynolds	31-12-78
494 (514)	F. J. C. Lilley	Civil eng. & public works contrs.	J. Aitken, *T. M. Bisset*	31- 1-79
495 (508)	Donald MacPherson Group	Paint & other surface coatings	R. Chester, *H. K. Cushing*	29-10-78
496 (480)	Trident Television	Television programme contractors etc.	G. E. Ward Thomas (M.D.)	30- 9-78
497 (478)	Amos. Hinton & Sons	Retail food stores	D. A. Hinton, *W. P. C. Hinton*	3- 3-79
498 (477)	Polaroid (U.K.)	Photographic & optical eqpmt. distbn.	H. Allen	31-12-77
499 (475)	Caravans International	Caravan manufacturers	S. Alper, *E. J. B. Timlin*	31- 8-78
500 (507)	Amalg. Power Engineering	Steam turbines, diesel engines, etc.	H. A. Whittall, *J. G. Ryder*	31-12-78

NOTES: *Total tangible assets less current liabilities (other than bank loans and overdrafts and future tax).   †As percentage of capital employed at beginning of the year.   ‡As at 13 July 1979.   §Appendix on page 70 gives list of Managing Directors whose names cannot be fitted into the main text.   ‖M.D. = Managing Director; J.M.D. = Joint Managing Director; A.C. = Acting Chairman; C.E. = Chief Executive.   ¶As percentage of capital employed at end of the year.   N/A Not available.   ¹UK only.   [34]Now a sub. co. of Associated Dairies Group Ltd.   [36]Now a sub. co. of Hawker Siddeley Group Ltd.

TURNOVER Total £000	Export £000	*CAPITAL EMPLOYED £000	Rank Latest year	Rank Previous year	NET PROFIT BEFORE INTEREST AND TAX Latest year £000	Rank	Previous year £000	% to turnover Latest year	†% to capital employed Latest year	Previous year	**No. of employees	‡Equity market cap. £M.
73,421	—	30,516	440	459	4,888	462	3,915	6·7	19·4	18.9	2,144	17·5
73,397	1,837	23,490	530	460	4,378	486	3,488	6·0	17·5	12·9	3,028[1]	15·4
72,630	14,367	30,262	444	585	6,801	370	6,121	9·4	30·5	34·3	1,510[1]	USA
72,339	728	23,094	535	633	4,951	459	2,307	6·8	32·9	14·7	1,469[1]	UQ
72,264	11,378	50,978	312	278	3,646	548	4,230	5·0	6·8	9·0	4,272	USA
72,077	—	37,524	386	326	272	957	3,652	0·4	0·6	9·0	3,490[1]	UQ
71,929	1,323	29,138	455	434	7,137	357	6,559	9·9	25·7	¶23·6	2,925[1]	I
71,901	913	12,041	768	748	984	880	1,430	1·4	9·1	14·8	874[1]	USA
71,722	6,529	34,124	406	449	6,796	371	5,407	9·5	26·0	25·2	2,518	USA
71,451	25,300	43,347	351	352	8,519	318	10,530	11·9	22·6	34·4	2,369[1]	35·8
71,324	—	151,089	143	153	28,630	120	21,103	40·1	23·8	26·5	—	UQ
71,014	406	19,239	601	597	6,014	402	4,055	8·5	35·1	27·1	4,169	17·1
70,841p.a.	2,671p.a.	19,574	593	677	3,303p.a.	595	2,395	4·7	25·2p.a.	17·6	3,220[1]	11·5
70,800	26,123	42,779	354	462	8,532	317	5,291	12·1	¶19·9	24·9	5,906	17·1
70,789	5,074	30,933	433	407	6,177	393	2,530	8·7	24·4	13·5	1,050[1]	UQ
70,741p.a.	70,655p.a.	18,734	614	537	Loss 13,906p.a.	1000	Loss 2,906p.a.	—	—	—	5,553[1]	UQ
70,700	26	13,104	739	706	5,058	455	2,738	7·2	41·1	26·4	3,824	6·5
70,454	12,288	35,694	398	455	6,613	379	5,389	9·4	25·9	21·8	4,239	21·1
70,341	6,806	70,434	255	218	Loss 8,789	999	468	—	—	0·7	2,093[1]	USA
69,976	6,418	24,474	516	530	5,669	419	4,279	8·1	27·5	22·3	4,922[1]	10·1
69,761	7,214	52,419	307	319	6,859	367	4,735	9·8	15·7	12·9	4,418[1]	65·9
69,627	11,016	25,460	505	547	6,074	398	4,705	8·7	30·4	27·5	2,671[1]	35·6
69,376	10,657	32,957	424	409	4,398	482	3,422	6·3	14·3	11·6	3,721[1]	11·6
69,266	511	997	992	989	216	961	343	0·3	15·4	28·4	574	USA
68,981	15,258	49,193	317	330	7,388	348	6,881	10·7	17·5	19·2	4,865[1]	—[36]
67,887	5,996	32,878	420	396	5,457	997	267	0·0	0·0	0·9	4,542	USA
67,824	199	27,527	474	505	9,536	299	5,234	14·1	43·5	26·8	4,164	53·0
67,712	—	21,433	564	745	1,094	869	2,781	1·6	6·9	35·2	2,537	UQ
67,696	3,433	36,432	391	430	5,572	425	6,169	8·2	19·4	28·7	2,351[1]	13·5
67,550	0	33,736	412	384	11,939	246	9,690	17·7	35·5	31·0	2,633[1]	29·3
67,465	5,883	22,621	543	516	4,211	494	4,001	6·2	19·6	21·0	3,169	16·9
67,198	3,047	33,144	417	564	1,364	837	3,501	2·0	7·1	20·3	193[1]	UQ
66,981	—	513,889	39	—	5,988	404	61,691	8·9	1·2	¶12·0	—	FR
66,624	7,914	44,966	344	590	5,860	410	3,082	8·8	33·3	25·4	3,913	14·0
66,520	8,454	18,919	610	533	1,797	768	1,774	2·7	8·8	9·5	3,566	6·6
66,386	6,956	25,540	502	502	5,115	451	5,051	7·7	23·1	28·6	1,199	UQ
66,333	0	22,357	547	510	1,599	798	1,731	2·4	7·4	10·0	668[1]	G
66,164	1,545	131	999	998	23	970	44	0·0	17·2	29·7	—	UQ
65,991	12,630	15,851	677	642	1,445	827	2,636	2·2	9·8	18·3	3,078[1]	USA
65,965	5,259	17,381	640	641	2,619	668	3,064	4·0	17·8	24·0	3,322[1]	7·1
65,813	1,864	9,582	833	833	3,418	576	1,310	5·2	42·6	16·0	3,197	UQ
65,694	318	16,833	650	646	5,044	456	3,840	7·7	34·8	36·5	2,501	—[34]
65,500	8,600	6,177	912	916	1,291	845	1,196	2·0	27·0	29·4	186[1]	2·9
65,496	1,300	16,958	648	662	4,260	493	3,165	6·5	30·7	37·7	2,365	14·4
65,490	3,348	24,091	522	501	4,764	464	3,903	7·3	21·5	23·3	2·712[1]	18·1
65,356	1,380	28,383	464	464	9,044	306	7,621	93·8	36·5	51·0	2,052[1]	29·6
65,338	—	8,549	855	876	1,322	841	1,788	2·0	20·0	31·6	2,342	4·3
65,163	42,000	27,251	479	515	5,423	435	10,183	8·3	25·3	48·3	1,648	USA
64,951	8,466	12,007	769	735	3,785	532	4,708	5·8	33·8	51·7	2,950	5·8
64,771	28,059	30,415	441	436	7,355	349	6,867	11·4	27·6	35·2	3,684	13·7

The following letters in the Market Capitalisation column denote unquoted companies and country of control: FR = France. G = Germany. I = Ireland. UQ = Unquoted. USA = United States of America.

Rank by turn-over	COMPANY	Main activity	Chairman and Managing Directors (in italics) §‖	Accounting period ended
501 (490)	Sale Tilney & Co.	Industrial plant mfrs, food distbtrs.	R. King, *R. T. Allsop*	30–11–78
502 (469)	Mersey Docks and Harbour	Operation of port facilities, etc.	Sir Arthur Peterson, *J. B. Fitzpatrick*	31–12–78
503 (492)	HAT Group	Specialist sub-contrs. to bldg. ind.	A. C. V. Telling, *D. M. Telling*	28– 2–78
504 (493)	Watson & Philip	Distribution of foodstuffs	D. C. Greig, *H. V. Gardner*	27–10–78
505 (489)	Lennons Group	Retail foodstuffs, wine & spirits	D. P. Lennon, *J. W. Bolton*	1– 4–78
506 (534)	Sheepbridge Engineering	Engineering	Lord Aberconway, *H. Gunner*	31– 3–79
507 (461)	Uniroyal	Rubber, plastic & chemical products	D. Beretta, *A. J. Stuart*	1– 1–78
508 (460)	F. H. Lloyd Holdings	Steel founders & mnfrs. of eng. prods.	R. H. Foster	31– 3–79
509 (462)	Arthur Lee & Sons	Steel manufacturing	H. P. Forder, *P. W. Lee*	30– 9–78
510 (472)	Telefusion	Renting, retail sale of radio & TV	J. N. Wilkinson (M.D.)	29– 4–78
511 (558)	Gillette UK	Razor & blade manufacturers, etc.	R. H. Burton, *R. S. Mills*	30–11–77
512 (623)	James Miller & Partners	Bldg. & civil engineering	J. Miller (M.D.)	31–12–77
513 (520)	Y. J. Lovell (Holdings)	Building contractors, etc.	Sir Peter Trench, *N. E. Wakefield*	30– 9–78
514 (685)	Rionda, De Pass	Sugar dealers	J. M. Fox, *R. M. Beatson*	31–12–77
515 (927)	Henry Stephens & Sons (Lon.)	Importers & exporters	J. E. Aldridge (A.C., M.D.)	31– 7–77
516 (556)	Wm. Low & Co.	Supermarket operators	A. M. Drysdale	2– 9–78
517 (543)	Lopex	A marketing communications group	C. J. N. Sykes	31–12–78
518 (515)	Selincourt	Textiles, lace & fashion garments	L. L. Leighton, *D. V. Pick*	31– 1–79
519 (516)	Rush & Tompkins Group	Propty., invest., bldg. & civil eng., etc.	D. J. Palmar.	31–12–78
520 (564)	Texas Instruments	Electronic component manufacturers	J. W. W. Peyton, *R. W. Wilmot*	31–12–78
521 (524)	Wm. Collins & Son (Holding)	Publishers, etc.	W. J. Collins, *D. W. Nickson*	31–12–78
522 (464)	M. Golodetz	Produce brokers	N/A	31–12–77
523 (511)	Aspro-Nicholas	Pharmaceuticals, chemists, etc.	R. R. Walker	30– 6–78
524 (542)	Rentokil Group	Timber preservation, pest control, etc.	W. H. Westphal, *B. McGillivray*	31–12–78
525 (485)	Revertex Chemicals	Rubber latex & synthetic resins	Sir Campbell Adamson, *K. Bushell*	31–12–78
526 (513)	Carlsberg Brewery	Brewers	P. J. Svanholm, *M. C. Iuul*	30– 9–77
527 (505)	Central Manfg. & Trading Grp.	Asbestos, rubber, plastics & all prod.	N. A. Hickman	31– 7–78
528 (799)	Citroën Cars	Vehicle importers & distributors	X. Karcher, *P. Brun-Wibaux*	31–12–77
529 (502)	Ward & Goldstone	Manfrs. of cables, elec. access., etc.	S. Goldstone, *M. H. Goldstone*	31– 3–78
530 (547)	Conder International	Construction of pre-fab buildings	R. T. Cole	31–12–78
531 (540)	Dorada Holdings	Motor sales & sevice, engineers, etc.	T. Kenny, *T. G. Shipton*	31–12–78
532 (510)	Prestige Group	Domestic houseware manufacturers	D. J. T. Lawman (M.D.)	31–12–77
533 (498)	Sulzer Bros. (UK)	General eng., paper mach., pumping in.	P. J. Strangeway, *W. R. Walton*	31–12–78
534 (509)	Quaker Oats	Grocery products, chemicals & toys	R. G. Lagden, *G. J. Yapp*	30– 6–78
535 (563)	Barr & Wallace Arnold Trust	Holidays & travel, motor dlrs., etc.	J. M. Barr	31–12–78
536 (575)	Lilly Industries	Pharmaceuticals, etc.	M. Perelman, *R. A. Bailey*	31–12–77
537 (619)	Saatchi & Saatchi Company	Advertising agency	J. K. Gill	30– 9–78
538 (550)	A. Oppenheimer & Co.	Export merchants & agents	J. Levison, *R. P. Adler* (J.C.)	31–12–76
539 (500)	Hestair	Special vehicles, consumer prodts, etc.	D. Hargreaves	31– 1–79
540 (657)	Smith Kline & French Labs.	Pharmaceutical manufacturers	J. M. Weaver, *L. N. A. Flockhart*	30–11–78
541 (422)	General Motors Scotland	Earthmoving equipment manfrs.	G. B. Heaney (M.D.)	31–12–77
542 (554)	Edgar Allen, Balfour	Steel makers & engineers	J. D. Oakley, *G. W. Wise*	1– 4–78
543 (578)	Marshall's Universal	General industrial group	R. L. Doughty, *J. A. Oliver*	31–12–78
544 (487)	Sedgwick Forbes Bland Payne	Insurance brokers, underwtg. agents	N. Mills, *P. T. Wright*	31–12–78
545 (652)	M & R–Martini & Rossi	Wine merchants	*Duke of Marlborough, I. G. Cottle*	31–12–77
546 (603)	Sandvik	Steel products	G. V. L. Ollen	31–12–77
547 (681)	John Silver Holdings	Meat importers & wholesalers	M. J. Silver (M.D.)	1– 7–78
548 (727)	P. L. Group (Foods)	Traders of oil & fat products	I. S. Hutcheson	2– 4–78
549 (560)	United Newspapers	Newspaper proprietors	Lord Barnetson (M.D.)	31–12–78
550 (612)	Lookers	Motor vehicle distbs. and engineers	R. E. Tongue, *W. K. Martindale*	30– 9–78

NOTES: *Total tangible assets less current liabilities (other than bank loans and overdrafts and future tax).   †As percentage of capital employed at beginning of the year.   ‡As at 13 July 1979.   §Appendix on page 70 gives list of Managing Directors whose names cannot be fitted into the main text.   ‖M.D. = Managing Director; J.M.D. = Joint Managing Director; A.C. = Acting Chairman. J.C. = Joint Chairman; C.E. = Chief Executive.   ¶As percentage of capital employed at end of the year.   N/A Not available.   ¹UK only.   ²Acting as principal. £7m, acting as agent, £11m.

TURNOVER Total £000	Export £000	*CAPITAL EMPLOYED £000	Rank Latest year	Rank Previous year	NET PROFIT BEFORE INTEREST AND TAX Latest year £000	Rank	Previous year £000	% to turnover Latest year	†% to capital employed Latest year	†% to capital employed Previous year	No. of **employees	‡Equity market cap. £M.
64,439	4,992	18,148	622	679	2,724	661	2,410	4·2	21·0	19·1	873[1]	9·3
64,418	—	89,341	210	176	3,383	586	8,833	5·3	3·5	9·6	8,094	—
64,357	586	12,912	748	709	2,138	735	3,126	3·3	17·6	34·5	9,743	13·6
64,218	0	5,486	930	923	909	891	1,193	1·4	20·0	33·1	848	3·8
64,118	0	8,194	870	774	1,697	783	1,766	2·6	17·1	33·2	1,989	9·4
63,836	12,825	33,243	415	492	5,312	441	5,855	8·3	17·9	26·1	5,391	36·4
63,654	20,028	26,811	485	441	2,084	742	3,524	3·3	10·0	22·2	2,969[1]	USA
63,510	8,338	33,955	409	408	3,586	555	5,341	5·6	11·1	17·4	5,261	14·9
63,418	3,379	31,363	430	423	2,978	626	4,701	4·7	10·1	18·0	2,375[1]	6·2
63,398	579	25,241	507	494	2,972	628	3,952	4·7	13·3	20·4	3,265[1]	20·2
62,933	28,625	35,377	401	432	5,451	433	1,774	8·7	19·1	6·6	3,144	USA
62,775	—	18,225	621	653	2,870	648	3,213	4·6	20·1	28·3	2,545	UQ
62,670	0	20,207	586	574	2,626	667	2,201	4·2	14·2	17·4	2,226	7·9
62,653	0	2,003	982	985	684	914	1,023	1·1	38·6	15·4	—	USA
62,166	5,451	735	994	997	367	945	108	0·6	85·2	27·6	—	UQ
62,074	0	6,991	890	868	1,485	823	1,833	2·4	12·9	33·7	3,478	8·3
62,003	—	9,040	842	826	2,428	696	1,958	3·9	29·4	22·9	700[1]	UQ
61,915	8,017	29,443	451	486	5,732	415	5,436	9·3	25·1	27·0	3,664[1]	13·7
61,231	0	38,520	381	339	2,300	711	2,554	3·8	5·8	7·7	1,946[1]	15·2
60,638	13,193	20,751	574	527	971	885	Loss 104	1·6	4·7	—	2,655[1]	USA
60,631	12,267	45,748	339	327	5,374	437	4,414	8·9	14·1	12·5	2,929[1]	17·3
60,600	18,000[2]	6,083	913	855	1,591	800	2,889	2·6	22·0	61·0	—[1]	UQ
60,583	7,934	25,540	501	487	8,218	323	6,224	13·6	36·0	29·2	1,261[1]	AUS
60,440	4,092	29,063	456	475	10,824	269	8,775	17·9	45·9	42·6	3,078[1]	97·2
60,348	7,314	22,492	544	538	3,304	594	3,491	5·5	16·3	20·5	1,884	7·1
60,277	—	42,368	356	346	5,990	403	5,083	9·9	14·9	20·0	730	DEN
60,094	1,040	32,223	423	442	4,398	483	4,619	7·3	16·5	20·5	2,385[1]	21·2
60,003	629	18,613	615	816	3,067	620	803	5·1	22·2	9·6	264[1]	FR
59,999	12,444	28,451	462	456	3,806	527	4,511	6·3	13·4	22·7	6,584[1]	15·1
59,896	15,982	9,698	830	806	808	904	2,017	1·3	9·3	28·0	1,892[1]	UQ
59,772	769	11,811	773	761	1,933	756	1,696	3·2	18·8	16·5	1,634	3·9
59,515	9,739	25,068	508	498	7,318	351	6,667	12·3	32·9	33·8	3,850	36·3
59,512	6,735	14,016	714	645	3,300	596	977	5·5	22·6	4·9	1,700[1]	SWZ
59,371	3,587	21,739	559	544	3,413	577	2,331	5·7	17·0	15·0	1,709	USA
59,356	29	12,699	744	739	2,699	663	1,923	4·5	24·5	26·5	1,824	7·2
59,134	32,272	42,920	352	404	10,085	284	10,332	17·1	32·1	34·6	2,340	USA
59,120	—	2,517	975	983	1,910	758	1,211	3·2	107·3	83·1	644	7·0
58,997	1,325	19,678	591	612	6,476	382	4,603	11·0	40·0	33·3	1,301	UQ
58,968	16,770	19,766	589	625	1,134	862	5,040	1·9	7·3	43·0	3,075	7·1
58,816	20,887	44,417	347	467	21,585	156	11,103	36·7	87·3	76·0	1,110[1]	USA
58,642	27,590	41,775	358	309	7,563	344	7,717	12·9	16·6	23·0	2,097[1]	USA
58,538	11,040	37,618	385	357	3,230	609	1,931	5·5	8·7	5·2	4,545[1]	12·9
58,489	266	16,059	671	661	4,527	474	3,822	7·7	32·5	39·6	2,203	7·4
58,379	—	40,409	369	386	25,256	140	23,387	43·3	75·5	82·4	2,188[1]	168·2
58,064	3	11,864	772	752	2,895	645	1,536	5·0	19·8	14·5	229	IT/SWZ
58,047	7,599	30,808	437	461	5,449	434	3,522	9·4	21·9	15·3	2,138	SW
57,732	672	3,285	963	976	981	881	730	1·7	42·7	35·8	174	UQ
57,723	2,332	91,620	777	917	2,176	731	1,908	3·8	28·7	40·0	236	UQ
57,396	466	27,400	476	465	6,859	368	5,576	12·0	28·0	25·3	5,447	25·4
57,272	126	12,368	762	776	2,278	715	1,779	4·0	23·1	27·7	1,093	3·9

The following letters in the Market Capitalisation column denote unquoted companies and country of control: AUS = Australia.   DEN = Denmark.   FR = France.
IT/SWZ = Italy/Switzerland.   SW. = Sweden.   SWZ = Switzerland.   UQ = Unquoted.   USA = United States of America.

Rank by turn-over	COMPANY	Main activity	Chairman and Managing Directors (in italics) §‖	Accounting period ended
551 (525)	Diamond Shamrock Europe	Chemicals for industrial purposes	F. A. Russell	30–11–78
552 (450)	Bryant Holdings	Bldg. contrs. & civil eng., prop. devpt.	A. C. Bryant (M.D.)	31– 5–78
553 (592)	Lee Cooper Group	Casual clothing mfrs. & distributors	H. C. Cooper, *P. Pouillot*	31–12–78
554 (429)	European Grain & Shipping	Merchants & brokers	H. André	31–12–77
555 (533)	Senior Engineering Group	Traders in engineering products	R. Smith, *G. R. Deveson*	31–12–78
556 (574)	NSS Newsagents	Retail newsagents	P. H. Byam-Cook, *R. G. Schweitzer*	1–10–78
557 (633)	Marshall of Cambridge (Enrg.)	General engineering	Sir Arthur Marshall (J.M.D.), *J. H. Huntridge*	31–12–77
558 (594)	Wilkins & Mitchell	Power presses and domestic appliances	H. R. Wilkins (M.D.)	30–12–78
559 (595)	Jonas Woodhead & Sons	Vehicle suspension specialists	E. S. Simpson (M.D.)	31– 3–78
560 (602)	Hewlett-Packard	Electronic apparatus manufacturers	F. Mariotti, *D. A. Baldwin, P. Carmichael*	31–10–78
561 (670)	E.R.F. (Holdings)	Commercial vehicle manufacturers	E. P. Foden (M.D.)	1– 4–78
562 (506)	Ogilvy & Mather	Marketing and advertising	J. Benson, *R. Venables*	31–12–76
563 (501)	Aberdeen Construction Grp.	Civil engineering & building	W. Tinch (M.D.)	31–12–78
564 (580)	Roche Products	Chemical manufacturers	F. Gerber, *W. W. Gerard*	31–12–77
565 (589)	T. C. Harrison	Ford, Vauxhall, Bedford, JCB main dlrs.	T. C. Harrison, *E. Harrison, J. F. Harrison*	31–12–78
566 (583)	Air Products	Industrial gases & equipment manfrs.	A. W. Walker, *L. L. Phannestiel, B. Street*	30– 9–78
567 (662)	Sony (U.K.)	Distrbs. of electrical goods	A. Morita, *W. H. Fulton*	31–10–77
568 (576)	SKF (U.K.)	Ball & roller bearing manfrs.	Sir John King, *H. C. Franklin*	31–12–77
569 (518)	Alfred Herbert	Machine tools manfrs. & distributors	P. Rippon	31–12–78
570 (601)	H. & J. Quick Group	Passenger & commercial vehicle dlrs.	N. Quick (M.D.)	31–12–78
571 (739)	MFI Furniture Centres[35]	Retailers of h'hold furniture, etc.	A. C. Southon, *N. A. V. Lister, J. W. Seabright*	27– 5–78
572 (466)	Hecht, Heyworth & Alcan	Rubber merchants	D. A. E. Beech	31–12–77
573 (630)	Pentos	Publishing, building, eng., etc.	T. A. Maher	31–12–78
574 (512)	Augustus Barnett & Son	Wine & spirit merchants	B. L. Barnett	29– 1–77
575 (607)	Blagden & Noakes (Holdings)	Steel drum manfrs. & reconditioners	J. K. Noakes	31–12–78
576 (541)	Metal Closures Group	Metal & plastic packagings	J. Boden	31–12–78
577 (579)	Liverpool Daily Post & Echo	Newspaper printing & publishing	H. B. Chrimes, *I. G. Park*	30–12–78
578 (718)	J. C. Bamford Excavators	Manfrs. of hydr. earth moving eqpmt.	A. P. Bamford (M.D.)	31–12–76
579 (584)	Alfred Preedy & Sons	Wholesale & retail tobacconists	H. L. Preedy	25– 3–78
580 (553)	McCorquodale & Co.	Printers & stationers	A. McCorquodale, *J. L. Wood*	30– 9–78
581 (581)	H. Samuel	Multiple retail jewellers	R. R. S. Edgar (J.M.D.), *R. Collingwood*	28– 1–78
582 (545)	British Enkalon	Man-made fibre producers	J. M. Ritchie, *A. S. Lobban*	31–12–78
583 (559)	H. & R. Johnson-Richards Tiles[38]	Ceramic tile manufacturers	W. K. Roberts	31– 3–78
584 (598)	Rohm & Haas (U.K.)	Chemical manufacturers	A. M. Levantin, *E. J. Cullen*	31–12–77
585 (247)	D'Arcy-MacManus and Masius[22]	Advertising & marketing advisors	A. J. Abrahams, *A. L. Clark, M. Johnson*	31–12–77
586 (591)	Pritchard Services Group	Bldg. maint. & security services, etc.	P. R. Pritchard (M.D.)	31–12–78
587 (654)	W. R. Grace	Manfrs. of chemical products	P. R. Johnston	31–12–77
588 (621)	Seddon Diesel Vehicles	Vehicle manufacturers	R. J. Pielstiker, *W. N. White*	31–10–77
589 (532)	Bison Group	'Bison' structural precast concrete	Sir Kenneth Wood, *G. Wigglesworth*	31–12–77
590 (614)	K Shoes	Manufacturers & sale of footwear	S. Crookenden, *G. O. Probert*	30– 9–78
591 (555)	Gonzalez Byass & Co.	Wine & spirit producers & shippers	G. W. Hawkings-Byass	31–12–77
592 (—)	Harris Queensway Group	Rtlrs. of carpets & h/hold furniture	P. C. Harris	23–12–78
593 (573)	Fodens	Commercial vehicle manufacturers	L. J. Tolley, *D. C. Foden, S. P. Twemlow*	1– 4–78
594 (639)	Clayton Denwandre Holdings	Vehicle equipment manufacturers, etc.	Lord Orr-Ewing, *J. W. Kinchin*	31–12–77
595 (536)	Star Diamond Co.	Dealing in diamonds	S. Hirschel (M.D.)	24– 5–78
596 (673)	Reo Stakis Organisation	Hoteliers and caterers, etc.	R. Stakis, *J. F. Loughray*	1–10–78
597 (585)	British Olivetti	Business machinery & systems mfrs.	E. Lolli, *K. Walkerden*	31–12–77
598 (606)	Corning	Glass manufacturers	O. Ames (M.D.)	4–12–77
599 (568)	Proprietors of Hay's Wharf	Goods handling & distribution, etc.	Sir David H. Burnett, *D. S. Clarabut*	30– 9–78
600 (599)	Scapa Group	Paper-machine clothing mfrs., etc.	T. D. Walker, *R. W. Goodall, J. Haythornwaite*	31– 3–78

NOTES: *Total tangible assets less current liabilities (other than bank loans and overdrafts and future tax).   †As percentage of capital employed at beginning of the year.   ‡As at 13 July 1979.   §Appendix on page 70 gives list of Managing Directors whose names cannot be fitted into the main text.   ‖M.D. = Managing Director; J.M.D. = Joint Managing Director; A.C. = Acting Chairman; C.E. = Chief Executive.   ¶As percentage of capital employed at end of the year.   N/A Not available.   ¹UK only.   [22]Previous-year figures relate to Masius Wynne-Williams & D'Arcy-Macmanus (Holdings) Ltd., the UK parent company which no longer produces consolidated accounts. For this reason and because alterations have been made to the partnership agreement, the figures are not comparable with those of the previous year.   [35]Now a sub. co. of Norcros Ltd.   [38]Now a sub. co. of MFI Furniture Group Ltd.

TURNOVER Total £000	Export £000	*CAPITAL EMPLOYED £000	Rank Latest year	Rank Previous year	NET PROFIT BEFORE INTEREST AND TAX Latest year £000	Rank	Previous year £000	% to turnover Latest year	†% to capital employed Latest year	Previous year	No. of **employees	‡Equity market cap. £M.
57,224p.a.	18,032p.a.	23,595	527	578	995p.a.	877	220	1·7	5·8p.a.	1·2	1,237	USA
57,000	220	18,423	618	517	3,571	556	3,116	6·3	16·7	18·2	2,029	11·0
56,843	1,378	20,894	572	650	7,233	354	4,533	12·7	50·2	38·0	2,296	20·9
56,782	37,844	4,442	947	971	559	932	452	1·0	24·3	13·2	60[1]	SWZ
56,733	5,360	28,098	469	452	5,218	445	5,425	9·2	20·2	23·8	3,559[1]	14·9
56,646	0	10,393	811	803	3,740	536	3,264	6·6	42·7	46·1	3,83a	18·4
56,620	5,846	13,795	721	732	1,769	770	1,149	3·1	15·6	12·1	2,904[1]	UQ
56,617p.a.	6,012p.a.	8,194	871	854	1,611p.a.	795	746	2·8	20·0p.a.	10·2	3,139	2·8
56,600	6,521	26,760	487	484	5,507	428	5,252	9·7	23·8	28·4	4,109[1]	13·4
56,511	12,003	23,183	534	588	5,339	440	5,014	9·4	30·2	32·6	1,207	USA
56,306	5,177	10,189	818	822	3,592	554	2,060	6·4	43·0	29·8	1,395[1]	7·4
56,146	—	6,357	906	880	1,980	749	1,710	3·5	40·4	33·8	633[1]	USA
56,137	0	20,382	582	572	3,365	588	3,961	6·0	18·0	24·0	3,428	9·3
56,088	19,462	41,510	363	290	621	922	Loss 14,674	1·1	1·2	—	1,780	SWZ
56,058	80	17,612	632	701	3,330	593	2,619	5·9	26·8	39·2	1,372	10·2
55,822	12,185	67,988	259	379	10,097	283	9,069	18·1	17·9	26·5	2,255[1]	USA
55,444	7,814	13,040	742	825	3,409	578	1,668	6·1	27·4	20·2	895[1]	JAP
55,214	19,941	46,564	335	313	Loss 3,704	994	Loss 277	—	—	—	3,826	SW
55,166	10,712	58,590	291	273	Loss 1,569	989	1,734	—	—	3·4	5,180	UQ
55,116	15	4,772	943	900	1,426	828	1,376	2·6	24·9	33·7	1,019	2·3
55,043	214	10,609	797	894	5,370	438	1,937	9·8	91·5	43·8	1,531	—[35]
54,847	450	6,580	901	798	862	898	627	1·6	9·7	12·7	—	FR
54,840	6,461	17,879	627	622	4,945	460	4,060	9·0	31·2	27·5	2,774[1]	27·7
54,645p.a.	0	1,834	987	981	407p.a.	944	Loss 627p.a.	0·7	14·2p.a.	—	532	SPN
54,523	2,804	19,648	592	575	5,188	447	4,273	9·5	28·3	35·1	2,393[1]	14·0
54,481	4,595	29,039	457	448	5,948	407	5,553	10·9	22·6	23·4	3,030[1]	22·3
54,404	221	22,140	552	536	4,103	502	4,133	7·5	20·1	22·0	3,158[1]	14·2
54,353	83	36,577	389	451	8,193	324	2,872	15·1	31·7	12·5	1,063	UQ
54,254	0	7,159	885	895	1,320	842	1,244	2·4	22·5	24·2	1,888	6·8
53,997	3,977	31,322	431	420	4,713	466	3,744	8·7	15·9	13·2	4,622[1]	17·0
53,922	1,314	36,765	388	406	10,493	277	9,127	19·5	33·8	33·4	4,505	98·8
53,606	8,940	22,731	539	438	1,063	873	Loss 164	2·0	4·2	—	2,857	5·9
53,592	8,904	38,865	378	382	5,967	406	4,819	11·1	17·6	15·6	4,368	—[38]
53,587	29,099	31,185	432	431	5,639	421	4,397	10·5	19·7	14·6	835[1]	USA
53,409	—	4,677	944	808	2,150	734	3,816	4·0	¶46·0	62·3	496	USA
53,383	—	12,693	754	830	3,116	616	2,730	5·8	38·4	37·8	14,023[1]	9·1
53,211	23,276	28,328	465	703	11,354	255	7,362	21·3	91·6	64·8	1,435[1]	USA
53,136p.a.	3,906p.a.	14,847	696	683	2,910p.a.	641	255	5·5	22·5p.a.	1·8	1,924[1]	USA
53,031p.a.	1,082p.a.	15,434	685	632	776p.a.	906	3,079	1·5	5·1p.a.	¶20·4	2,927	SAR
53,018	3,025	20,471	577	583	4,005	511	2,414	7·6	22·3	15·0	5,682[1]	16·7
53,007	221	30,182	448	389	3,113	617	2,346	5·9	9·3	8·1	153[1]	BAH
52,978	0	9,283	837	—	5,144	450	1,599	9·7	60·5	¶18·8	1,308	37·9
52,785	13,155	19,080	605	635	3,828	525	3,139	7·3	25·7	19·8	2,957[1]	9·2
52,762	7,327	27,358	477	556	4,300	492	3,069	8·1	21·9	18·2	4,763[1]	USA
52,720	47,906	11,104	786	909	975	882	986	1·8	18·3	22·2	—	UQ
52,712	0	16,674	655	681	3,121	615	1,943	5·9	24·1	17·9	3,978	19·1
52,642	19,827	17,806	629	532	1,494	821	1,589	2·8	7·3	10·0	2,611	IT
52,619	21,016	30,600	439	433	1,416	831	3,414	2·7	5·0	16·8	4,176[1]	USA
52,500	258	52,664	305	320	6,047	401	4,947	11·5	13·9	9·7	3,264[1]	24·5
52,361	11,969	41,323	364	365	7,964	331	8,374	15·2	22·1	27·9	4,200	26·7

The following letters in the Market Capitalisation column denote unquoted companies and country of control: BAH = Bahamas. FR = France. IT = Italy. JAP = Japan. SAR = Saudi Arabia. SPN = Spain. SW = Sweden. SWZ = Switzerland. UQ = Unquoted. USA = United States of America.

Rank by turn-over	COMPANY	Main activity	Chairman and Managing Directors (in italics) §‖	Accounting period ended
601 (689)	T. Cowie	Motor vehicle dealers, finance, etc.	T. Cowie (M.D.)	30– 9–78
602 (523)	M. J. Gleeson (Contractors)	Civil eng. & building contractors	J. P. Gleeson (M.D.)	30– 6–78
603 (320)	Oce-Van Der Grinten Finance	Reprographic eqpt. manfrs., etc.	J. J. Kaptein	30–11–78
604 (551)	Usborne & Son (London)	Grain importers	D. W. Frame (M.D.)	31– 3–78
605 (675)	Batleys of Yorkshire	Cash & carry wholesalers	L. Batley, *A. R. G. McCullen*	29– 4–78
606 (569)	LEP Group	Intnl. transport & travel agents, etc.	R. J. D. Leeper (M.D.)	31–12–77
607 (586)	Chamberlain Phipps	Shoe components and plastics, etc.	W. R. F. Chamberlain	31– 3–78
608 (537)	Petrola (UK)	Dealers in crude oil	S. J. Latsis, *J. F. Jarvis-Smith*	31–12–74
609 (546)	GEI International	Engineering	T. Kenny, *J. O. Sewell*	31– 3–79
610 (743)	Control Data	Computer systems	*J. H. Ward*	30–11–78
611 (611)	Howard Tenens Services	Distribution & eng. services	E. C. Morris, *D. F. F. Barrett*	31– 3–78
612 (567)	J. Gerber & Co.	Confirming house	K. P. Van Ek (M.D.)	31–12–78
613 (677)	Black & Edgington	Mnfrs. of tents, marquees, canvas gds.	R. G. Duthie (J.M.D.), *D. G. Moodie*	31–12–78
614 (669)	Silentnight Holdings	Bedding & upholstery manufacturers	R. Smith, *H. Crowther, K. C. Murray*	27– 1–79
615 (528)	Whitecroft	Textiles, bldg. & eng. sup., eng., constn.	J. Tavare (M.D.)	31– 3–78
616 (632)	Napier Brown & Co.	Sugar & dried fruit merchants	F. Ridgwell	31–12–77
617 (618)	Ruston-Bucyrus	Manfrs. of excavators and cranes	W. B. Winter, *N. J. Verville*	31–12–77
618 (597)	Elbar Industrial	Vehicle distbn., agricultural mchy., etc.	A. L. Hood, *K. Williams*	31–12–78
619 (682)	Colgate-Palmolive	Toilet & domestic cleaning products	S. M. Ford (M.D.)	30– 9–78
620 (605)	British Vita Co.	Manfrs. of polymeric products, etc.	F. A. Parker	31–12–78
621 (565)	May & Hassell	Timber importers	J. H. B. Atley, *P. J. Atley*	31– 3–78
622 (762)	G. Percy Trentham	Building & civil eng. contractors	G. D. Trentham	31–12–78
623 (620)	Adwest Group	Engineers, etc.	F. V. Waller (M.D.)	30– 6–78
624 (879)	Argos Distributors[24]	Retailers	P. J. Ricketts, *T. V. McAuliffe, J. M. Phillips*	5–11–77
625 (642)	Butterfield-Harvey	Engineering, factoring, processing	T. F. Honess	1– 4–78
626 (631)	Wolverhampton & Dudley Brws.	Brewers	E. J. Thompson (M.D.)	30– 9–78
627 (724)	Hanger Investments	Motor dealers	P. D. Adams (J.M.D.), *J. G. Dickson*	31–12–78
628 (637)	BPM Holdings	Printers & publishers	Sir Michael Clapham	1– 7–78
629 (629)	Fine Art Developments	Greeting card mfrs., mail order, etc.	F. R. Kerry, *D. T. Barnes*	31– 3–79
630 (624)	James Neill Holdings	Tool manufacturers, general engineer	J. H. Neill	31–12–78
631 (604)	Willis Faber	Insurance brokers	A. R. Taylor	31–12–78
632 (671)	R. G. Carter (Holdings)	Builders	S. H. Tuddenham (A.C.,M.D.)	31–12–78
633 (635)	Redfearn National Glass	Glass container manufacturers	J. L. C. Pratt (M.D.)	1–10–78
634 (561)	R. H. Thompson Group	Provision merchants	D. J. N. Thompson, *R. M. Thompson, J. S. C. Tidmarsh*	28– 1–78
635 (649)	Christie-Tyler	Manfrs. of furniture & upholstery	G. M. Williams (M.D.)	30– 4–78
636 (634)	A. C. Cossor	Electronic equipment, etc.	Lord Sherfield	30–11–77
637 (701)	Motherwell Bridge (Hldgs.)	Heavy engineering	A. B. Miller, *H. Porter, L. H. Lister*	31–12–77
638 (557)	Lockwoods Foods	Fruit & vegetable, etc., canners	P. B. Lockwood, *N. G. Horton-Mastin, W. P. Lockwood*	31– 5–78
639 (571)	Cameron Iron Works	Mrfs. of valves, oilfield eqpt., etc.	H. Allen	30– 6–78
640 (—)	Manor National Group Motors	Sales & servicing of motor vehicles	R. A. Stoodley (M.D.)	31–12–78
641 (622)	Myson Group	Heating, ventilating & air conditng.	R. E. Myson (M.D.)	31–12–78
642 (656)	Matthew Clark & Sons (Hldgs.)	Wine & spirit shippers & merchants	F. W. Gordon Clark	30– 4–78
643 (648)	Anderson Strathclyde	Mining & industrial eqpt. mfrs.	R. H. Thorpe (M.D.)	31– 3–78
644 (683)	MAT Transport Intl. Group	Transport & ancillary services	Sir Leonard Neal, *P. A. Kunzler*	30– 9–77
645 (693)	Collett, Dickenson, Pearce In.	Advertising agency	J. W. Pearce, *J. M. Salmon*	31–12–78
646 (864)	Cyanamid of Great Britain	Pharmaceutical products	D. R. B. Banks	30–11–78
647 (600)	Readson	Textile manufacturers	E. Dodson, *T. Weatherby*	31– 3–78
648 (857)	CBS United Kingdom	Records & music	M. L. Oberstein	31–10–77
649 (696)	United Gas Industries	Gas appliances and meters etc.	H. T. Nicholson	2– 4–78
650 (638)	Parker Timber Group	Timber mchts., manfrs. of timber prods.	K. Whitby, *H. Sherwood*	31– 3–78

NOTES: *Total tangible assets less current liabilities (other than bank loans and overdrafts and future tax).   †As percentage of capital employed at beginning of the year.   ‡As at 13 July 1979.   §Appendix on page 70 gives list of Managing Directors whose names cannot be fitted into the main text.   ‖M.D. = Managing Director; J.M.D. = Joint Managing Director; A.C. = Acting Chairman; C.E. = Chief Executive.   ¶As percentage of capital employed at end of the year.   N/A Not available.   ¹UK only.
[24]Now a sub. co. of BAT Industries Ltd.

TURNOVER		*CAPITAL EMPLOYED			NET PROFIT BEFORE INTEREST AND TAX						**No. of employees	‡Equity market cap. £M.
Total £000	Export £000	£000	Rank Latest year	Previous year	Latest year £000	Rank	Previous year £000	% to turnover Latest year	†% to capital employed Latest year	Previous year		
52,263	0	17,026	645	710	2,760	658	2,311	5·3	22·8	23·4	1,002	5·4
52,000	951	12,566	757	782	744	909	1,438	1·4	7·9	17.1	2,952[1]	3·3
51,780	10,130	35,130	403	305	2,500	686	5,257p.a.	4·8	¶7·1	¶11.5p.a.	3,249[1]	HOL
51,746	2,669	2,322	978	949	575	931	380	1·1	18·2	17·1	—	UQ
51,584	0	3,708	952	946	598	925	531	1·2	17·1	24·3	370	3·6
51,545	0	38,041	382	369	5,500	429	4,700	10·7	15·5	18·0	5,814	21·0
51,442	7,853	13,466	732	688	3,678	544	2,683	7·1	28·7	23·3	2,835	11·6
51,433	—	144	998	999	14	972	30	0·0	9·5	25·6	—	LU
51,338	6,416	28,510	460	443	6,826	369	6,148	13·3	25·7	28·5	2,600[1]	23·4
51,186	5,377	16,648	656	529	3,804	528	3,157	7·4	20·8	15·3	1,092	USA
51,186	465	18,316	620	584	1,834	766	442	3·6	10·3	2·4	2,831	5·7
51,098	2,044	6,644	898	922	1,515	816	1,568	3·0	30·9	35·7	—	UQ
51,092	5,884	30,869	435	489	3,297	598	3,399	6·5	14·6	21·7	3,680[1]	14·6
50,935	1,973	35,106	694	712	4,504	477	3,465	8·8	37·7	42·2	3,136	15·4
50,816	3,786	10,652	438	445	5,091	453	5,993	10·0	19·2	21·7	3,847[1]	22·0
50,618	—	1,249	991	993	202	962	187	0·4	33·3	50·8	—	UQ
50,583	23,729	39,851	371	399	10,499	276	8,470	20·8	32·7	¶26·4	2,100	USA
50,096	1,518	16,157	667	722	2,757	659	2,640	5·5	23·7	42·5	1,323	7·8
50,026	4,457	18,335	619	615	3,453	569	1,545p.a.	6·9	17·8	9·6p.a.	1,282	USA
49,874	2,783	25,566	500	521	7,786	334	6,679	15·6	36·9	42·0	2,561[1]	23·8
49,710	107	31,794	427	400	1,726	779	2,952	3·5	14·0	14·0	1,673[1]	5·3
49,687	0	8,405	857	871	973	884	819	2·0	14·4	12·2	1,480	UQ
49,504	6,556	27,578	472	513	7,072	360	6,020	14·3	32·8	32·9	3,667[1]	30·7
49,315	0	7,494	879	927	1,358	838	55	2·8	32·1	2·9	1,006[1]	—[24]
48,898	7,440	22,194	550	545	3,227	610	2,188	6·6	15·8	11·1	3,085[1]	10·8
48,886	0	36,193	393	416	7,424	347	5,949	15·2	24·6	24·7	4,960	47·6
48,843	0	18,533	616	742	3,707	541	2,039	7·6	34·0	27·0	787	7·3
48,808	76	13,577	728	746	4,183	498	2,023	8·6	38·7	20·2	3,650[1]	9·1
48,430	2,100	23,946	523	555	6,340	388	5,342	13·1	32·2	37·5	2,954[1]	27·7
48,372	17,130	49,032	318	329	3,400	562	5,255	7·1	8·1	14·1	4,929	11·7
48,284	—	69,104	258	233	19,812	168	20,628	41·0	29·9	37·0	2,758[1]	82·0
48,214	38	7,287	882	901	796	905	440	1·7	14·0	8·6	2,980	UQ
48,045	685	26,177	496	620	4,421	479	4,852	9·2	25·7	36·9	2,708	14·3
48,035	619	4,933	940	945	Loss 231	976	535	—	—	14·1	900[1]	UQ
48,005	1,371	6,315	909	903	1,948	754	2,631	4·1	34·6	58·5	2,858	8·5
47,833	15,416	22,459	545	589	3,823	526	3,415	8·0	21·7	19·0	3,480[1]	USA
47,827	11,719	19,198	603	648	4,120	501	4,685	8·6	28·5	43·0	2,935[1]	UQ
47,705	956	24,867	511	579	3,595	553	3,479	7·5	19·9	18·0	2,307[1]	5·4
47,288	35,455	41,739	359	349	7,077	359	8,689	15·0	18·6	25·7	1,760	USA
47,179	78	11,032	791	—	1,605	796	1,215	3·4	¶14·5	¶11·0	1,143	3·7
46,908	4,733	20,432	579	543	2,927	640	1,588	6·2	14·6	8·2	2,608[1]	8·6
46,776	308	10,643	795	786	2,096	738	2,229	4·5	22·5	31·1	313	6·2
46,769	9,844	34,203	405	435	4,568	472	3,629	9·8	16·5	14·2	4,269[1]	24·7
46,541	0	5,115	934	921	1,547	810	47p.a.	3·3	33·9	1·3p.a.	1,062[1]	UQ
46,365	—	2,729	971	974	1,615	794	1,370	3·5	77·0	78·7	281[1]	3·8
46,196	21,791	33,077	418	446	8,853	310	7,804	19·2	29·8	29·5	1,535	USA
46,095	4,165	16,131	668	639	3,396	583	3,278	7·4	22·9	30·0	2,981	UQ
45,914	3,928	7,124	887	965	7,462	345	3,122	16·3	187·9	126·6	1,690[1]	USA
45,811	4,422	15,866	676	613	2,680	664	2,085	5·9	16·6	13·3	3,554[1]	9·1
45,755	236	18,792	613	606	2,604	670	3,051	5·7	15·7	27·9	1,462	9·9

The following letters in the Market Capitalisation column denote unquoted companies and country of control: HOL = Holland.   LU = Luxembourg.   UQ = Unquoted.
USA = United States of America.

Rank by turn-over	COMPANY	Main activity	Chairman and Managing Directors (in italics) §‖	Accounting period ended
651 (666)	Sidney C. Banks	Grain merchants & seed specialists	J. B. Godber, *M. C. Banks, R. L. Banks*	31– 5–78
652 (894)	Motorola	Manfrs. & distbs. of electrical goods	M. W. Larkin	31–12–77
653 (680)	Renwick Group	Motor & fuel disbn., travel agents, etc.	C. W. Wilton, *K. E. Holmes*	1– 4–78
654 (661)	British Tissues	Paper manufacturers	R. V. Olsen	31–12–77
655 (713)	Hoveringham Group	Extraction & processg. of aggregates	G. H. C. Needler	31 12–78
656 (800)	Ryland Vehicle Group	Vehicle distributors	W. J. Whale	30– 4–78
657 (593)	Charles Hurst	Vehicle distbn. & service	C. T. Hurst, *C. A. Stuart, S. Magowan*	31–12–78
658 (700)	Surridge Dawson (Holdings)	Newsagents, booksellers, stationers	G. P. C. Krayenbrink (Board Chairman) *(see page 70)*	1– 1–78
659 (721)	Tilbury Contracting Group	Civil eng., bldg. & public wks. contrs.	J. P. S. Edge-Partington, *C. Brand*	31–12–78
660 (889)	A. H. Philpot and Sons	Farming & agricultural products	H. R. Philpot	30– 9–77
661 (645)	Associated Octel Company	Manfr. & sale of antiknock compounds	*W. C. Greaves*	31–12–77
662 (566)	Courts (Furnishers)	Retailers of house furniture, etc.	E. G. Cohen, *P. C. Cohen, B. J. R. Cohen*	31– 3–78
663 (655)	Waring & Gillow (Holdings)	Retail furnishers, clothing manfrs.	M. Cussins, *J. R. Cussins*	31– 3–78
664 (570)	Thomas Roberts (Westminster)	Timber, road materials, etc.	Mrs. P. M. Roberts, *B. Kilpatrick*	31– 3–78
665 (733)	Charles Barker ABH Intl.	Advertising practitioners	J. V. Wellesley	31–12–78
666 (577)	British Bata Shoe Co.	Footwear manufacturers	T. J. Bata	31–12–77
667 (749)	Reads	Metal container manfrs.	M. White, *W. S. Kratzer*	25–11–77
668 (—)	OCS Group[27]	Cleaning & security services, etc.	D. Goodlife, *G. Goodlife*	31– 3–78
669 (643)	A. Cohen & Co.	Metal refiners, non-ferrous alloys	R. H. Cohen, *M. Pylkkanen, C. A. Cohen*	31–12–77
670 (692)	Bowthorpe Holdings	Electrical engineers, etc.	R. A. Parsons (M.D.)	31–12–78
671 (842)	Pattullo, Higgs & Co.	Agricultural merchants	J. D. Langlands (M.D.)	30– 6–77
672 (837)	Robert Horne & Co.	Paper merchants	K. E. Horne, *M. T. Bairstow, W. D. Musgrove*	30– 9–78
673 (613)	Hollis Bros. & E.S.A.	Timber, sawmillers, flooring contrs.	G. S. Mitchell (M.D.)	31– 3–78
674 (777)	Arlington Motor Holdings	Motor dealers, etc.	N. C. N. Housden, *J. M. Heywood*	31– 3–78
675 (617)	Cruden Investments	Building contractors	A. C. Bennett, *M. R. A. Matthews*	31– 3–78
676 (640)	Barton & Sons	Tubing manufacturers & engineers	J. M. Wardle	31–12–78
677 (694)	Cam Gears	Motor steering gears	D. S. Leese, *R. A. Pinnington*	31–12–77
678 (615)	St. Regis International	Cartons, cases, paper, etc.	Lord Robens, *H. L. Hazell*	31–12–77
679 (735)	Van Leer (UK)	Packaging manufacturers	J. C. Prichard, *J. Schuringa*	31–12–77
680 (707)	Libby, McNeill & Libby	Canned food manufacturers	H. J. Thrall	31–12–77
681 (636)	Barker & Dobson Group	Confectioners, tobacconists, grocers	R. W. Aitken	1– 4–78
682 (—)	J. Soufflet (UK)	Grain merchants	M. Soufflet, *C. F. Haycroft*	30– 6–77
683 (651)	Favor Parker	Animal feed manufacturers	H. G. Parker	31– 1–78
684 (784)	Derek Crouch	Opencast mining, civil eng., bldg. cnst.	D. C. H. Crouch	31–12–78
685 (803)	Highland Distilleries	Malt whisky distillers	J. A. R. MacPhail, *J. M. Goodwin*	31– 8–78
686 (698)	Siebe Gorman Holdings	Diving, survival & safety eqpmt., etc.	G. C. D'Arcy Biss, *E. B. Stephens*	1– 4–78
687 (672)	Brown & Tawse	Steel & tube stckhldrs. & engineers	S. D. Rae (M.D.)	31– 3–78
688 (668)	Haverhill Meat Products	Bacon curing	E. R. Griffiths	5– 3–78
689 (807)	Lin-Pac Containers	Packaging manufacturers	H. E. Cornish (M.D.)	31–12–76
690 (703)	Armitage Shanks Group	Sanitary pottery & fittings mfrs.	K. Campbell, *K. L. Shanks, L. Clarke*	1– 4–78
691 (726)	Eaton	Engineers	Sir Leonard Crossland, *H. T. Holland*	31–12–77
692 (688)	Ellis & Everard	Building materials, chemicals, fuel	A. J. Everard	30– 4–78
693 (653)	Bemrose Corporation	Packaging, printing & publishing	G. Brunton	30–12–78
694 (738)	J. Hepworth & Son	Multiple tailors	R. E. Chadwick, *J. T. Rowlay*	31– 8–78
695 (715)	Bentalls	Department stores	J. D. Spooner, *L. E. Bentall*	3– 2–79
696 (702)	Avon Cosmetics	Manufacturers of cosmetics, etc.	J. E. Preston, *B. D. Crosby*	31–12–77
697 (850)	Danepak	Bacon processors	J. Esp. Sorensen, *B. Robinson*	1–10–77
698 (759)	National Panasonic (UK)	Importers of electrical goods	A. Imura	20– 9–78
699 (679)	Consolidated Pneumatic Tool	Pneumatic tool manufacturers, etc.	K. Lall	31–12–77
700 (706)	John Waddington	Manfrs. of games & pastimes, printers	V. H. Watson, *E. P. Rundle, J. Scott*	2– 4–78

NOTES: *Total tangible assets less current liabilities (other than bank loans and overdrafts and future tax).   †As percentage of capital employed at beginning of the year.   ‡As at 13 July 1979.   §Appendix on page 70 gives list of Managing Directors whose names cannot be fitted into the main text.   ‖M.D. = Managing Director; J.M.D. = Joint Managing Director; A.C. = Acting Chairman; C.E. = Chief Executive.   ¶As percentage of capital employed at end of the year.   N/A Not available.   ¹UK only.
[27]Company incorporated 11.2.77.

TURNOVER		*CAPITAL EMPLOYED			NET PROFIT BEFORE INTEREST AND TAX						**No. of employees	‡Equity market cap. £M.
Total £000	Export £000	£000	Rank Latest year	Previous year	Latest year £000	Rank	Previous year £000	% to turnover Latest year	†% to capital employed Latest year	Previous year		
45,754	5,494	4,005	950	932	610	923	644	1·3	15·4	25·3	159	3·4
45,711	22,976	16,429	660	690	3,298	597	400	7·2	26·0	4·3	953	USA
45,613	4,076	5,728	921	897	1,577	804	1,168	3·5	27·0	22·9	1,708[1]	3·2
45,599	582	20,432	578	559	3,297	599	479	7·2	17·0	2·5	2,184[1]	UQ
45,592	—	27,266	478	581	5,754	414	3,978	12·6	31·9	26·6	1,872	15·9
45,441	255	11,957	771	892	2,233	723	1,363	4·9	37·5	30·3	927	UQ
45,439	247	9,116	841	802	1,110	865	1,443	2·4	12·6	21·5	893	1·2
45,358	—	3,603	957	954	1,603	797	1,145	3·5	55·2	48·8	895	UQ
45,253	561	14,306	707	711	2,578	673	2,131	5·7	21·3	21·0	1,763	5·9
45,244	17,372	1,933	985	956	480	937	178	1·1	17·0	12·6	115	UQ
44,993	—	36,767	387	401	7,198	355	7,197	16·0	22·5	23·0	2,810[1]	UQ
44,937	0	24,299	517	473	5,526	427	5,324	12·3	23·0	28·5	2,070[1]	20·2
44,935	823	19,188	604	614	3,798	530	3,097	8·5	23·6	21·6	3,465	20·7
44,653	617	19,530	596	549	1,143	858	2,179	2·6	5·7	12·6	1,929[1]	UQ
44,479	—	1,920	986	980	1,071	871	526	2·4	56·3	41·8	495[1]	UQ
44,382	9,169	14,540	702	531	2,943	635	4,862	6·6	14·3	32·3	3,082[1]	UQ
44,376	312p.a.	24,102	521	617	5,479p.a.	431	2,818	12·3	34·3p.a.	23·2	—	USA
44,079	141	18,910	611	—	3,978	515	—	9·0	¶21·0	—	20,260	UQ
44,030	5,611	12,389	760	696	2,294	712	2,539	5·2	18·4	27·3	241[1]	5·0
43,988	6,905	27,537	473	495	6,895	365	6,158	15·7	30·9	32·3	2,086[1]	34·0
43,950	563	4,564	946	944	838	901	292	1·9	23·7	10·1	256	UQ
43,900	220	6,702	896	926	1,853	764	1,437	4·2	37·2	33·4	448	UQ
43,489	2,188	17,825	628	576	2,574	674	3,303	5·9	14·1	27·4	2,505	5·9
43,409	349	14,415	705	890	1,867	763	1,285	4·3	30·6	18·4	907	4·3
43,407	—	3,973	951	938	510	935	1,448	1·2	13·2	38·9	2,761[1]	UQ
43,347	2,560	22,622	542	528	4,197	495	3,964	9·7	20·3	19·9	2,454	12·0
43,283	17,424	9,424	834	834	5,615	423	4,775	13·0	70·1	38·8	2,475[1]	USA
43,081	1,517	36,533	390	359	8,972	308	5,030p.a.	20·8	26·0	17·1p.a.	2,526	USA
43,017	3,625	21,409	565	738	2,585	672	3,054	6·0	23·4	31·1	2,079[1]	HOL
43,003p.a.	2,929	18,954	609	734	882p.a.	896	1,085	2·1	7·8p.a.	8·1	734	SWZ
42,882	2,664	5,028	937	910	663	918	Loss 117	1·5	12·8	—	2,756	13·1
42,863	604	260	997	—	337	948	151p.a.	0·8	¶129·6	¶100·7p.a.	—	FR
42,803p.a.	0	5,305	932	919	Loss 168p.a.	975	1,384	—	—	53·2	249[1]	UQ
42,790	0	24,689	514	724	3,541	557	2,397	8·3	30·6	26·9	2,072	14·8
42,617	1,632	28,292	466	477	4,598	470	3,830	10·8	19·5	21·1	292	56·8
42,538	6,167	23,060	536	569	5,022	458	4,589	11·8	26·7	28·9	2,970	21·2
42,470	188	17,153	643	618	3,768	533	3,630	8·9	23·6	31·9	1,043	13·2
42,467	—	7,184	884	867	1,512	818	1,823	3·6	22·2	26·8	1,719	UQ
42,332	1,814	21,468	562	607	4,641	469	4,118	11·0	31·9	36·3	2,238[1]	UQ
42,310	7,177	22,851	538	523	2,992	625	2,783	7·1	14·2	15·3	3,081[1]	16·7
42,179	23,270	44,804	346	415	2,493	688	4,739	5·9	8·3	17·4	5,286	USA
42,023	337	9,364	835	751	1,292	844	1,424	3·1	12·2	16·7	1,102	6·4
42,019	6,536	22,008	556	577	2,895	644	2,165	6·9	15·9	14·2	3,073[1]	8·4
41,786	64	62,820	273	241	6,063	399	4,848	14·5	9·8	13·2	4,132	34·1
41,713	137	17,959	625	611	2,942	639	2,600	7·1	18·0	17·8	3,163	18·7
41,702	7,489	9,601	832	791	4,539	473	4,416	10·9	49·8	44·3	1,916[1]	USA
41,683	—	8,332	862	898	1,114	863	536	2·7	18·3	9·2	1,084[1]	DEN
41,581	858	6,856	892	913	3,431	573	3,274	8·3	68·5	¶146·4	143[1]	JAP
41,405	9,287	33,201	416	402	3,290	600	6,627	7·9	10·3	25·7	1,914	USA
41,379	3,124	23,497	529	563	2,943	638	3,852	7·1	15·3	25·3	3,346	10·4

The following letters in the Market Capitalisation column denote unquoted companies and country of control: DEN = Denmark.   FR = France.   HOL = Holland.
JAP = Japan.   SWZ = Switzerland.   UQ = Unquoted.   USA = United States of America.

Rank by turn-over	COMPANY	Main activity	Chairman and Managing Directors (in italics) §‖	Accounting period ended
701 (732)	Agfa-Gevaert	Marketing of sensitised materials	A. Beken, *G. Ahrens*	31–12–77
702 (705)	Harris & Sheldon Group	Lifts, kitchen furniture, advtg. eqpmt.	J. D. Miller	31–12–78
703 (768)	Ferguson Industrial Hldgs.	Bldrs. & plumrs. mchts., ironmongery, etc.	D. S. Vernon	28– 2–78
704 (834)	Sketchley	Dry cleaning, overall service, textiles	G. Wightman	30– 3–79
705 (711)	Star Aluminium Co.	Mfrs. & marketers of aluminium foil	Sir Richard Powell, *D. Fredjohn*	31–12–78
706 (719)	Joseph Stocks & Sons (Hldgs.)	Wholesale provision merchants	D. W. Ostenfeld	31– 3–78
707 (725)	Plantation Holdings	Light eng., scientific inst., plantatns.	S. W. Livesey	31–12–78
708 (802)	Carnation Foods Co.	Manfrs. of evaporated milk, etc.	A. L. Merry	30– 9–77
709 (769)	LWT (Holdings)	ITA programme contractors	J. Freeman	23– 7–78
710 (830)	Forth Wines	Wholesale wine & spirit merchants	P. T. Bell (J.M.D.), *J. M. Cran*	30– 9–78
711 (710)	Ofrex Group	Office & ed. eqpt. supplies	G. Drexler, *A. G. Andrews*	31–12–78
712 (625)	Otis Elevator Co.	Lift & escalator manfrs.	P. J. A. Fougeron, *J. N. Cunningham*	30–11–78
713 (801)	W. Canning	Electrical & mechanical engineers	A. R. Houseman	31–12–78
714 (820)	Bullough	Engineering	B. P. Jenks, *D. B. Battle*	31–10–78
715 (678)	Homfray & Co.	Carpet manufacturers	D. E. Gillam, *C. Croft*	30– 9–78
716 (709)	Hopkinsons Holdings	Boiler mountings, valves, etc. manfrs.	F. R. Bentley, *J. F. Goulding*	2– 2–79
717 (806)	Walter Lawrence	Building contractors, etc.	J. A. B. Redgrave	30– 6–78
718 (737)	UKO International	Ophthalmic lens mfrs., catering eqpmt.	Sir Ian Morrow	31– 3–78
719 (756)	Fenwick	Departmental stores	J. J. Fenwick (M.D.)	27– 1–78
720 (716)	Burnett & Hallamshire Hldgs.	Construction, mining, oil, etc.	N. F. Swiffen, *G. Helsby*	31– 3–79
721 (521)	Drake & Scull Holdings	Elec., mechanical & constr. engineers	M. C. Abbott	31–10–78
722 (764)	Akzo Chemie UK (Holdings)	Chemical manufacturers	Dr. E. M. Hunt (M.D.)	31–12–77
723 (641)	Armour Foods (UK)	Meat and food importers	U. G. Harlow (M.D.)	31–12–78
724 (714)	Ley's Foundries & Engrg.	Malleable castings & engineering	F. D. Ley	30– 9–78
725 (722)	British Sidac	Transparent cellulose film makers	P. S. C. Ellis, *F. Warren*	31–12–77
726 (659)	Polygram Leisure	Gramophone record, etc. distributors	S. L. G. Gottlieb	31–12–77
727 (824)	Pioneer Concrete (Holdings)	Concrete manufacturers	R. F. Crocker (M.D.)	30– 6–78
728 (734)	Ault & Wiborg Group	Printer's inks & rollers, paints, etc.	C. F. Strang, *P. V. Clarke*	31–12–78
729 (660)	Airfix Industries	Toys, gen. housewares, packaging, etc.	R. R. M. Ehrmann, *D. R. Sinigaglia*	31– 3–78
730 (911)	RCA	Electronic engineers	P. Potashner, *J. M. Sheasby*	31–12–78
731 (867)	Alfa Romeo (Great Britain)	Motor car importers & distributors	G. De Bona, *C. Cattaneo*	31–12–78
732 (717)	Brintons	Woven carpet manufacturers	Sir Tatton Brinton (J.M.D.) *(see page 70)*	2– 7–77
733 (776)	MK Electric Holdings	Manfrs. of electric plugs, sockets, etc.	D. L. M. Robertson, *L. G. Hazzard*	1– 4–78
734 (676)	Sidlaw Industries	Jute spinning & manufacturing, etc.	Sir John Carmichael	29– 9–78
735 (582)	Gibbons Dudley	Engineering, refractories, etc.	R. D. Turner, *J. B. Pearson, G. J. Stanley*	31–12–78
736 (774)	Weetabix	Manfrs. of breakfast cereal foods	W. A. George (M.D.)	31– 7–78
737 (658)	Bambergers[29]	Timber, etc. importers, builders mchts.	C. D. Woodburn-Bamberger (J.M.D.) *(see page 70)*	31– 3–78
738 (741)	Galliford Brindley	Civil engineering contractors, etc.	P. Galliford	30– 6–78
739 (757)	Greene, King & Sons	Brewers, maltsters, wine & spirit mch.	Sir Hugh Greene, *W. J. Bridge*	30– 4–78
740 (684)	Carless, Capel & Leonard	Refiners of hydrocarbon solvents	J. T. Leonard	31– 3–79
741 (783)	Johnson & Johnson	Surgical & baby products manfrs., etc.	A. M. Quilty, *P. McKenna*	1– 1–78
742 (644)	Ratcliffs (Great Bridge)	Brass & copper rolled strip manfrs.	F. R. Ratcliff (J.M.D.), *E. H. Ratcliff, D. M. Ratcliff*	31–12–78
743 (814)	Caffyns	Automobile agents & engineers	Sir Edward Caffyn *(see page 70)*	31– 3–78
744 (712)	Esperanza	International services, copper	Lord Kissin, *R. B. Loder*	31– 3–78
745 (744)	Royal Worcester	Table & ornamental ware, electronics	Lord Nelson of Stafford, *L. T. Davies, J. E. Herrin*	31–12–78
746 (720)	MacMillan Bloedel Containers	Fibreboard container manufacturers	D. L. McLaughlin, *J. D. Bence*	31–12–77
747 (760)	Reader's Digest Association	Publishers	V. Ross (M.D.)	30– 6–78
748 (664)	Spear & Jackson Internl.	Mfrs. of steel, saws & hand tools	S. M. De Bartolome, *L. A. Grosbard*	30–12–78
749 (695)	J. Murphy & Sons	Building, civil engineering, etc.	J. Murphy, *J. Clifford*	31–12–77
750 (788)	Walmsley (Bury) Group	Papermaking & pulp machinery manfrs.	A. Green, *A. J. Pettengell*	30– 9–78

NOTES: *Total tangible assets less current liabilities (other than bank loans and overdrafts and future tax). †As percentage of capital employed at beginning of the year. ‡As at 13 July 1979. §Appendix on page 70 gives list of Managing Directors whose names cannot be fitted into the main text. ‖M.D. = Managing Director; J.M.D. = Joint Managing Director; A.C. = Acting Chairman; C.E. = Chief Executive. ¶As percentage of capital employed at end of the year. N/A Not available. ¹UK only. [29]Now a sub. co. of International Timber Corpn. Ltd. [33]Now in voluntary liquidation after scheme of reconstruction.

TURNOVER Total £000	Export £000	*CAPITAL EMPLOYED £000	Rank Latest year	Previous year	NET PROFIT BEFORE INTEREST AND TAX Latest year £000	Rank	Previous year £000	% to turnover Latest year	†% to capital employed Latest year	Previous year	**No. of employees	‡Equity market cap. £M.
41,249	—	14,426	704	736	1,262	850	1,045	3·1	11·3	9·2	839[1]	B/G
41,113	3,813	23,224	533	522	4,306	491	3,804	10·1	19·6	23·4	3,963	17·3
41,102	696	12,112	767	793	2,040	745	1,580	5·0	22·5	21·4	1,674	11·0
40,972	34	19,496	597	673	5,032	457	3,967	12·3	31·7	30·1	5,753[1]	29·2
40,952	3,297	29,953	449	391	285	956	3,308	0·7	0·9	12·8	—	SWZ
40,803	0	2,669	974	987	596	926	595	1·5	34·9	41·8	224	1·3
40,702	8,214	26,595	490	504	4,379	485	4,236	10·8	19·9	22·2	2,287[1]	—[33]
40,670	14,711	12,878	749	728	2,194	728	2,309	5·4	19·1	22·1	696	USA
40,572	1,797	24,223	520	534	5,857	411	5,642	14·4	28·7	30·5	1,526	25·8
40,519	—	977	993	994	244	958	284	0·6	30·7	49·2	—	UQ
40,339	8,810	23,771	524	526	5,173	448	4,096	12·8	25·0	29·4	2,699[1]	19·2
40,115p.a.	9,258p.a.	11,369	780	599	3,718p.a.	538	3,237	9·3	28·7p.a.	18·9	3,304	USA
40,059	5,205	15,442	684	684	1,699	782	1,864	4·2	13·2	22·1	2,189	6·1
40,025	6,759	20,403	581	691	5,169	449	3,210	12·9	40·7	31·0	2,521	21·9
40,004	9,112	24,694	513	440	1,513	817	2,160	3·8	5·6	9·4	1,955[1]	4·3
39,976	8,290	25,491	503	463	3,424	575	4,506	8·6	13·8	20·1	3,968[1]	8·0
39,841	1,174	13,536	730	801	1,496	820	1,573	3·8	17·0	22·5	1,977[1]	3·7
39,812	3,417	26,965	483	506	4,406	480	4,977	11·1	20·1	28·7	4,287[1]	20·1
39,513	0	16,023	672	637	3,926	519	2,866	9·9	26·5	22·9	2,455[1]	UQ
39,502	12	16,511	659	665	3,136	614	2,749	7·9	22·8	25·2	1,256	20·1
39,498	7,639	2,328	977	963	2,526	682	2,624	6·4	96·1	74·6	3,740	6·0
39,412	15,500	17,597	633	649	2,318	709	3,035	5·9	16·1	43·9	800[1]	HOL
39,380	167	6,498	903	882	503	936	530p.a.	1·3	8·0	8·3p.a.	168	USA
39,364	8,272	19,320	600	567	1,198	855	1,689	3·0	6·3	9·4	3,635	4·1
39,340	13,864	17,864	636	587	1,582	802	2,334	4·0	8·9	14·9	2,529[1]	B
39,210	2,023	13,434	733	784	Loss 601	979	359	—	—	3·8	1,599[1]	G
39,186	—	10,218	817	829	2,969	630	2,136	7·6	36·5	33·3	620	AUS
38,964	2,623	14,747	699	705	3,394	584	2,441	8·7	27·6	23·6	1,635	9·7
38,865	8,773	27,142	481	500	3,610	551	5,037	9·3	16·3	26·3	2,731	10·6
38,851	12,945	13,969	716	820	3,257	606	1,516	8·4	33·6	18·1	1,512	USA
38,799	1,084	8,950	843	874	452	942	151	1·2	6·8	3·4	140[1]	IT
38,786	5,453	19,070	606	610	2,118	736	3,460	5·5	12·9	25·8	2,502	UQ
38,777	7,599	26,831	484	520	6,171	395	6,097	15·9	29·2	36·2	4,704[1]	36·1
38,687	2,770	21,831	558	535	1,717	780	1,955	4·4	8·4	8·8	3,044[1]	4·5
38,655	3,533	33,000	419	429	4,136	500	4,288	10·7	14·3	17·5	2,566[1]	17·4
38,621	4,326	20,583	575	594	2,265	719	1,559	5·9	13·0	14·0	1,877[1]	UQ
38,588	0	12,375	761	685	1,654	788	2,403	4·3	12·9	22·9	336	—[29]
38,582	144	8,662	850	886	2,553	678	2,413	6·6	41·5	47·7	2,110	7·8
38,560	0	19,568	594	596	4,364	488	3,736	11·3	25·2	27·3	1,457	37·8
38,494	4,819	14,819	697	725	3,046	622	2,053	7·9	26·3	20·2	324	20·1
38,442	8,300	22,215	549	552	3,759	534	3,176	9·8	19·0	18·4	1,959	USA
38,426	10,279	10,555	800	772	1,797	769	1,684	4·7	18·1	16·0	812[1]	4 1
38,363	11	10,304	813	821	1,266	848	973	3·3	15·1	12·4	1,707	3·5
38,362	4,195	15,303	687	666	3,449	570	5,726	9·0	25·2	56·1	1,270[1]	11·9
38,307	8,302	22,072	555	509	3,517	561	1,599	9·2	16·2	7·8	4,430[1]	11·0
38,289	—	12,915	747	766	4,087	505	4,676	10·7	40·2	40·2	1,510	CAN
38,147	4,240	9,309	836	847	2,312	710	1,708	6·1	29·9	24·1	1,129	USA
38,080	5,090	14,541	701	600	2,509	684	2,179	6·6	14·7	10·6	1,973[1]	7·2
38,036	—	10,529	802	817	1,526	815	965	4·0	18·2	11·0	2,757	UQ
37,816	9,883	22,374	546	488	2,483	690	2,549	6·6	10·9	10·5	1,497[1]	USA

The following letters in the Market Capitalisation column denote unquoted companies and country of control: AUS = Australia.　B = Belgium.
B/G = Belgium/Germany.　CAN = Canada.　G = Germany.　HOL = Holland.　IT = Italy.　SWZ = Switzerland.　UQ = Unquoted.
USA = United States of America.

Rank by turn-over	COMPANY	Main activity	Chairman and Managing Directors (in italics) §‖	Accounting period ended
751 (704)	Mothercat	Pipeline contractors, etc.	Mrs L. E. Bustani, *S. H. Shammas*	31–12–77
752 (708)	J. E. England & Sons (Wlgtn.)	Produce merchants & growers	J. R. England (J.M.D.), *J. H. L. England*	31–12–78
753 (667)	Walter Runciman & Co.	Shipping & freight agents, etc.	W. G. Runciman	31–12–78
754 (793)	Valour Co.	Makers of heat apparatus, engineers	M. Montague, *R. J. Ing, K. R. Stockwell*	31– 3–78
755 (750)	Siemens	Selling org. for Siemens products	H. M. Threlfall, *H. W. Vahl*	30– 9–78
756 (841)	Borden (UK)	Mfrs. of synthetics	H. A. Collinson, *K. M. Cole*	31–12–77
757 (863)	City Electrical Factors	Electrical wholesalers & manfrs.	R. C. Clifton (M.D.)	31– 3–77
758 (690)	William Grant & Sons	Distillers of scotch whisky, etc.	A. G. Gordon (M.D.)	31–12–77
759 (763)	George Mellis & Son	Grocers	D. W. Mellis (J.M.D.), *G. M. Mellis*	30– 4–78
760 (665)	Richardsons, Westgarth & Co.	Marine, turbine, electrical & gen. eng.	A. D. McN. Boyd	31–12–78
761 (753)	Associated Paper Industries	Paper manufacturers	K. L. Young, *J. A. Graham*	30– 9–78
762 (748)	H. P. Bulmer Holdings	Manufacturers of cider, etc.	P. J. Prior, *G. B. Nelson*	28– 4–78
763 (745)	Corah	Mnfrs. & distr. of clothing & fabrics	G. N. Corah (J.M.D.), *L. O. Helgeson*	29–12–78
764 (829)	Short Brothers	Aircraft & missile manfrs.	Sir George Leitch, *P. F. Foreman*	31– 8–77
765 (846)	Wagon Industrial Holdings	Engineering	C. L. Smith	31– 3–78
766 (—)	WGI	Mech., civil, structural, process eng.	D. R. Brooks (M.D.)	31– 3–79
767 (—)	Sun Valley Poultry	Poultry products	U. Corbett, *R. A. Corbett*	28– 1–78
768 (766)	Frederick Parker	Engineers	K. J. Parker (M.D.)	30– 9–78
769 (798)	Montedison UK	Plastic raw materials, etc.	*F. G. Pace*	31–12–77
770 (787)	Telephone Rentals	Communication & alarm equipment	E. H. Cooper, *R. A. Sly*	31–12–78
771 (731)	Inver House Distillers	Whisky distillers	K. J. Newman, *T. F. Flynn*	31–12–77
772 (782)	Carborundum Co.	Mnfrs. of abrasives, resistant mats.	K. A. Mack, *T. A. Egan*	31–12–77
773 (755)	Lister & Co.	Textile manufacturers	I. E. Kornberg, *J. A. Kornberg, M. H. E. Dracup*	31– 3–78
774 (691)	Wigglesworth & Co.	Merchanting of fibres & machinery	A. E. Simons, *V. J. Landon* (J.C.)	30– 9–78
775 (794)	Ellis & Goldstein (Holdings)	Wholesale manfrs. of coats, costumes	A. J. Philpott, *B. Barnett*	31– 1–79
776 (—)	IDC Group	Design & construction of buildings	H. Hicks	31–10–78
777 (758)	Gieves Group	Motor dealers, tailoring, book manfg.	M. E. A. Keeling	31– 1–79
778 (773)	D. C. Thomson & Co.	Printers & publishers	B. H. Thomson (J.M.D.), *D. B. Thomson*	31– 3–78
779 (754)	Richards & Wallington Inds.	Plant hirers	W. R. Richards (M.D.)	31–12–78
780 (815)	Star Paper	Paper manufacturers	T.-E. Lassenius, *E. V. Olander*	31–12–77
781 (747)	Austin Reed Group	Menswear retailers & manfrs.	B. St. G. A. Reed	31– 1–79
782 (723)	Anglo-European Foods Group	Frozen food wholesalers	C. I. Thompson	31–12–77
783 (887)	Scotia Investments	Leisure industry, insce. broking, etc.	Lord Merrivale of Walkhampton (*see page 70*)	31– 7–78
784 (538)	Humphreys & Glasgow	Engineers	A. Congreve (*see page 70*)	31– 3–78
785 (818)	Holt Lloyd International	Mfrs. of car-care products, etc.	T. Heywood (M.D.)	24– 2–79
786 (839)	Minet Holdings	Insurance brokers	J. Wallrock	31–12–78
787 (832)	Guardian & Manchester Ev. Ns.	Newspaper & magazine publishers	P. W. Gibbings	1– 4–78
788 (813)	Sandoz Products	Dyestuffs, chemicals & pharmctls.	Sir Richard Powell	31–12–78
789 (740)	Tunnel Holdings	Manfrs. of cement & allied products	J. D. Birkin (M.D.)	26– 3–78
790 (884)	Frankipile	Foundation engineers	W. R. Rowland, *T. W. Dawkins*	31–12–76
791 (300)	Barrow Hepburn Group	Merchanting & consumer products, etc.	R. Smith	31–12–78
792 (437)	Sheffield Smelting Co.	Precious metals	D. Bryars	31–12–77
793 (804)	Cincinnati Milacron	Manfrs. of machine tools, etc.	C. R. Meyer, *J. G. Campbell*	31–12–77
794 (819)	Spirax-Sarco Engineering	Specialists in fluid control eqpmt.	A. C. Brown (M.D.)	31–12–78
795 (627)	Hardy & Co. (Furnishers)	Retail house furnishers	P. C. Harris, *A. Behar*	1– 4–78
796 (647)	G. D. Searle & Co.	Ethical pharmaceuticals	*Chairmanship rotates between Directors*	31–12–77
797 (728)	Robinson & Sons	Surgical dressing manfrs. etc.	R. B. Robinson, D. C. Robinson	1– 1–78
798 (781)	Ransomes, Sims & Jefferies	Machinery manfrs. & property devlprs.	G. W. Bone, *R. L. Dodsworth*	30–12–78
799 (790)	Allied Textile Companies	Textiles	J. E. Lumb	30– 9–78
800 (817)	Unwins Wine Group	Off licence operators	*M. A. Wetz, R. J. A. Rotter, M. J. C. Wetz*	28– 2–78

NOTES : *Total tangible assets less current liabilities (other than bank loans and overdrafts and future tax).   †As percentage of capital employed at beginning of the year.   ‡As at 13 July 1979.   §Appendix on page 70 gives list of Managing Directors whose names cannot be fitted into the main text.   ‖M.D. = Managing Director; J.M.D. = Joint Managing Director; A.C. = Acting Chairman; C.E. = Chief Executive.   ¶As percentage of capital employed at end of the year.   N/A Not available.   ¹UK only.

| TURNOVER | | *CAPITAL EMPLOYED | | | NET PROFIT BEFORE INTEREST AND TAX | | | | †% to capital employed | | **No. of employees | ‡Equity market cap. £M. |
Total £000	Export £000	£000	Rank Latest year	Rank Previous year	Latest year £000	Rank	Previous year £000	% to turnover Latest year	Latest year	Previous year		
37,763	0	26,231	494	508	8,262	322	12,054	21·9	38·0	100·8	—	LEB
37,749	828	1,744	988	986	62	968	479	0·2	3·5	35·0	306	1·3
37,670	3,478	55,792	297	308	2,151	733	5,024	5·7	4·7	12·5	1,695[1]	6·1
37,580	3,396	12,229	765	733	2,279	714	1,890	6·1	20·1	16·2	2,432[1]	9·0
37,528	4,204	17,025	646	668	994	878	1,749	2·6	7·3	13·4	985	G
36,992	6,846	15,155	693	689	2,233	722	2,174	6·0	17·6	27·9	1,606[1]	USA
36,921	95	8,363	861	846	2,968	631	2,536	8·0	38·3	35·1	—	UQ
36,919	12,571	38,030	383	348	7,014	362	5,406	19·0	21·8	18·9	812	UQ
36,910	15	4,950	938	936	475	938	603	1·3	12·2	18·0	766[1]	UQ
36,814	858	13,993	715	621	1	974	2,152	0·0	0·0	13·4	2,371	3·8
36,673	3,474	14,789	698	758	2,159	732	2,157	5·9	20·7	23·9	1,605[1]	6·5
36,660	2,091	26,228	495	485	2,401	701	4,507	6·5	10·5	26·4	2,009[1]	18·1
36,635	2,593	17,445	637	608	3,687	543	3,563	10·1	22·2	23·3	4,107	10·3
36,608	25,084	26,552	491	539	Loss 4,929	996	Loss 3,977	—	—	—	6,386[1]	UQ
36,577	6,451	16,090	670	674	3,932	517	2,740	10·7	29·9	24·1	2,445[1]	15·7
36,361	2,192	12,788	751	—	2,254	720	1,281	6·2	25·3	16·0	2,358[1]	7·0
36,274	645	10,435	807	—	1,753	773	2,920	4·8	23·9	73·6	1,676	UQ
36,227	26,600	21,446	563	550	5,284	443	5,290	14·6	26·7	31·9	1,698[1]	UQ
36,203	84	16,725	652	623	1,266	849	1,769	3·5	8·1	20·2	—	IT
36,116	453	43,843	350	344	10,928	266	9,559	30·3	28·0	27·1	1,874[1]	73·7
36,092	8,041	25,723	499	499	2,323	707	Loss 1,888	6·4	10·5	—	738	USA
36,070	8,985	26,788	486	553	5,553	426	5,194	15·4	28·1	28·1	2,366	USA
35,982	3,656	21,554	560	537	2,180	729	396	6·1	10·7	2·2	3,693[1]	9·5
35,798	793	5,539	929	924	916	890	1,059	2·6	20·4	24·9	—	UQ
35,686	4,395	11,203	784	799	1,896	761	1,287	5·3	21·3	15·0	4,412	6·0
35,582	261	6,731	895	—	1,371	836	711	3·9	20·1	10·2	1,012	2·9
35,523	3,694	10,296	814	770	1,906	760	1,462	5·4	19·1	18·8	1,689[1]	5·3
35,490	1,465	35,886	394	419	6,574	380	6,920	18·5	22·1	25·9	3,045	UQ
35,478	3,489	41,716	360	360	5,293	442	4,894	14·9	14·3	13·8	2,286[1]	10·4
35,453	4,318	16,714	654	708	2,220	724	1,036	6·3	18·2	9·4	1,352	FIN
35,341	4,155	23,689	525	571	4,038	510	3,082	11·4	21·6	17·0	1,988	10·1
35,210	1,498	3,313	962	967	550	934	576	1·6	¶22·9	24·0	567	UQ
35,179	0	5,679	924	778	2,766	657	2,078	7·9	37·1	21·8	463	
35,161	5,427	6,354	907	907	1,578	803	1,860	4·5	29·1	45·2	1,722[1]	UQ
35,149	3,952	10,020	822	819	3,642	549	3,017	10·4	43·5	46·1	724[1]	24·4
35,112	—	39,522	374	398	17,630	180	15,026	50·2	54·6	68·2	1,435	55·7
35,081	894	8,598	852	857	1,813	767	73	5·2	25·3	0·9	2,749	UQ
35,004	6,012	13,760	723	702	1,529	814	2,359	4·4	12·3	19·2	890	SWZ
34,836	435	46,884	334	332	6,670	376	6,437	19·1	16·0	17·2	1,536	25·3
34,820	261	13,945	717	740	2,871	647	1,099	8·2	26·1	13·0	576	B
34,810	7,664	14,574	700	482	2,948	634	5,568	8·5	¶20·2	21·9	758	7·9
34,769	3,468	14,099	712	667	1,691	784	634	4·9	12·5	6·7	970[1]	USA
34,733	13,396	22,154	551	507	2,943	636	2,864	8·5	13·5	13·7	2,371[1]	USA
34,707	5,967	26,518	492	542	6,375	387	5,519	18·4	31·6	33·0	2,769	39·0
34,629	0	18,867	612	468	Loss 1,094	985	905	—	—	3·8	2,254	28·4
34,497	18,152	28,412	463	368	2,447	694	2,088	7·1	6·9	6·4	2,185	USA
34,408	3,865	18,065	624	580	2,280	713	1,780	6·6	14·1	12·9	3,723	UQ
34,405	8,578	36,430	392	405	3,446	572	3,211	10·0	12·2	12·9	2,801[1]	8·9
34,403	13,582	13,195	737	699	2,804	652	3,002	8·2	22·6	27·9	2,303	8·7
34,389	0	3,041	966	958	61	969	487	0·2	2·2	19·8	1,007	UQ

The following letters in the Market Capitalisation column denote unquoted companies and country of control: B = Belgium.　FIN = Finland.　G = Germany.　IT = Italy.　LEB = Lebanon.　SWZ = Switzerland.　UQ = Unquoted.　USA = United States of America.

Rank by turn-over	COMPANY	Main activity	Chairman and Managing Directors (in italics) §‖	Accounting period ended
801 (828)	Triplex Foundries Group	Foundries, engineering, etc.	R. Harrison (M.D.)	31– 3–78
802 (792)	Henry Wigfall & Son	Multiple shop retlrs. of elec. goods	F. C. B. Morrell, *R. W. Morrell*	1– 4–78
803 (—)	Brown & Jackson	Bldg. & civil eng. contrs., etc.	B. S. A. Duffy (J.M.D.), *C. J. C. Bailey (J.M.D.)*	31–12–78
804 (779)	Redman Heenan International	Specialised engineering products	A. Murray	30– 9–78
805 (795)	Roussel Laboratories	Pharmaceutical & chemical products	J. G. Machizaud, *G. E. Powderham*	31–12–78
806 (—)	Bartella	Metal merchants	K. Hannan, *N. Tom*	30– 6–77
807 (843)	Aaronson Bros.	Veneer merchants	*Chairmanship rotates between certain Dirs.*	30– 9–78
808 (825)	Maynards	Confectioners	H. P. Salmon (J.M.D.), *R. W. Ramsdale*	24– 6–78
809 (872)	Mixconcrete (Holdings)	Concrete & building material supps.	J. Mackaness	30–11–78
810 (811)	Crest Nicholson	Housing, leisure & engineering	D. L. Donne	31–10–78
811 (831)	Caltex (UK)	Petroleum distributors	W. E. Tucker, *S. Hollin*	31–12–77
812 (808)	J. & J. Dyson	Refractory mats. & fire resisting gd.	G. A. Lomas, *E. Bales, F. J. Houghton*	31– 3–78
813 (—)	Habitat Design Holdings	Retailers of household goods	T. O. Conran, *M. E. Tyson*	25– 6–78
814 (922)	J. E. Lesser & Sons (Hldgs.)	Construction and development	C. L. Lesser, *M. M. Lesser*	31–12–77
815 (686)	Phoenix Timber Co.	Timber etc., importers, mchts, etc.	A. B. Gourvitch (M.D.)	31– 3–78
816 (775)	Luncheon Vouchers	Luncheon voucher service	B. K. Beaumont	31–12–77
817 (874)	Unitech	Electronics, etc.	P. A. M. Curry	3– 6–78
818 (826)	Letraset International	Type transfer & instant lettering	W. Fieldhouse	30– 4–78
819 (974)	Electrocomponents	Electronic component mfrs. & distbtrs.	R. A. Marler	31– 3–78
820 (—)	Total Oil Marine	Oil & gas exploration, devmt. & prod.	R. Granier de Lilliac, *D. Renouard*	31–12–78
821 (827)	Laurence Scott	Elect. machinery & control gear mfrs.	P. M. Tapscott, *W. McCraith*	31– 3–78
822 (917)	Crown Cork Co.	Mfrs. of bottletops, etc.	A. H. F. Hayward (M.D.)	31–12–77
823 (847)	E. M. Denny (Holdings)	Meat importers, etc.	J. F. L. Denny	1–10–77
824 (767)	Concentric	Controls & assemblies for industry	D. F. Dodd	30– 9–78
825 (797)	Towers & Co.	Wholesale distrbs. of meat & poultry	J. B. Buxton	30– 9–77
826 (878)	Tecalemit	Engineering	N. J. Bennett, *J. M. Bennett*	31– 3–78
827 (983)	Colt International & Assoc.	Heating & ventilation equipment	A. O'Hea (M.D.)	29–12–78
828 (796)	Bellway Holdings	Building, devmt. & property invest.	J. Bell, *K. Bell*	31– 7–78
829 (881)	Nabisco	Cereal, biscuit & cake mix manfrs.	R. E. Woodcock	30–11–77
830 (—)	N. G. Bailey & Co.	Electrical engineers & contrs.	D. W. Gillespie, *N. S. Bailey*	28– 2–78
831 (785)	Manganese Bronze Holdings	Castings, components, bldg. prods., etc.	R. Dennis Poore	31– 7–78
832 (833)	AM Intl. Information Sys.	Office machinery manufacturers	*H. H. Egginton*	30– 6–78
833 (770)	Ruberoid	Bituminous building materials, etc.	T. Kenny, *J. A. Roberts*	31–12–78
834 (—)	Arthur Bartfeld Group	Mchntg. & preparation of furs, skins	A. Bartfeld, *P. N. Bartfeld*	30– 4–78
835 (752)	Booth (International Hldgs)	Hide & skin merchants and tanners	G. W. Wilks, *J. S. M. Booth*	31–12–78
836 (765)	Percy Bilton	Prop. inv. & devmt., bldg. & civil eng.	P. Bilton, *A. G. Smith, R. W. A. Groom*	31–12–78
837 (891)	Diploma	Electnc. compts., engineering, etc.	A. J. C. Thomas	30– 6–78
838 (851)	Cowan, De Groot	Toy & fancy goods, electrical dealrs.	D. Cowan (J.M.D.), *I. Williams*	30– 4–78
839 (699)	York Trailer Holdings	Commercial trailer mfrs. & marketers	F. W. Davies	31–12–78
840 (—)	London Export Corpn. (Hldgs.)	Importers & exporters	J. Perry, *G. M. Perry, S. Perry*	31– 5–78
841 (—)	Carron Company (Holdings)	Mnfrs. of metal, plastic & eng. prods.	C. S. R. Stroyan, *J. Lambie*	31–12–78
842 (805)	Alfred Booth & Co.	Builders and developers, etc.	R. H. Amis	31–12–77
843 (736)	Turriff Corporation	Engineering contractors, etc.	W. G. Turriff, *M. Greenburg*	31–12–78
844 (809)	Time Products	Horological & assoc. activities	M. J. Margulies	31– 1–79
845 (821)	Parkland Textile (Holdings)	Worsted combers, spinners & manfrs.	J. L. Hanson, *B. J. Spencer*	2– 3–79
846 (—)	Wigmore Holdings	Advertising agency	A. B. Brooker	31– 3–78
847 (853)	H. Brammer & Co.	Transmission belting, bearing distbn.	J. E. Head	31–12–78
848 (789)	Garner Scotblair	Tanners & leather manfrs.	Sir Kenneth Newton (M.D.)	31– 1–79
849 (895)	James Burrough	Gin distillers	A. Burrough	28– 2–79
850 (991)	Champion Sparking Plug Co.	Spark plug manufacturers	R. A. Stranahan, Jr., *R. V. Senez*	31–12–77

NOTES: *Total tangible assets less current liabilities (other than bank loans and overdrafts and future tax).   †As percentage of capital employed at beginning of the year.   ‡As at 13 July 1979.   §Appendix on page 70 gives list of Managing Directors whose names cannot be fitted into the main text.   ‖M.D. = Managing Director; J.M.D. = Joint Managing Director; A.C. = Acting Chairman; C.E. = Chief Executive.   ¶As percentage of capital employed at end of the year.   N/A Not available.   ¹UK only.
²⁵Now a sub. co. of Exchange Telegraph Co. (Holdings) Ltd.   ³³Now in voluntary liquidation after scheme of reconstruction.

| TURNOVER | | *CAPITAL EMPLOYED | | | NET PROFIT BEFORE INTEREST AND TAX | | | | | | **No. of | ‡Equity |
Total £000	Export £000	£000	Rank Latest year	Rank Previous year	Latest year £000	Rank	Previous year £000	% to turnover Latest year	†% to capital employed Latest year	Previous year	employees	market cap. £M
34,381	961	10,671	794	789	2,974	627	2,371	8·6	32·4	29·8	3,165	7·0
34,354	0	23,240	532	540	2,565	676	2,415	7·5	12·7	11·9	2,561	13·5
34,309	295	8,407	856	—	1,411	833	280	4·1	¶16·8	9·8	1,420	5·3
34,270	11,518	11,645	776	768	2,943	637	2,730	8·6	29·2	32·3	2,501[1]	12·1
34,210	11,500	27,189	480	511	3,786	531	3,125	11·1	17·5	16·2	1,003[1]	G
34,205	8	2,742	970	—	682	915	471	2·0	29·7	24·8	—	UQ
34,203	6,441	22,115	553	582	4,062	508	3,417	11·9	22·6	22·8	971[1]	17·7
34,164	1,517	7,504	878	878	1,532	813	1,650	4·5	23·6	28·8	2,122[1]	7·7
34,073	68	8,895	847	853	2,274	717	1,435	6·7	30·6	21·3	1,021	6·0
34,036	9,810	13,869	718	757	3,018	623	2,098	8·9	28·9	23·6	1,457[1]	16·0
34,003	9,573	4,789	942	845	290	955	Loss 228	0·9	3·7	—	148[1]	USA
33,903	9,881	18,089	623	626	3,376	587	2,972	10·0	21·8	21·8	2,177	6·8
33,903	2,766	7,134	886	—	2,561	677	1,751	7·6	38·6	32·2	1,119[1]	UQ
33,863	10,949	15,220	690	652	1,453	825	1,095	4·3	10·2	7·6	993[1]	UQ
33,827	207	16,201	666	644	1,158	857	3,284	3·4	7·9	26·9	1,300[1]	3·6
33,805	117	282	996	995	Loss 516	977	383	—	—	90·3	—	UQ
33,765	1,993	10,130	820	827	3,476	565	2,574	10·3	42·2	38·0	2,019	26·5
33,568	7,194	13,726	725	687	7,706	338	6,819	23·0	60·4	64·2	1,311	52·3
33,556	1,618	14,358	706	795	7,596	342	4,537	22·6	84·4	73·0	1,063	87·0
33,494	56	273,627	81	—	5,619	422	32,104	16·8	2·1	14·4	281	FR
33,486	5,002	20,218	585	603	2,494	687	3,087	7·4	14·9	22·2	4,029[1]	6·1
33,355	5,337	15,492	683	726	1,933	755	1,410	5·8	16·7	14·6	1,119[1]	USA
33,344	242	8,268	866	866	922	887	849	2·8	13·5	14·1	600	AUS
33,233	4,158	10,425	810	779	1,568	806	2,438	4·7	16·3	29·4	2,357	8·1
33,126	1,845	4,935	939	940	455	941	419	1·4	12·1	¶11·2	388	NZ
32,998	4,500	16,379	663	660	4,062	509	3,143	12·3	28·9	26·0	2,727[1]	16·4
32,878	2,458	17,377	641	718	3,277	602	3,025	10·0	23·4	25·7	1,818	UQ
32,852	2	31,512	428	373	4,459	478	1,325	13·6	12·8	5·9	1,407[1]	—[33]
32,752	2,866	8,018	873	883	1,038	875	743	3·2	16·4	12·1	2,290	USA
32,707	347	5,863	919	—	1,039	874	774	3·2	23·6	26·2	3,045[1]	UQ
32,701	3,330	17,211	642	630	3,285	601	3,467	10·0	21·5	26·4	2,543	4·3
32,550	8,578	13,642	726	640	1,737	778	Loss 64	5·3	11·7	—	2,590	USA
32,479	2,060	8,930	845	823	1,566	807	1,188	4·8	18·9	16·1	1,620	4·5
32,449	19,263	5,926	917	—	895	893	990	2·8	18·1	31·3	—	UQ
32,353	3,937	8,399	858	840	895	894	1,343	2·8	11·4	21·0	791[1]	2·4
32,347	0	61,136	281	247	7,685	339	7,453	23·8	12·8	12·8	929	81·6
32,280	1,700	15,201	691	676	4,738	465	4,229	14·7	36·1	39·4	1,656	33·5
32,171	1,009	11,446	779	813	2,203	727	2,070	6·8	26·1	37·2	812	9·8
32,169	8,537	11,092	787	714	1,563	808	3,019	4·9	15·0	46·6	1,723[1]	5·0
32,095	12,214	5,619	927	—	766	907	716	2·4	23·2	28·0	—	UQ
32,022	2,711	12,920	746	—	1,687	785	876	5·3	13·9	8·1	1,856	7·1
32,006	107	6,342	908	889	833	902	1,605	2·6	13·6	25·6	2,382[1]	UQ
31,951	0	6,363	905	912	1,410	834	1,181	4·4	28·1	23·8	1,122[1]	4·1
31,938	924	19,568	595	657	5,216	446	4,017	16·3	36·8	37·5	1,148[1]	36·9
31,800	6,598	16,106	669	663	3,010	624	2,742	9·5	21·8	25·4	1,949	6·2
31,753	—	3,325	960	—	1,106	867	693	3·5	30·9	22·9	432	—[25]
31,731	1,499	15,249	689	698	5,483	430	4,577	17·3	44·1	50·6	1,516[1]	35·2
31,687	10,900	11,266	783	814	1,643	790	1,586	5·2	19·5	24·7	900	5·3
31,634	16,569	11,317	782	763	3,354	590	3,127	10·6	32·7	33·1	516	UQ
31,615	15,003	9,878	825	841	4,341	490	4,179	13·7	55·5	49·9	1,574	USA

The following letters in the Market Capitalisation column denote unquoted companies and country of control: AUS = Australia. FR = France. G = Germany. NZ = New Zealand. UQ = Unquoted. USA = United States of America.

Rank by turn-over	COMPANY	Main activity	Chairman and Managing Directors (in italics) § ‖	Accounting period ended
851 (812)	Stanley Tools	Hand tool manufacturers	S. H. Davies (M.D.)	5–11–77
852 (934)	Sotheby Parke Bernet Group	Fine art auctioneers	P. C. Wilson	31– 8–78
853 (876)	Midland News Association	Newspaper proprietors	M. Graham, *L. J. Stallard*	31–12–78
854 (771)	Reed & Smith Holdings²³	Paper manufacturers, etc.	D. Harrison	31–12–76
855 (772)	Hercules Powder Co.	Chemical manufacturers	*E. G. Bruce*	30–11–77
856 (948)	Braby Leslie	Civil & mechanical engineering	E. R. Izod	31– 3–78
857 (761)	Rexmore	Textiles, timber & p.v.c. products, etc.	A. Rosenblatt, *M. Rosenblatt*	31– 3–78
858 (838)	Prosper De Mulder	Animal by-product manufacturers	P. F. De Mulder	31– 3–78
859 (—)	Horizon Travel	Air holiday operators	B. W. Tanner (M.D.)	30–11–78
860 (848)	Mettoy Co.	Toy manufacturers	A. Katz, *P. H. Katz*	31–12–78
861 (845)	Macmillan	Publishers	M. V. Macmillan, *F. H. Whitehead*	31–12–77
862 (942)	Leyland Paint and Wallpaper	Manfrs. of paint, wallcoverings, etc.	P. W. A. Simmonds, *B. Jones*	30–12–78
863 (859)	Brit. Steam Specialties Grp.	Pipeline equipment suppliers	Mrs. H. P. Waudby, *R. Sellick*	31– 3–78
864 (844)	J. & W. Henderson (Holdings)	Building trades' merchants	G. L. Grant (J.M.D.), *J. Duncan*	31– 3–78
865 (780)	Lancer Boss Group	Fork lift truck mfrs. & distributors	G. N. Bowman-Shaw	31– 3–78
866 (836)	P. Leiner & Sons	Gelatine manufacturers	L. Leiner	31– 3–78
867 (—)	Clifford's Dairies	Milk distbn. dairy prods., groceries	G. Clifford, *J. Clifford*	31–12–78
868 (—)	Audiotronic Holdings	Distrs. of hi-fi & other audio eqpmt.	G. Rose, *D. G. Smith*	4– 3–78
869 (949)	Tunnel Refineries	Starch manufacturers, etc.	R. I. Foden, *B. J. Smartt*	27– 8–77
870 (860)	Deritend Stamping Co.	Forgings, pressings, castings, elects.	D. J. Mead (M.D.)	28– 2–79
871 (897)	Braid Group	Vehicle distributors, etc.	D. C. Bamford, *W. C. G. Cartwright*	30– 9–78
872 (—)	Status Discount	Retail discount stores	E. D. Healey, *A. J. Cooper*	30–11–78
873 (890)	William Leech (Builders)	House-building & development	J. R. Adamson (M.D.)	28– 2–78
874 (870)	Tullis Russell & Co.	Paper manufacturers	D. F. O. Russell, *R. MacGregor, R. J. Wylie*	31– 3–78
875 (791)	Textron	Manfr. of ball bearings, zips, pens, etc.	J. B. Collinson, *R. P. Straetz*	30–11–76
876 (959)	William Moss Group	Builders & contractors	T. F. James	31–12–78
877 (869)	Martonair International	Pneumatic control equipment manfrs.	G. Godwin, *R. C. Cartwright*	31– 7–78
878 (905)	Wm. Donald (W'sale Meat Ctrs)	Wholesale meat contractors, farmers	W. S. Donald (M.D.)	31– 3–78
879 (786)	W. J. Oldacre (Holdings)	Animal feed manufacturers	W. J. Oldacre (M.D.)	31– 5–78
880 (—)	Kiril Mischeff (Holdings)	Foodstuffs capital equipt, warehsg.	R. Mischeff	30– 6–77
881 (—)	Blyth, Greene, Jourdain & Co.	Indl. hldgs. and general merchants	J. M. Blyth Currie (M.D.)	31–12–77
882 (840)	Clifford Motor Components	Component manufacturers	L. J. Tebodo, *L. T. Davies, J. E. Herrin*	24–12–77
883 (923)	Ash & Lacy	Metal stockholders & perforators	J. F. Vernon (M.D.)	29–12–78
884 (—)	Walkers Crisps	Manfrs. of potato products	R. E. Gerrard, *A. Reeve*	3–12–77
885 (888)	Lonsdale Universal	Printers & stationers, etc.	N. G. Ramseyer, *A. K. W. Edwards*	30– 9–78
886 (960)	National Carbonising Co.	Producers of smokeless fuel, etc.	M. A. Gaze	31– 3–78
887 (—)	George Ewer & Co.	Motor coach props. & motor trade dis.	H. G. Ewer (M.D.)	9– 9–78
888 (925)	Hogg Robinson Group	Insurers & Lloyds brokers	M. P. Abbott (M.D.)	31– 3–78
889 (986)	D. B. Marshall (Newbridge)	Broiler chicken breeders	D. B. Marshall, *W. M. Marshall, D. E. Roberts*	30– 9–77
890 (896)	Bodycote International	Textiles & industrial clothing, etc.	J. C. Dwek (M.D.)	31–12–78
891 (928)	Wates Construction	Building contractors	M. E. Wates, *P. S. Lord*	1– 1–78
892 (904)	William R. Warner & Co.	Manufacturing chemists	J. T. Beasley (M.D.)	30–11–77
893 (893)	James Beattie	Retail department stores	J. Beattie, *S. Wyeth*	31– 1–79
894 (—)	HTV Group	Television programme contractors	Lord Harlech	31– 7–78
895 (947)	Avana Group	Cake manfrs., bakers & confectioners	Sir Julian Hodge, *J. S. Randall*	1– 4–78
896 (—)	Lancia (England)	Motor vehicle distributors	W. A. Davis, *A. J. Hemelik*	31–12–77
897 (951)	Cosalt	Ships chandlery, caravan mfrs., etc.	J. M. T. Ross	31–12–78
898 (—)	General Mills UK	Toy manufacturers, chemicals, travel	R. B. Simpson (M.D.)	1– 5–77
899 (816)	Brittains	Fine papermakers, etc.	K. R. Latchford, *S. Mallinson*	31–12–77
900 (—)	Scotcros	Packaging, drink, food & transport	W. R. Alexander, *A. Mitchell*	31– 3–79

NOTES: *Total tangible assets less current liabilities (other than bank loans and overdrafts and future tax).   †As percentage of capital employed at beginning of the year.   ‡As at 13 July 1979.   §Appendix on page 70 gives list of Managing Directors whose names cannot be fitted into the main text.   ‖M.D. = Managing Director; J.M.D. = Joint Managing Director; A.C. = Acting Chairman.   ¶As percentage of capital employed at end of the year.   N/A Not available.   ¹UK only.   ²³Now a sub. co. of St. Regis International Ltd.

TURNOVER Total £000	Export £000	*CAPITAL EMPLOYED £000	Rank Latest year	Rank Previous year	NET PROFIT BEFORE INTEREST AND TAX Latest year £000	Rank	Previous year £000	% to turnover Latest year	†% to capital employed Latest year	Previous year	** No. of employees	‡Equity market cap. £M.
31,595	13,319	21,888	557	566	3,710	539	3,399	11·7	19·4	19·2	2,233[1]	USA
31,482	—	16,643	657	655	7,137	358	5,167	22·7	50·2	48·6	672[1]	37·6
31,481	0	9,270	838	828	3,755	535	2,757	11·9	45·9	33·7	1,619	UQ
31,406	835	9,886	824	775	736	910	213	2·3	7·8	2·6	1,572	—[23]
31,392	8,117	13,033	743	678	3,430	574	3,000	10·9	36·4	41·1	406	USA
31,376	5,710	9,196	840	879	2,509	683	1,651	8·0	39·1	30·0	1,559	6·7
31,336	3,948	8,319	863	807	1,227	853	1,286	3·9	14·7	15·7	1,614	6·6
31,294	0	7,320	881	877	3,082	618	2,115	9·8	47·1	41·4	760	UQ
31,269	0	6,577	902	—	2,953	633	1,023	9·4	127·9	46·5	289[1]	12·2
31,169	12,746	17,690	630	680	3,994	514	3,129	12·8	30·8	26·7	3,389	9·4
31,153	8,256	14,045	713	719	4,087	506	3,420	13·1	35·0	37·5	703[1]	UQ
31,147	6,303	10,126	821	852	2,875	645	1,776p.a.	9·2	37·8	25·6p.a.	1,699	9·1
31,144	2,069	10,540	801	815	2,484	689	2,031	8·0	29·5	26·7	1,144[1]	11·9
31,141	14	7,111	888	887	1,008	876	1,049p.a.	3·2	16·4	23·0p.a.	501	I
31,088	19,485	11,794	774	717	4,378	487	2,894	14·1	54·8	45·9	981[1]	UQ
31,006	14,518	15,102	695	694	1,450	826	1,975	4·7	11·5	21·6	740[1]	UQ
30,995	—	10,723	793	—	1,654	789	1,032	5·3	21·7	15·3	1,239	6·5
30,984p.a.	3,969p.a.	4,264	948	—	Loss 1,357p.a.	988	1,180	—	—	32·2	483[1]	1·2
30,949	2,057	16,718	653	762	2,634	666	2,795	8·5	25·7	41·4	538	UQ
30,911	2,976	13,575	729	727	1,501	819	1,830	4·9	13·0	18·4	2,333	5·6
30,877	0	8,594	853	856	1,113	864	1,048	3·6	15·4	19·4	952	2·1
30,866	0	7,518	877	—	3,929	518	2,008	12·7	101·2	37·6	529	28·4
30,820	0	20,953	511	595	2,908	642	3,366	9·4	16·8	28·1	1,978[1]	13·2
30,793	5,825	32,549	422	428	3,188	612	2,666	10·4	11·0	11·0	1,573[1]	UQ
30,683	9,127	25,940	497	450	2,391	702	3,226	7·8	9·9	16·2	3,750[1]	USA
30,524	1,076	7,623	875	920	170	805	805	0·6	3·7	21·0	1,553	UQ
30,469	7,301	20,295	584	598	5,113	452	3,961	16·8	29·8	29·2	1,458[1]	23·4
30,459	2,672	5,916	918	930	292	954	444	1·0	7·1	12·4	375	UQ
30,348	—	3,610	956	962	670	917	657	2·2	25·2	39·9	265	UQ
30,316	209	3,503	958	—	582	929	481	1·9	35·1	¶29·0	—	UQ
30,227	11,403	13,867	719	—	2,019	748	1,607	6·7	15·1	13·7	820[1]	UQ
30,207	3,310	15,509	682	654	2,326	706	4,053	7·7	16·4	27·0	3,051	USA
30,204	250	11,356	781	744	2,094	739	1,665	6·9	19·3	15·9	847	7·5
30,184	124	6,811	893	—	4,684	467	3,855	15·5	69·5	58·6	1,045	USA
30,180	1,517	12,184	766	777	2,180	730	1,880	7·2	22·1	17·8	2,256	6·5
30,162	5,194	9,791	829	760	107	967	488	0·4	1·0	7·4	944	8·5
30,133p.a.	—	7,233	883	—	1,423p.a.	829	1,048	4·7	22·0p.a.	20·4	706	6·5
30,053	—	24,961	509	519	9,638	296	8,196	32·1	45·6	64·8	3,150	32·3
30,015	46	13,281	736	729	1,625	793	1,198	5·4	14·3	13·3	1,879	UQ
29,865	594	15,173	692	731	2,413	700	2,249	8·1	21·2	21·4	1,772[1]	8·3
29,845	—	5,054	936	931	824	903	510	2·8	20·6	6·1	1,437	UQ
29,828	13,510	8,208	869	831	4,899	461	2,720	16·4	60·6	27·5	1,386[1]	USA
29,706	0	9,663	931	835	3,352	591	2,576	11·3	42·0	29·6	2,055	20·5
29,684	1,741	12,709	753	—	3,612	550	3,241	12·2	37·5	34·4	1,156	14·4
29,612	382	11,071	789	747	2,595	671	2,017	8·8	24·0	29·7	1,776	21·1
29,598	941	11,970	770	—	414	943	160	1·4	6·2	3·4	158	IT
29,512	7,587	14,459	703	713	2,541	680	2,609	8·6	21·3	31·5	1,413	5·3
29,446	2,788	19,437	599	—	1,339	839	287	4·5	9·7	¶2·1	1,622	USA
29,441	6,950	14,105	711	658	1,558	809	1,175	5·3	12·4	10·4	1,778	2·3
29,428	615	8,949	844	—	1,751	775	1,076	6·0	22·8	25·2	762[1]	7·1

The following letters in the Market Capitalisation column denote unquoted companies and country of control: I = Ireland.   IT = Italy.   UQ = Unquoted. USA = United States of America.

Rank by turn-over	COMPANY	Main activity	Chairman and Managing Directors (in italics) §‖	Accounting period ended
901 (865)	Walter Alexander	Coachbuilding, fuel oil distbn., etc.	W. R. Alexander	31– 3–78
902 (861)	Strong & Fisher (Holdings)	Clothing & fashion, leather tanners	E. D. G. Davies, *R. J. Strong*	31– 5–78
903 (916)	Boustead	Plantations, eng., metals, etc.	A. Charton	31–12–78
904 (913)	Camford Engineering	General engineering	L. J. Citroen, *D. Keech*	30– 9–78
905 (730)	Ocean Wilsons (Holdings)	Shipping services, port activities	Earl of Dartmouth	31– 1–78
906 (989)	Home Charm	Wallpaper, DIY, etc., suppliers.	H. E. Fogel (M.D.)	30–12–78
907 (822)	Pfizer	Chemical & pharmaceutical mfrs.	W. J. Wilson (M.D.)	30–11–77
908 (875)	Twinlock	Business information systems, etc.	A. K. L. Stephenson, *B. J. Holland*	2– 3–79
909 (687)	Leigh & Sillavan Group	Metal merchants and manufacturers	A. E. Whitworth	31– 3–79
910 (994)	MDW Holdings	Bldg. & civil eng. contractors	H. A. Whitson, *J. C. K. Murray*	31–12–78
911 (823)	East Lancashire Paper Group	Paper manufacturers, etc.	C. G. Seddon, *J. C. Seddon*	31–12–78
912 (—)	Hyster	Mechanical handling equipment manfrs.	A. E. Whitworth (C.E.)	31–12–77
913 (944)	Thomas Witter & Co.	Floor & wall covering manufacturers	H. Bowser, *J. Jackson*	30–11–78
914 (930)	TPT	Paper & plastic products mfrs.	W. D. Grove (M.D.)	31–12–77
915 (886)	Brunning Group	Advertising agency, etc.	G. B. Brunning (M.D.)	31– 3–79
916 (—)	Minories Garages	Motor dealers & engineers	W. Rankin	31–10–78
917 (—)	Comben Group	Estate develrs & house builders	L. Roydon, *T. R. Roydon*	31–12–78
918 (955)	Alexanders Holdings	Ford main dealers, etc.	J. B. T. Loudon, *H. Clayton, W. E. Burns*	30– 9–78
919 (—)	Geers Gross	Advertising agents & consultants	R. Gross	31–12–78
920 (—)	Siemssen, Hunter	Tobacco and publishing	R. Siemssen, *N. Freeman*	31–12–78
921 (877)	United Sterling Corpn.	Plastics raw materials	Lord Plurenden	31–12–77
922 (938)	Manders (Holdings)	Manfrs. of paint & printing ink	G. Norman (M.D.)	31–12–78
923 (835)	Warburtons	Bakers, manufacturing & wholesale	H. D. Warburton, T. H. Warburton, *J. P. Speak*	24– 9–77
924 (852)	Keep Brothers	Confirming house	P. G. Lloyd (M.D.)	30– 9–78
925 (945)	Armstrong Cork Co.	Thermoplastic flooring manfrs.	J. H. Binns, *R. Kemp*	31–12–77
926 (883)	Gordon & Gotch Holdings	Exporters of periodicals, books, etc.	Sir Anthony Percival, *C. C. Goodall*	31– 3–78
927 (—)	Young & Rubicam Holdings	Advertising and public relations	J. E. De Deo	31–12–77
928 (920)	Laws Stores	Grocers	W. G. McClelland (M.D.)	8– 4–78
929 (950)	Associated Book Publishers	Publishers & booksellers	P. H. B. Allsop, *M. R. Turner*	31–12–78
930 (943)	Stothert & Pitt	Engineers	Sir Ralph Bateman, *A. Cheetham*	1– 7–78
931 (885)	Leopold Lazarus	Metal merchants	F. A. Lissauer, *W. Griessmann*	31– 7–77
932 (900)	Longton Transport (Hldgs.)	Road transport, steel stkhg, veh. dist.	A. J. Dale	31– 3–78
933 (929)	Burco Dean	Manfrs. of domestic appliances, etc.	*D. B. Isherwood*	30– 9–78
934 (909)	Francis Industries	Engineering	D. M. Saunders	31–12–78
935 (957)	James Walker & Co.	Manfrs. of packings & jointings	D. Davies, *C. J. Higgins*	31– 3–78
936 (976)	Titaghur Jute Factory Co.	Manufacture of jute goods	H. J. Silverston	30– 6–78
937 (937)	Alfa Laval Co.	Centrifugal & agricultural engineer	Sir Archibald Ross, *B. R. Fagerström*	31–12–77
938 (—)	Wander	Ovaltine foods	A. C. E. Wander	31–12–77
939 (—)	Western Motor Holdings	Motor deliveries, sales & service	J. R. Smyth	31–12–78
940 (990)	Johnson Wax	Manufacturers of polish, etc.	S. C. Johnson, *G. R. Hudson*	30– 6–78
941 (—)	IAS Cargo Airlines	Air freight services	A. J. Stocks	31– 3–78
942 (921)	Highams	Textile manufacturers	W. M. Higham (J.M.D.), *J. H. F. Wilken*	31– 3–79
943 (901)	Graylaw Holdings	Prop. invest & garage proprietors	V. W. A. Gray (M.D.)	30– 6–76
944 (—)	Nacanco	Metal container manfrs.	*A. E. Church*	30–11–77
945 (892)	Fuerst Day Lawson Holdings	Commodity merchants	Mrs E. D. Lawson, *R. V. Neal*	31–12–77
946 (—)	Williamson Tea Holdings	Tea plantations	R. B. Magor	31–12–77
947 (987)	Mills & Allen International	Advertising, money broking, printing	Sir Ian Morrow, *C. R. Hollick*	30– 6–78
948 (968)	Brookton	Supermarkets, etc.	A. M. G. Weston	1–10–77
949 (868)	Lec Refrigeration	Refrigerator manufacturers	C. R. Purley (J.M.D.), *E. A. Cowen*	31–12–78
950 (964)	Evode Holdings	Mfrs. of adhesives, jointing cmpns., etc.	A. Simon (A.C.)	30– 9–78

NOTES: *Total tangible assets less current liabilities (other than bank loans and overdrafts and future tax).   †As percentage of capital employed at beginning of the year.   ‡As at 13 July 1979.   §Appendix on page 70 gives list of Managing Directors whose names cannot be fitted into the main text.   ‖M.D. = Managing Director; J.M.D. = Joint Managing Director; A.C. = Acting Chairman; C.E. = Chief Executive.   ¶As percentage of capital employed at end of the year.   N/A Not available.   ¹UK only.   ¹⁴Quotation suspended.

TURNOVER Total £000	Export £000	*CAPITAL EMPLOYED £000	Rank Latest year	Previous year	NET PROFIT BEFORE INTEREST AND TAX Latest year £000	Rank	Previous year £000	% to turnover Latest year	†% to capital employed Latest year	Previous year	**No. of employees	‡Equity market cap. £M.
29,361	1,864	13,788	722	755	2,540	681	2,088	8·7	24·3	26·7	1,678[1]	UQ
29,356	10,627	13,084	740	723	1,415	832	2,472	4·8	12·2	34·9	1,280	4·1
29,276	158	13,350	735	692	2,674	665	2,184	9·1	21·1	18·3	1,061	8·7
29,264	2,002	20,193	587	634	2,791	653	2,586	9·5	18·7	22·2	1,808	9·9
29,236	0	11,784	775	824	2,770	656	2,846	9·5	25·6	40·0	864	9·7
29,163	788	6,001	916	928	2,111	737	1,360	7·2	50·5	44·5	966	15·8
28,972	9,543	35,780	396	366	3,465	566	3,552	12·0	11·4	11·9	1,507	USA
28,910	4,523	12,965	745	756	2,418	699	1,661	8·4	23·1	14·4	2,370	UQ
28,748	1,777	4,813	941	942	2,968	632	Loss 220	10·3	122·6	—	125	UQ
28,700	—	5,629	926	915	1,107	866	691	3·9	23·0	15·1	837	2·9
28,627	620	10,242	816	790	1,572	805	1,424	5·5	17·2	15·2	1,544	3·7
28,625	19,882	14,261	709	—	2,445	695	671	8·5	23·4	6·8	963	USA
28,483	5,282	9,259	839	818	1,910	759	925	6·7	22·8	11·8	1,144[1]	4·3
28,455	913	12,668	755	693	3,954	516	3,721	13·9	31·2	39·0	1,030[1]	USA
28,439	563	5,655	925	918	895	895	902	3·1	18·8	20·2	830	1·8
28,411	0	8,028	872	—	1,275	846	850	4·5	19·7	17·2	658	UQ
28,389p.a.	—	28,833	458	—	3,232p.a.	608	2,238	11·4	19·6p.a.	11·9	1,166	14·2
28,358	—	6,027	914	925	916	889	695	3·2	21·1	18·8	519	2·5
28,342	—	1,987	984	—	625	921	285	2·2	31·5	85·1	—	2·5
28,287	819	6,674	897	—	1,335	840	929	4·7	29·8	28·1	602	4·0
28,277	5,042	9,871	826	792	849	899	1,816	3·0	9·3	22·1	1,017[1]	CI
28,204	1,385	22,273	548	546	3,524	560	2,535	12·5	17·6	19·2	1,338[1]	21·4
28,120	75	7,110	889	859	1,087	870	1,443	3·9	16·5	22·3	3,476	UQ
28,108	0	3,317	961	959	575	930	840	2·0	21·5	38·8	—	UQ
28,103	4,413	32,002	425	469	Loss 3,355	992	Loss 1,015	—	—	—	1,501	USA
28,082	22,445	5,703	922	899	1,136	861	991	4·0	19·8	18·3	510	3·3
28,074	466	2,203	980	—	920	888	651	3·3	49·3	30·8	349[1]	USA
28,039	—	3,217	965	948	314	951	472	1·1	9·4	17·8	1,177	UQ
27,929	4,680	10,528	803	787	3,487	564	2,733	12·5	37·6	33·7	524[1]	10·7
27,909	17,767	13,410	734	842	1,535	812	1,238	5·5	19·7	11·3	2,013	4·6
27,899	7,273	6,220	910	848	340	947	995	1·2	4·4	15·5	—	SWZ
27,870	0	12,793	750	785	1,630	792	1,850	5·8	17·2	23·5	1,006	5·3
27,800	1,529	10,485	805	780	1,954	753	1,469	7·0	20·4	15·8	1,933	5·9
27,749	1,773	12,722	752	764	1,960	751	2,033	7·1	19·1	21·3	2,125	4·9
27,721	6,330	19,932	588	561	3,536	559	3,489	12·8	18·3	18·0	2,373[1]	UQ
27,698	398	3,271	964	906	Loss 570	978	Loss 1,294	—	—	—	17,096	0·3
27,475	2,770	8,552	854	796	1,850	765	1,483	6·7	20·7	17·0	1,006[1]	SW
27,465	9,492	10,636	796	—	2,025	747	2,954	7·4	22·1	49·0	695	SWZ
27,434	9	10,483	806	—	675	916	942	2·5	8·5	13·5	1,282	2·0
27,372	8,758	11,072	788	836	3,142	613	1,828	11·5	39·6	27·7	749[1]	USA
27,371	—	5,735	920	—	1,247	851	1,021	4·6	33·0	24·6	315[1]	UQ
27,327	776	9,834	827	844	1,965	750	1,378	1·2	25·2	19·2	2,200	3·9
27,310	—	35,689	399	395	1,709	781	1,979	6·3	5·2	6·9	662[1]	UQ
27,261	1,918	13,821	720	—	3,250	607	447	11·9	34·5	9·2	802	USA
27,231	14,484	2,195	981	975	320	950	559	1·2	15·4	29·6	—	UQ
27,120	—	12,468	759	—	7,733	335	5,870	28·5	79·3	76·3	—	3·9
26,910	984	8,272	865	911	5,696	417	4,212	21·2	112·5	87·4	919[1]	20·3
26,895	—	1,992	983	982	328	949	352	1·2	18·2	21·5	661[1]	UQ
26,845	5,699	8,895	846	788	1,642	791	1,821	6·1	17·9	26·8	1,787	3·6
26,761	1,373	8,389	859	843	1,481	824	1,634	5·5	19·0	27·8	1,060[1]	—[14]

The following letters in the Market Capitalisation column denote unquoted companies and country of control: CI = Channel Islands.　SW = Sweden.　SWZ = Switzerland.
UQ = Unquoted.　USA = United States of America.

Rank by turn-over	COMPANY	Main activity	Chairman and Managing Directors (in italics) §‖	Accounting period ended
951 (977)	Edbro (Holdings)	Engineers	L. V. D. Tindale, *C. Taylor*	31– 3–78
952 (—)	John Wood Group (Aberdeen)	Eng., fishing & North Sea oil	J. Wood, *I. C. Wood*	31–12–77
953 (985)	Atlas Express Group	Carriers, etc.	R. H. Farmer (M.D.)	31–12–77
954 (871)	Tremletts Holdings	Engineering, timber & furniture	R. Smith, *D. J. Eccleston*	31– 3–77
955 (—)	Constantine Holdings	Property, transport services, etc.	H. N. Constantine, *J. Constantine*	31–12–77
956 (981)	H. E. Samson	Suppliers of cut steel	H. E. Samson	31– 3–78
957 (—)	Barretts & Baird (Wholesale)	Slaughterers, meat wholesalers, etc.	R. J. Barrett	29–12–77
958 (—)	Superdrug Stores	Drug stores	R. Goldstein, *R. S. Goldstein, P. D. Goldstein*	3– 3–79
959 (—)	Johnson Group Cleaners	Dyers and cleaners	J. L. Crockatt, *P. Bollom*	30–12–78
960 (973)	C. E. Heath & Co.	Insurance brokers, u/w agents	F. R. D. Holland	31– 3–79
961 (—)	Sandell Perkins	Timber products	C. R. Carr, *T. I. Perkins*	31– 3–78
962 (—)	Norton Abrasives	Abrasive manufacturers	*D. S. Fowlie*	31–12–77
963 (—)	Bernard Wardle & Co.	Vinyl coated fabrics, pvc sheeting	D. A. Boothman, *J. W. Sharpe*	3–12–78
964 (—)	Transparent Paper	Cellulose wrapping mfrs.	Lord Kenyon, *M. R. Fairbarns*	31– 3–79
965 (—)	British Midland Airways	Airline operators	M. D. Bishop	31–12–77
966 (—)	Eva Industries	Agricultural tools, engineering	T. R. Astley (M.D.)	31– 3–78
967 (—)	Fiat Allis UK	Construction machy. mfrs.	M. Pittaluga, *D. C. Hemmings*	31–12–77
968 (993)	Carr's Milling Industries	Flour millers, bakers, etc.	I. C. Carr	2– 9–78
969 (992)	H. A. Job	Milk distributors, etc.	A. L. Roberts, *S. Roberts*	29– 4–78
970 (908)	Edrington Holdings	Scotch whisky industry	Miss E. G. Robertson	31–12–77
971 (958)	Sheffield Twist Drill & St.	Manfrs. of engineers small tools	J. L. Dickinson, *K. G. T. Clephane*	31–12–78
972 (899)	Wrigley Co.	Chewing gum manufacturers	G. T. Morgan	31–12–77
973 (918)	Ronson Products	Lighters, razors & domestic applncs.	*A. A. F. van Cüylenburg*	31–12–78
974 (—)	Willett & Son (Corn Merchns.)	Corn merchants	C. J. Tilley (J.M.D.), *J. R. V. Wright*	7– 4–77
975 (—)	Wilson (Connolly) Holdings	Housing est. bldrs., ind. bldg. contrs.	J. A. Leavey, *L. A. Wilson, M. E. D. Robinson*	31–12–78
976 (972)	Berry Bros. & Rudd	Wine and spirit merchants	A. A. Berry	31– 3–78
977 (854)	James Latham	Timber importers & merchants	E. M. L. Latham (*see page 70*)	31– 3–78
978 (855)	Bulmer & Lumb (Holdings)	Worsted spinners	J. H. Nunnerley, *Sir William Bulmer*	1– 4–79
979 (751)	Colombo Commercial (Produce)	Produce merchants	E. W. Miller, *J. R. M. Collins*	31–12–77
980 (935)	British Mohair Spinners	Combing, dyeing & spinning	T. W. Hibbert, *G. Litten*	31–12–78
981 (—)	Jessups (Holdings)	Motor vehicle dealers, etc.	A. Jessup (M.D.)	31– 8–78
982 (953)	Biro Bic	Manufacturers of ball point pens	F. W. G. Bolt (M.D.)	31–12–77
983 (—)	J. Marr and Son	Trawler owners	G. A. Marr	31– 3–77
984 (—)	Jones, Stroud (Holdings)	Fabrics & materials for text. & elec.	P. L. Jones, *D. L. Jones*	31– 3–78
985 (984)	C. G. Hacking & Sons	Produce merchants	P. Manby, *C. G. Hacking*	30– 6–78
986 (—)	J. B. Holdings	Constructional & mechanical engrs.	W. G. S. Johnston, *A. J. D. Ferguson*	31–12–78
987 (—)	B. H. Blackwell	Retail booksellers	R. Blackwell	31– 8–77
988 (967)	Home Brewery Co.	Brewers	B. H. Farr	30– 9–78
989 (919)	Bell & Howell	Scientific instrument manfrs.	G. E. A. Perutz, *W. J. Donaldson*	31–12–77
990 (961)	Davies Turner & Co.	Shipping & forwarding agents, etc.	U. G. E. Stephenson (J.M.D.), *K. A. Hewett*	31– 3–78
991 (933)	P. Panto & Co.	Whsle, tobacconists, confectioners, etc.	P. Panto, *I, Panto* (M.D.)	22–12–78
992 (—)	National Car Parks	Car park managers	R. F. Hobson, *Sir Donald Gosling*	31–12–78
993 (—)	Playboy Club of London	Opertrs. of clubs (gaming, restaurant)	V. A. Lownes (M.D.)	30– 6–78
994 (—)	Alpine Holdings	Double glazing, aluminium windows	J. G. Gulliver, *M. A. Grant*	31– 1–79
995 (—)	R. & G. Cuthbert	Nurserymen and seedsmen	C. T. Clague (M.D.)	31–12–77
996 (—)	United Scientific Holdings	Optical, scientific, electronic equip.	J. D. Robertshaw, *P. K. Levene*	30–9–78
997 (—)	A. Goldberg & Sons	Departmental stores	Mark Goldberg (M.D.)	31– 3–79
998 (—)	Erith & Co.	Builders' merchants	G. Fisher, *G. P. Davies*	31–12–78
999 (—)	Shaw Carpets	Tufted carpet manufacturers	J. W. H. Hartley	28– 4–78
1000 (915)	Peek Holdings	Distbn. & storage of food products	Viscount Slim	31–12–75

NOTES: *Total tangible assets less current liabilities (other than bank loans and overdrafts and future tax). †As percentage of capital employed at beginning of the year. ‡As at 13 July 1979. §Appendix on page 70 gives list of Managing Directors whose names cannot be fitted into the main text. ‖M.D. = Managing Director; J.M.D. = Joint Managing Director; A.C. = Acting Chairman; C.E. = Chief Executive. ¶As percentage of capital employed at end of the year. N/A Not available. ¹UK only.

TURNOVER Total £000	Export £000	*CAPITAL EMPLOYED £000	Rank Latest year	Rank Previous year	NET PROFIT BEFORE INTEREST AND TAX Latest year £000	Rank	Previous year £000	% to turnover Latest year	†% to capital employed Latest year	†% to capital employed Previous year	**No. of employees	‡Equity market cap. £M.
26,733	8,601	16,424	661	730	3,853	522	3,699	14·4	33·9	49·0	1,551[1]	13·3
26,674	3,414	15,970	673	—	3,462	568	2,708	13·0	27·6	29·2	1,567	UQ
26,637	—	5,698	923	935	747	908	675	2·8	19·0	18·0	2,063[1]	UQ
26,623	1,936	10,574	799	753	2,208	725	2,029	8·3	23·2	¶21·3	1,698[1]	DEN
26,619p.a.	—	12,608	756	—	1,753p.a.	772	1,420	6·6	13·7p.a.	12·6	946	UQ
26,615	1,646	3,382	959	955	847	900	605	3·2	29·2	26·0	—	UQ
26,578	1,936	2,687	973	—	300	953	288	1·1	14·7	17·6	332	UQ
26,535	0	7,335	880	—	2,086	741	1,383	7·9	39·3	44·9	1,200	UQ
26,527	—	17,919	626	—	3,668	545	2,332	13·8	26·6	19·0	5,286	16·2
26,458	—	29,216	452	470	16,141	199	14,733	61·0	66·1	78·2	1,269[1]	49·7
26,457	162	8,602	851	—	2,061	744	2,129	7·8	28·3	44·5	891[1]	UQ
26,442	10,980	13,059	741	—	2,322	708	1,828	8·8	18·8	19·3	1,406[1]	USA
26,439	2,075	13,750	724	—	1,417	830	1,406	5·4	15·5	15·8	1,454	5·8
26,308	4,686	8,261	867	—	1,139	860	1,233	4·3	14·4	19·8	1,401[1]	4·5
26,276	—	2,864	969	—	1,488	822	176	5·7	67·1	8·8	939	UQ
26,275	5,961	15,840	679	—	3,362	589	2,607	12·8	27·2	33·4	2,570	8·9
26,238	23,276	14,284	708	—	2,335	705	3,612	8·9	21·9	41·3	587[1]	IT
26,097	398	7,597	876	869	1,099	868	885	4·2	16·3	17·6	777	4·3
26,073	0	5,105	935	929	1,584	801	1,332	6·1	38·3	36·9	1,380	UQ
26,045	1,214	48,268	322	338	5,593	424	5,747	21·5	14·0	19·4	739[1]	UQ
25,921	8,636	23,453	531	481	2,739	660	3,059	10·6	11·8	17·4	2,442[1]	SW
25,906	4,229	13,480	731	700	3,656	547	4,530	14·1	29·4	43·3	600[1]	USA
25,898	10,789	9,916	823	767	474	939	1,279	1·8	4·7	13·5	2,874	USA
25,868	—	1,402	990	—	237	960	273	0·9	26·8	34·9	—	UQ
25,844	0	19,202	602	—	3,491	563	2,482	13·5	22·4	18·2	531	8·5
25,840	22,989	8,888	848	858	1,219	854	653	4·7	17·1	10·1	—	UQ
25,840	137	11,045	790	737	1,319	843	2,057	5·1	11·8	22·8	497[1]	4·2
25,835	2,201	8,317	864	863	2,270	718	2,288	8·8	32·7	32·6	1,520	5·0
25,828	—	585	995	996	14	971	116	0·1	2·5	36·4	—	BAH
25,817	8,916	15,336	686	659	3,054	621	2,724	11·8	21·8	21·6	1,847	5·2
25,780	338	8,376	860	—	1,271	847	984	4·9	19·8	19·6	491	1·9
25,754	2,513	13,595	727	669	3,271	603	2,770	12·7	24·2	27·5	325[1]	FR
25,715	552	17,689	631	—	2,351	703	503	9·1	13·6	3·2	1,595	UQ
25,591	2,429	15,292	688	—	2,784	654	2,580	10·9	20·3	23·4	2,094[1]	8·6
25,466	15,126	1,604	989	992	308	952	197	1·2	33·4	22·5	—	UQ
25,401	6,956	12,333	763	—	2,611	669	2,713	10·3	23·9	29·3	935[1]	5·8
25,393	16,480	6,980	891	—	2,235	721	1,601	8·8	39·4	33·9	851[1]	UQ
25,381	0	19,068	607	591	3,538	558	3,521	13·9	20·1	22·4	1,578	UQ
25,345	1,079	10,426	808	783	862	897	1,999	3·4	9·1	30·4	641	USA
25,298	0	2,242	979	969	687	912	659	2·7	29·2	37·6	492[1]	UQ
25,277	0	3,655	954	957	240	959	405	0·9	8·6	13·9	472	0·9
25,258	0	11,148	785	—	3,597	552	3,389	14·2	37·0	33·6	2,765	UQ
25,252	—	18,999	608	—	13,354	229	12,623	52·9	116·7	999·3	1,036	UQ
25,221	72	2,907	968	—	1,920	757	947	104·1	7·6	56·4	716	13·6
25,210	128	6,795	894	—	906	892	415p.a.	3·6	15·4	7·7p.a.	1,046	SW
25,159	11,422	10,170	819	—	4,003	512	2,776	15·9	80·7	85·8	1,420	32·4
25,109p.a.	0	16,826	651	—	2,480p.a.	691	1,907	9·9	18·9p.a.	17·6	1,622	10·6
25,103	156	5,543	928	—	1,231	852	854	4·9	34·1	23·5	546	4·9
25,053	5,933	6,408	904	—	990	879	467	3·8	12·7	7·7	819	5·3
25,046p.a.	10p.a.	6,219	911	885	Loss 607p.a.	980	—[15]	—	—	—	1,086	0·3

The following letters in the Market Capitalisation column denote unquoted companies and country of control: BAH = Bahamas.   DEN = Denmark.   FR = France. IT = Italy.   SW = Sweden.   UQ = Unquoted.   USA = United States of America.

Appendix to Table 1: Managing directors

Rank in table	Company	Managing Directors
1	British Petroleum Co.	*J. Birks, C. C. F. Laidlaw, J. W. R. Sutcliffe, P. I. Walters, M. M. Pennell, R. W. Adam*
19	Inchcape & Co.	*Sir Michael Parsons, J. W. Ritchie, J. M. H. Millington-Drake*
26	Marks & Spencer	*M. M. Sacher, R. Greenbury, W. B. Howard, H. N. Lewis, Sir Derek Rayner*
32	P. & O. Steam Navigation Co.	*R. B. Adams, H. F. Spanton, O. Brooks*
36	Tube Investments	*R. M. Bagnall, T. E. Barnsley*
55	EMI	*Lord Delfont (Chief Executive), R. Brooke*
74	George Wimpey	*T. T. Candlish, C. J. Chetwood, S. S. Jardine, P. J. Ward*
136	Taylor Woodrow	*R. E. Aldred, N. C. Baker, B. S. L. Trafford, F. R. Gibb*
152	British Sugar Corpn	*J. M. Beckett (Chief Executive)*
192	Croda International	*D. Mather, G. R. Hembrough, D. Jewsbury*
219	Lead Industries Group	*R. G. Harper, M. J. G. Henderson, C. A. Kelly*
320	Illingworth, Morris & Co.	*D. Hanson, P. Hardy, J. L. Hopkinson, J. D. P. Tanner*
338	London Brick Co.	*M. O. Wright, J. Bristow, D. H. Lawrence*
344	Magnet & Southerns	*P. H. Doughty, P. T. Duxbury, C. E. Illingworth, G. A. B. Storey*
358	Borg-Warner	*G. C. Hartman, G. S. McNally, S. R. Walsh, P. G. W. Whybrow (J.M.D.)*
658	Surridge Dawson (Holdings)	*P. J. M. Surridge (Executive Chairman), P. G. Durance*
732	Brintons	*T. A. Tolley, H. F. Lowe*
737	Bambergers	*L. A. Woodburn-Bamberger*
743	Caffyns	*A. M. Caffyn, A. E. F. Caffyn, R. J. M. Caffyn*
783	Scotia Investments	*A. T. Dembeniotis, P. Frohlich*
784	Humphreys & Glasgow	*F. W. Edwards, R. Langford, W. Richardson, D. D. Young*
977	James Latham	*C. G. A. Latham, D. R. Latham, J. M. Latham, R. H. Bridle*

2 The 50 largest acquisitions and mergers*

Rank (total consideration)	Acquiring company	Acquired company	VALUE OF CONSIDERATION FOR EQUITY NOT ALREADY OWNED			
			Total £000	Cash £000	Equity £000	Other £000
1	Associated Dairies Group	Associated Dairies Ltd	210,204	—	210,204	—
2	George Wimpey Ltd	George Wimpey & Co.	180,480	—	180,480	—
3	Costain Group	Richard Costain	116,066	—	116,066	—
4	Tenneco International Holdings	Albright & Wilson	114,980	114,980	—	—
5	Harrisons & Crosfield	Harrisons Malaysian Estates	111,617	—	111,617	—
6	International Thomson Group	Thomson Organisation	62,265	3,306	33,061	25,898
7	Allied Breweries	J. Lyons & Co.	56,718	—	56,718	—
8	Marchwiel	Marchwiel Holdings	47,701	—	44,210	3,491
9	Hawker Siddeley Group	Carlton Industries[1]	43,695	43,695	—	—
10	Hawker Siddeley Group	Westinghouse Brake & Signal Co.	39,065	—	39,065	—
11	Norcros	H. & R. Johnson—Richards Tiles	34,390	14,193	20,197	—
12	Imperial Group	J. B. Eastwood	30,806	30,806	—	—
13	Dawson International	John Haggas	25,969	12,465	13,504	—
14	Northern Foods	Pork Farms	22,818	10,680	12,138	—
15	Rank Organisation	Leisure Caravan Parks	19,908	19,908	—	—
16	Greenall Whitley & Co.	James Shipstone & Sons	18,954	11,469	7,485	—
17	Letraset International	Stanley Gibbons International	18,419	12,785	5,634	—
18	Harrisons & Crosfield	Sabah Timber	13,003	—	13,003	—
19	Letraset International	J. & L. Randall	11,823	1,178	10,645	—
20	Raybeck	Bourne & Hollingsworth	11,119	11,119	—	—
21	Associated Dairies Group	Allied Retailers	9,804	5,149	4,655	—
22	Dana Engineering	Turner Manufacturing	9,425	9,425	—	—
23	Johnson & Firth Brown	Weston-Evans Group	8,155	4,174	3,981	—
24	Linfood Holdings	Wheatsheaf Distribution & Trading	7,749	1,867	3,579	2,303
25	International Timber Corpn	Bambergers	7,311	2,329	4,982	—
26	Bowater Corpn	Crossley Building Products	6,427	6,427	—	—
27	Associated Engineering	Fluidrive Engineering Co.	6,298	—	6,298	—
28	Scapa Group	Bury & Masco (Holdings)	6,136	2,772	3,364	—
29	Associated Dairies Ltd.	Wades Departmental Stores	5,699	5,699	—	—
30	Cement-Roadstone Holdings	J. & W. Henderson (Holdings)	5,652	5,652	—	—
31	Aurora Holdings	Samuel Osborn & Co.	5,329	—	5,329	—
32	J. H. Fenner & Co. (Holdings)	James Dawson & Son	5,224	—	5,224	—
33	Vantona Group	J. Compton Sons & Webb (Holdings)	5,189	5,189	—	—
34	Rockware Group	Alida Packaging Group	3,582	3,582	—	—
35	Ladbroke Group	Myddleton Hotels	3,527	3,527	—	—
36	LWT (Holdings)	Hutchison	3,500	3,500	—	—
37	Manor National Group Motors	Oliver Rix	3,438	—	1,442	1,996
38	Alfred Preedy & Sons	Midland Educational Co.	3,240	2,597	643	—
39	Unigate	Carding Group	3,067	3,067	—	—
40	Whitecroft	Randalls Group	2,917	1,542	1,375	—
41	Northern Foods	Ch. Goldrei Foucard & Son	2,390	2,390	—	—
42	Ferguson Industrial Holdings	Peerage of Birmingham	2,153	986	1,167	—
43	S. & W. Berisford	Turner Curzon	1,739	1,739	—	—
44	Crown House	Best and May	1,703	289	1,414	—
45	Black & Edgington	Gailey Group	1,611	—	1,611	—
46	Simon Engineering	Gordon-Johnson-Stephens Holdings	1,581	1,581	—	—
47	Kaye Organisation	Bonser Engineering	1,545	1,545	—	—
48	Associated Portland Cement Mnfrs	BCA	1,479	1,479	—	—
49	Central Manufacturing & Trading Group	G. R. Francis Group	1,394	1,394	—	—
50	Mitchell Cotts Group	Mitchell Cotts Transport	1,247	—	1,247	—

NOTES: *This table covers the fiscal year 1978/79 and includes companies listed in Table 1 of last year's *Times 1000*. Acquisitions of unquoted companies are not included and alternative offers have been ignored and consideration calculated on the basic offer.
[1]Offer was made for 51.9% of shares.

3 Largest shareholdings table*

Rank in 1978/9 '1000	Company	Date	Nominal equity capital £000	Prudential Assurance	Legal & General Assurance	Britannic Assurance	Norwich Union Life Ins.	Pearl Assurance	Co-Op. Ins.	**Nominees	Others
				%	%	%	%	%	%	%	%
2	'Shell' Transport & Trading	31.3.79	138,104	2.9	—	—	—	—	—	—	—
3	BAT Industries	23.5.79	90,874	1.71	—	—	—	—	—	1.62	(a) 1.14 (b) 2.02
4	Imperial Chemical Industries	1.1.79	570,465	2.86	—	—	—	—	—	2.50	(c) 1.66 (d) 18.45
5	Unilever Ltd.	31.3.79	45,767	3.77	—	—	1.08	—	—	—	(d) 18.45
6	Imperial Group	30.4.79	176,577	2.22	1.51	—	—	—	—	3.55	(b) 1.23 (d) 18.45
7	BL	31.3.79	578,700	—	—	—	—	—	—	—	(e) 98.89
10	General Electric Co.	30.3.79	137,175	5.92	—	—	—	—	—	—	(f) 1.24
11	Rio Tinto-Zinc Corporation	3.4.79	62,794	3.07	—	—	—	—	—	12.08	—
12	Bowater Corporation	31.3.79	149,759	3.01	—	—	—	1.48	—	12.45	(g) 1.14 (b) 1.21
14	Grand Metropolitan	2.4.79	220,956	2.68	1.03	—	1.19	—	—	6.41	(b) 1.39
15	Guest, Keen & Nettlefolds	1.5.79	151,334	2.85	1.23	1.36	—	1.27	—	1.21	(b) 2.53 (h) 3.71 (j) 2.00 (k) 1.31 (n) 1.14 (p) 1.11
16	Courtaulds	31.3.79	68,311	2.22	—	—	—	—	—	1.13	(b) 1.35
18	Rothmans International	31.3.79	19,556	2.12	—	—	—	—	—	14.56	(q) 43.78
19	Reed International	6.4.79	111,746	3.60	—	—	1.80	1.05	1.07	6.70	(b) 2.48
22	Dunlop Holdings	20.4.79	66,226	2.22	—	1.62	—	—	—	7.11	(r) 1.23
23	S. & W. Berisford	31.3.79	20,287	4.93	—	—	—	2.24	1.16	4.36	(s) 2.55 (t) 1.70 (u) 1.05 (v) 1.23
24	Inchcape & Co.	31.3.79	80,828	2.58	—	—	1.27	—	—	10.48	(w) 1.75 (x) 3.36 (y) 1.12
25	Tate & Lyle	7.3.79	54,559	3.50	—	—	—	—	1.00	2.18	(b) 1.20
26	Marks & Spencer	—	324,914	6.31	—	—	—	—	—	—	(b) 1.56
27	Lonrho	31.3.79	47,260	—	—	—	—	—	—	1.02	(z) 21.40 (aa) 13.90 (bb) 1.70
29	Ranks Hovis McDougall	5.5.79	68,395	2.77	1.39	—	—	1.53	—	16.71	(b) 2.57 (r) 1.09 (cc) 1.11 (dd) 1.47
30	Allied Breweries	31.3.79	131,570	3.68	1.36	—	—	—	—	—	—
31	C. T. Bowring & Co.	2.1.79	27,185	—	—	—	1.15	1.15	—	11.27	(ee) 1.17
32	Amalgamated Metal Corpn	6.2.79	6,285	1.34	—	—	—	1.12	—	—	(ff) 1.27 (gg) 76.64
33	Thorn Electrical Industries	29.3.79	35,096	3.79	—	—	—	1.56	1.20	—	(hh) 1.19 (b) 1.89 (jj) 1.39 (kk) 2.07
34	BICC	16.2.79	74,657	3.49	1.41	1.61	—	1.25	1.31	5.94	(b) 1.31 (nn) 1.05
35	Burmah Oil Co.	31.3.79	143,972	—	—	—	—	—	—	14.89	—
36	Sears Holdings	29.3.79	224,269	2.62	—	—	1.03	1.35	—	6.79	(b) 1.58
37	P. & O. Steam Navigation Co.	6.6.79	141,158	1.27	1.05	—	—	—	1.11	11.82	(b) 1.22
39	Consolidated Gold Fields	31.3.79	36,905	2.56	—	—	—	—	—	10.62	—
40	Tozer, Kemsley & Millbourn	31.3.79	9,975	2.11	—	—	—	—	—	4.99	(pp) 9.99 (r) 1.20 (cc) 1.57 (t) 4.01 (jj) 1.00 (v) 1.21 (qq) 3.34
41	Hawker, Siddeley Group	27.3.79	49,263	2.95	—	—	1.28	—	—	7.36	(rr) 1.08
42	Bass	23.3.79	69,450	4.41	—	1.73	—	—	—	7.19	(b) 1.08 (ss) 1.26

NOTES: *Based on holdings of 1% or more. **This column is the sum of nominee holdings of 1% or more. It is possible that by aggregating the true beneficial interests of nominee holders of less than 1%, undisclosed holdings of 1% or more may exist.
(a) Imperial Investments Ltd. (b) National Coal Board Pensions Fund Nominees Ltd. (c) Bank of England. (d) Trustees of the Leverhulme Trust. (e) National Enterprise Board. (f) Royal Insurance Co. Ltd. (g) Airways Pension Fund Trustees Ltd. (h) Post Office Pension Funds. (j) British Rail Pension Fund. (k) ICI Pension Funds. (n) Eagle Star Insurance. (p) Commercial Union Assurance. (q) Rothmans Tobacco (& Holdings) Ltd. (r) Church Commissioners for England. (s) E. S. Margulies. (t) ITC Pension Trust Ltd. and another. (u) Scottish Amicable Life Assurance Society. (v) Sun Alliance and London Assurance Co. Ltd. (w) Glenapp Estate Co. Ltd. (x) Inchcape Family Investments Ltd. (y) John W. M. M. Richard and others. (z) Gulf Fisheries Co. W.L.L. (aa) R. W. Rowland. (bb) Thomas Tilling Ltd. (cc) Eagle Star Insurance Co. Ltd. (dd) Official Custodian for Charities. (ee) Mrs V. M. Eveson. (ff) J. D. Bannerman. (gg) Preussag AG. (hh) United Kingdom Temperance & General Provident Institution. (jj) Royal London Mutual Insurance Society Ltd. (kk) Sir Jules Thorn and other. (nn) Merchant Navy's Officers' Pension Fund Trustee Ltd. (pp) Barclays Bank International Ltd. (qq) Westments Ltd. (rr) British Petroleum Pension Trust. (ss) Royal Insurance Co. Ltd.

When your company stops earning its keep we start to earn ours.

A fire or flood in your factory or office is bad enough in itself, but even more trouble may come later.

Just how soon will you be able to start up again after the calamity, and what can you tell the staff about their jobs and their wages?

What happens to your customers and the contracts you have to complete?

The GRE Business Interruption Policy will help to see that you do not lose financially during the time it takes to put matters right.

It'll pay for temporary accommodation, for extra overtime and sub-contracted work, and pay salaries as well.

Most important of all it'll help to meet all your expenses and still leave you with the profit you would have anticipated.

So if you'd like to take some of the worries out of your business life contact your local GRE branch or your usual insurance adviser.

And find out how well we can work together.

GRE Guardian Royal Exchange Assurance

Head Office: Royal Exchange, London EC3V 3LS

GREAT INSURANCE

The New Orient Express.
(London-Singapore in 9 hrs.)

Flying by Concorde to Singapore[†] costs only 15% more than First Class.

Concorde also flies to Bahrain in 4 hours. Dallas in 8 hours[*]. New York in 4 hours. Washington in 4¼ hours.

British airways Concorde

*Interchange with Braniff †In association with SIA

4 Nationalised inds., State holding cos.

| Rank | Name—*Chairman* | Turnover £000 | *Capital employed £000 | NET PROFIT BEFORE INTEREST & TAX | | | INTEREST PAID | | Employees |
				Latest year £000	†% To capital employed Latest year	Previous year £000	Latest year £000	Previous year £000	
1	Electricity Council & Boards *Sir Francis Tombs*	5,445,100	6,801,300	**862,300**	13·2	747,400	**442,900**	454,700	159,825
2	Post Office *Sir William Barlow*	4,619,000	7,469,300	**1,281,100**	18·6	1,108,700	**510,200**	390,400	410,977
3	National Enterprise Board *Sir Leslie Murphy*	4,157,600	1,823,300	**119,000**	7·8	115,400	**92,900**	86,800	278,514
4	British Steel Corporation *Sir Charles Villiers*	3,288,000	4,253,700	**Loss 77,200**	—	Loss 236,100	**207,700**	197,400	190,000
5	National Coal Board *Sir Derek Ezra*	2,989,400	1,924,200	**96,000**	6·4	99,000	**144,500**	91,700	300,000
6	British Gas Corporation *Sir Denis Rooke*	2,971,800	2,180,800	**618,200**	29·4	473,400	**98,100**	147,300	101,750
7	British Railways Board *Sir Peter Parker*	1,978,800	1,781,500	**58,300**	4·7	68,400	**49,100**	43,000	243,264
8	British Airways *R. Stainton*	1,640,300	792,800	**114,700**	13·8	62,000	**25,000**	23,000	57,741
9	British Aerospace *Lord Beswick*	894,492	326,560	**67,566**	23·4	72,696	**7,744**	10,111	72,010
10	British Shipbuilders *Sir Anthony Griffin*	730,507p.a.	98,664	**Loss101,877p.a.[1]**	—	—	**6,432**	—	86,600
11	S. of Scotland Electricity Board *R. Berridge*	463,410	712,630	**87,812**	12·2	89,911	**60,576**	67,392	13,739
12	National Bus Company *Lord Shepherd*	437,443	199,398	**28,335**	15·8	20,255	**12,980**	12,044	64,270
13	British National Oil Corporation *Lord Kearton*	431,827	763,879	**12,186**	2·1	6,125	**9,911**	8,006	897
14	National Freight Corporation *R. L. E. Lawrence*	394,000	129,600	**15,829**	11·7	8,100	**14,774**	16,506	39,847
15	London Transport Executive *R. Bennett*	334,617	933,567	**Loss 1,927[2]**	—	Loss 2,777[2]	N/A	N/A	59,998
16	British Broadcasting Corporation *Sir Michael Swann*	287,327	107,948	**2,311**	2·1	5,768	**545**	822	25,888
17	N. of Scotland Hydro-Electric Bd. *Lord Kirkhill*	172,694	553,178	**54,430**	11·0	46,839	**47,061**	41,501	4,059
18	British Airports Authority *N. J. Payne*	162,234	342,486	**35,256**	10·7	32,280	**3,964**	4,029	7,070
19	British Transport Docks Board *Sir Humphrey Browne*	117,694	176,968	**29,679**	17·5	29,046	**6,504**	6,852	11,609
20	Scottish Transport Group *Lord Donnet of Balgay*	105,722	92,835	**2,219**	3·2	1,648	**947**	975	14,112
21	Independent Broadcasting Authority *Lady Plowden*	22,637	42,605	**4,018**	9·8	2,814	**181**	184	1,200

NOTES: *Total tangible assets less current liabilities (other than bank loans and overdrafts). † As percentage of capital employed at beginning of year. [1] After £89,780,000 write-down of investments in sub. cos. in respect of losses incurred during period. [2] After interest. N/A Not available.

5 Clearing banks

| Rank | Name—*Chairman* | GROSS DEPOSITS | | TOTAL ASSETS | | NET PROFIT AFTER TAX | |
		Latest year £000	Previous year £000	Latest year £000	Previous year £000	Latest year £000	Previous year £000
1	Barclays Bank* *Sir Anthony Tuke*	**20,841,000**	19,348,000	**23,884,000**	22,077,000	**228,000**	118,200
2	National Westminster Bank** *R. Leigh-Pemberton*	**20,228,200**	17,602,637	**22,183,600**	19,187,765	**183,600**	108,830
3	Midland Bank *Lord Armstrong of Sanderstead*	**13,824,983**	11,754,188	**15,550,275**	13,382,640	**140,734**	88,633
4	Lloyds Bank[1] *Sir Jeremy Morse*	**13,520,610**	12,393,716	**14,762,762**	13,529,780	**127,699**	83,511
5	National & Commercial Banking Group *Sir Michael Young-Herries*	**3,782,778**	3,292,686	**4,439,045**	3,882,571	**32,058**	30,507
6	Bank of Scotland *Lord Clydesmuir (Governor)*	**2,027,740**	1,618,910	**2,393,452**	1,979,710	**21,344**	12,593
7	Co-operative Bank *Sir Arthur Sugden*	**401,994**	365,007	**458,948**	415,785	**2,634**	1,822

NOTES: *Including Barclays Bank Internationial Ltd., (see Table 9). **Including International Westminster Bank Ltd., (see Table 9). [1] Including Lloyds Bank International Ltd.

6 Finance houses

Rank	Name—*Chairman*	OUTSTANDING BALANCES		CAPITAL EMPLOYED		NET PROFIT BEFORE INTEREST AND TAX	
		Latest year £000	Previous year £000	Latest year £000	Previous year £000	Latest year £000	Previous year £000
1	Lombard North Central *Earl of Crawford and Balcarres*	992,146	900,968	1,040,763	912,671	109,348	110,263
2	United Dominions Trust *L. C. Mather*	463,100	488,100	848,100	906,200	83,600	112,900
3	Mercantile Credit Co. *A. Victor Adey*	424,356	291,482	885,424	621,080	75,607	68,166
4	Lloyds and Scottish Finance *G. Duncan*	407,881	292,870	580,924	431,022	59,455	51,619
5	Forward Trust *J. A. Cave*	342,062	268,979	409,414	321,063	42,274	37,033
6	Hodge Finance *R. A. S. Lane*	268,501	228,364	284,753	218,407	27,538 p.a.	23,925 p.a.
7	Bowmaker *P. Bowring*	206,445	147,747	286,417	212,263	29,200	23,257
8	Provident Financial Group *Lord Chelmer*	161,093	135,298	108,941	86,884	17,508	15,834
9	North West Securities *Lord Balfour of Burleigh*	148,863	119,168	260,817	201,851	24,340	20,806
10	First National Securities* —	128,442	124,281	129,437	127,310	19,241	20,223
11	Commercial Credit Services Holdings *R. J. Harrison*	56,677	56,403	71,709	62,851	6,603	5,480 p.a.
12	Wagon Finance Corpn. *S. M. de Bartolome*	49,498	37,363	32,957	27,141	5,786	4,698
13	British Credit Trust *J. P. Bourke*	48,981	32,942	46,469	26,473	5,069 p.a.	3,752
14	F. C. Finance *Sir Arthur Sugden*	43,778	35,925	77,018	74,516	6,161	5,704
15	HFC Trust *I. Martindale*	34,138	23,176	28,637	18,035	2,646	1,924
16	St. Margaret's Trust *D. B. Reid*	27,342	21,160	25,093	18,721	2,079	2,046
17	Wessex Finance Corpn. *P. N. Price*	24,436	24,050	25,401	25,232	2,159	Loss 1,124
18	AVCO Financial Services —	18,448	12,767	17,104	11,985	2,139	1,681
19	Boston Trust & Savings *I. Stepanian*	13,618	9,893	11,150	7,603	916	748
20	London Scottish Finance Corpn *R. H. Landman*	11,974	7,914	6,240	3,996	1,122	938
21	Shawlands Securities *N. R. Frizzell*	8,111	3,991	8,840	6,229	883	717
22	Wrenwood Finance Co. *F. I. C. Ellwood*	1,139	1,223	1,540	1,285	123 p.a.	113

NOTE: * Figures extracted from combined accounts of First National Securities Ltd. and other related companies (not prepared for statutory purposes).

The all-round strength of Bowring

In 1978 Bowring yet again had another record year. 1978 showed consistent high performance throughout the Group's world-wide operations. These include insurance broking—good progress; insurance underwriting—a significant advance; credit finance—Bowmaker outstandingly successful; engineering—continued improvement; merchant banking—Singer & Friedlander a strong advance; trading—profits up despite a downward trend; shipping—substantial reduction in operating loss.

Bowring

C.T. Bowring & Co. Ltd
The Bowring Building, Tower Place,
London EC3P 3BE
Tel: 01-283 3100   Telex: 882191

Awarded to
C.T. Bowring
(Insurance)
Holdings Ltd.

79

7 Accepting houses

Rank	Name—*Chairman*	*TOTAL ASSETS Latest year £000	Previous year £000	ACCEPTANCES Latest year £000	Previous year £000	NET PROFIT AFTER TAX Latest year £000	Previous year £000
1	Schroders *Earl of Airlie*	1,390,779	1,066,060	152,414	110,731	4,269	3,504
2	Kleinwort, Benson, Lonsdale *R. A. Henderson*	1,386,479	1,234,052	243,885	196,138	8,864	7,479
3	Hambros *J. O. Hambro*	1,249,636	1,165,510	274,667	257,960	7,035	4,851
4	Hill Samuel Group *Sir Kenneth Keith*	1,176,896	1,094,638	233,750	209,066	7,340	6,852
5	Samuel Montagu & Co. (Inc. Drayton) *P. Shelbourne*	1,086,790	898,539	69,817	57,139	2,000	1,659
6	Morgan Grenfell Holdings *J. E. H. Collins*	911,000	752,516	136,900	110,370	3,692	5,180
7	S. G. Warburg & Co. *Lord Roll of Ipsden, G. C. Seligman*	799,251	651,472	107,851	100,955	12,955	9,704
8	Lazard Brothers & Co. *D. Meinertzhagen*	577,571	517,870	64,261	51,161	3,656	3,807
9	N. M. Rothschild & Sons *Evelyn de Rothschild*	416,855	362,392	37,439	32,760	500	403
10	Baring Brothers & Co. *J. F. H. Baring*	320,503	284,118	65,888	42,145	650	650
11	Guinness Mahon & Co. *D. Robson*	237,854	198,474	28,659	30,540	1,600	1,200
12	Brown, Shipley Holdings *Lord Farnham*	218,251	196,289	34,643	25,557	1,651	1,693
13	Singer & Friedlander *A. N. Solomons*	192,701	173,381	48,669	31,803	1,740	1,187
14	Antony Gibbs Holdings *Sir Philip de Zulueta*	179,420	176,228	61,073	45,634	407	455
15	Arbuthnot Latham Holdings *A. R. C. Arbuthnot*	165,853	170,976	19,615	17,304	788	1,097
16	Charterhouse Japhet *M. H. W. Wells*	123,435	88,091	29,075	26,268	759 p.a.	815
17	Rea Brothers *W. H. Salomon*	80,002	77,372	13,198	11,655	451	501

NOTES: This table comprises all members of the Accepting Houses Committee.
*Excluding acceptances.

8 Discount houses

Rank	Name—*Chairman*	GROSS DEPOSITS Latest year £000	Previous year £000	TOTAL ASSETS Latest year £000	Previous year £000	NET PROFIT AFTER TAX Latest year £000	Previous year £000
1	Union Discount Co. of London *A. J. O. Ritchie*	1,311,763	948,506	1,331,917	968,439	1,803	6,114
2	Gerrard & National Discount Co. *R. G. Gibbs*	1,184,115	1,010,877	1,213,004	1,034,588	5,006	5,708
3	Alexanders Discount Co. *J. P. R. Glyn*	468,323	496,461	480,463	509,099	200	2,139
4	Cater Ryder & Co. *E. D. D. Ryder*	411,776	422,759	423,531	433,800	1,515	1,732
5	Smith St. Aubyn & Co. (Holdings) *J. F. E. Smith*	350,388	326,786	358,917	334,531	1,495	1,947
6	Clive Discount Holdings *N. H. Chamberlen*	336,947	395,278	345,766	403,425	1,384	2,119
7	Jessel Toynbee & Co. *M. R. Toynbee*	309,196	259,005	314,992	265,504	942	1,299
8	King & Shaxson *T. S. Hohler*	264,073	256,743	271,535	263,843	709	1,217
9	Allen Harvey & Ross *A. J. Buchanan*	225,436	249,801	231,590	255,989	586	1,201
10	Gillett Brothers Discount Co. *I. T. H. Logie*	211,754	237,151	217,421	243,029	213	1,014
11	Seccombe Marshall & Campion *D. G. Campion*	97,741	74,301	100,997	77,526	227	304

NOTE: This table comprises all members of the London Discount Market Association.

Money market experts

Clive Discount Co. Ltd.
(Members of the London Discount Market Association)

Specialist traders in:
Sterling certificates of deposit · Short term sterling deposits
Eligible and non-eligible bank bills · Treasury bills
Trade bills · Local authority bills and bonds

Clive Investments Ltd.

Fixed interest investment management for institutional
and private clients · Funds are managed
either on a discretionary or advisory basis.

If you would like to talk about any aspect of our market,
ring Michael Jameson-Till on 01-283 1101 or write to:
Clive Discount Co. Ltd., 1 Royal Exchange Avenue, London EC3V 3LU.

81

9 British banks trading mainly overseas

Rank	Name—*Chairman*	GROSS DEPOSITS		TOTAL ASSETS		NET PROFIT AFTER TAX	
		Latest year £000	Previous year £000	Latest year £000	Previous year £000	Latest year £000	Previous year £000
1	Barclays Bank International* *Sir Anthony Tuke*	**10,772,000**	10,355,000	**12,600,000**	12,173,000	**54,600**	49,300
2	Hong Kong and Shanghai Banking Corpn** *M. G. R. Sandberg*	**7,614,105**	6,801,046	**8,581,352**	7,772,298	**74,201**	59,391
3	Standard Chartered Bank *Lord Barber*	**7,608,546**	7,110,114	**9,369,215**	8,493,657	**53,672**[1]	54,510
4	Lloyds Bank International[2] *Sir Reginald Verdon-Smith*	**5,340,600**	4,841,900	**5,995,000**	5,463,000	**19,700**	18,500
5	International Westminster Bank[3] *Viscount Sandon*	**4,885,287**	4,296,818	**6,601,466**	5,298,133	**19,547**	16,801
6	Grindlays Holdings *N. J. Robson*	**2,817,464**	2,640,719	**2,960,150**	2,760,456	**12,111**	10,558
7	Bank of Tokyo and Detroit (International) *Y. Kashiwagi*	**153,169**	139,376	**175,485**	155,722	**1,867 p.a.**	1,016

NOTES: *Subsidiary of Barclays Bank Ltd.
** Incorporated in Hong Kong, a British Colony.
[1] Taken from proforma figures.
[2] Subsidiary of Lloyds Bank Ltd.
[3] Subsidiary of National Westminster Bank Ltd.

WHERE IN THE WORLD WILL YOU FIND STANDARD CHARTERED?

HERE, BUT NOT JUST HERE

Clements Lane is the nerve centre of the Standard Chartered world, but to our customers it's only one of 1500 Group addresses in 60 countries around the world.

This exceptional network could save you time and money for your business; if your bank can't offer you the same, come and see us at Clements Lane or ring Keith Skinner on 01-623 7500.

Standard Chartered
Bank Limited
helps you throughout the world

Head Office: 10 Clements Lane, London EC4N 7AB   Assets £12,000 million

Rank	Name	Managers	*Value of fund £000	Number of unit holders
1	Investment Trust Units	S. & P.	179,145	80,205
2	M. & G. Dividend	M. & G.	107,102	35,107
3	M. & G. General Trust	M. & G.	97,155	22,452
4	T.S.B. General	T.S.B.	87,871	37,218
5	Local Authorities' Property	L.A.M.	84,297	74
6	Charifund	M. & G.	77,759	3,950
7	Guardhill	G.R.E.	73,524	1,403
8	Unicorn Income	B.U.	65,187	18,981
9	Unicorn Capital	B.U.	64,071	36,040
10	Unicorn '500'	B.U.	61,297	25,905
11	Financial Securities	S. & P.	58,924	41,867
12	Scotbits	S.S.	58,025	55,913
13	Dollar Trust	H.S.	57,383	10,968
14	UK Equity	S. & P.	54,457	36,815
15	Scotyields	S.S.	54,441	37,220
16	Schroder Property Fund for Pension Funds & Charities	H.S.W.	53,394	212
17	Abbey General	A.M.	51,557	3,100
18	M. & G. American & General	M. & G.	51,276	14,741
19	Unicorn Extra Income	B.U.	48,424	21,082
20	Income	S. & P.	48,147	43,520
21	High Yield	S. & P.	46,697	33,220
22	Unicorn General	B.U.	43,457	61,192
23	High Return	S. & P.	43,019	13,764
24	M. & G. Extra Yield	M. & G.	42,223	12,500
25	Tyndall Capital	T.M.	41,800	8,312
26	Growth	N.W.	40,588	36,265
27	Commodity Share	S. & P.	40,250	23,248
28	M. & G. Recovery	M. & G.	39,949	12,828
29	M. & G. High Income	M. & G.	38,613	14,905
30	Hambro Accumulator Fund	A.H.G.	38,149	31
31	Universal Growth	S. & P.	37,760	22,187
32	Allied High Income	A.H.G.	36,175	17,979
33	Schroder Special Exempt Fund	H.S.W.	35,092	135
34	Practical	P.I.	34,882	3,700
35	Capital Units	S. & P.	33,961	31,344
36	Lloyds Bank Balanced	L.B.	33,640	25,589
37	Unicorn Financial	B.U.	32,882	14,166
38	Target Financial	T.T.M.	32,406	13,004
39	Lloyds Bank Income	L.B.	32,180	10,392
40	United States Growth	S. & P.	31,522	11,861
41	Allied Equity Income Trust	A.H.G.	30,984	10,010
42	Capital Trust	H.S.	30,186	3,701
43	M. & G. Second General Trust	M. & G.	29,578	8,112
44	Target Equity	T.T.M.	28,252	5,455
45	Norwich Union Group Trust Fund	N.G.T.	27,470	132
46	Prudential	P.	26,640	1,500
47	T.S.B. Scottish	T.S.B.	26,591	855
48	Local Authorities' Wider-Range	L.A.M.	26,511	90
49	Tyndall Income	T.M.	26,400	6,128
50	Target Preference	T.T.M.	25,907	21,680
51	Select International	S. & P.	25,630	4,418
52	High Income	B.T.M.	24,989	17,576
53	Henderson High Income	H.	24,618	10,167
54	British Trust	H.S.	24,284	12,844
55	Income Trust	H.S.	24,035	4,782
56	Allied First Trust	A.H.G.	23,792	13,187
57	Unicorn Growth Accumulator	B.U.	23,729	17,974
58	Hambro Smaller Companies	A.H.G.	22,999	3,075
59	Electrical & Industrial Development Trust	A.H.G.	22,977	8,968
60	Equity & Law	E. & L.	22,752	315
61	Growth	B.T.M.	22,487	20,059
62	Lloyds Bank Worldwide Growth	L.B.	22,042	27,886
63	Funds in Court Capital	P.T.	21,700	9,339
64	Metals Minerals & Commodities Trust	A.H.G.	21,565	15,245
65	Barclay Trust Investment Fund (Income)	B.U.	21,520	1,128
66	Allied Growth & Income Trust	A.H.G.	20,650	2,832
67	Gartmore High Income	G.F.M.	20,155	6,538
68	International Trust	H.S.	19,800	11,287
69	Scotshares	S.S.	19,440	26,699
70	Hambro Fund	A.H.G.	19,240	399
71	M. & G. Compound Growth	M. & G.	19,192	12,589
72	Allied Captital Trust	A.H.G.	18,859	4,971
73	Portfolio Investment Fund	N.W.	18,787	5,221
74	M. & G. Pension Exempt	M. & G.	18,674	192
75	Shield	B.T.M.	18,157	20,557

NOTE: *At 31 May 1979.

MANAGERS

A.H.G.	Allied Hambro Group
A.M.	Abbey Unit Trust Managers Ltd.
B.T.M.	Britannia Trust Management Ltd.
B.U.	Barclays Unicorn Ltd.
E. & L.	Equity & Law Unit Trust Managers
G.F.M.	Gartmore Fund Managers Ltd.
G.M.	Grieveson Management Co. Ltd.
G.R.E.	Guardian Royal Exchange Unit Managers Ltd.
H.	Henderson Unit Trust Management Ltd.
H.S.	Hill Samuel Unit Trust Managers Ltd.
H.S.W.	J. Henry Schroder Wagg & Co. Ltd.
L.A.M.	Local Authorities Mutual Investment Trust
L.B.	Lloyds Bank Unit Trust Managers Ltd.
M. & G.	M. & G. Group Ltd.
N.G.T.	Norwich General Trust Ltd.
N.W.	National Westminster Unit Trust Managers Ltd.
P.	Prudential Unit Trust Managers Ltd.
P.I.	Practical Investment Co. Ltd.
P.T.	Public Trustee Office
S. & P.	Save & Prosper Securities Ltd.
S.S.	Scotbits Securities Ltd.
T.M.	Tyndall Managers Ltd.
T.S.B.	T.S.B. Unit Trust Managers Ltd.
T.T.M.	Target Trust Managers Ltd.

The M&G Pension Fund Investment Service.

For some years now M&G have been providing an investment management service for the pension funds of companies and public corporations, as well as charitable foundations.

We are now extending this facility and taking on new clients for our Pension Fund Investment Service. Our independent status, wide contacts with stockbrokers and the very substantial volume of investments under M&G management place us in an ideal position to provide an investment service of this type.

For a copy of our new booklet "The M&G Pension Fund Investment Service," or to arrange an appointment to discuss the investment management of your Company's pension fund, please write to:

**David Morgan
M&G INVESTMENT MANAGEMENT LTD
Three Quays, Tower Hill
London EC3R 6BQ
Telephone: 01-626 4588**

THE M&G GROUP

11a   Insurance companies - Life

Rank	Name—*Chairman*	LIFE ETC. FUNDS Latest year £000	Previous year £000	INSURANCES IN FORCE Latest year £000	Previous year £000	NEW BUSINESS Latest year £000	Previous year £000
1	Prudential Corporation *R. H. Owen*	4,760,500	4,259,200	36,270,700	32,448,200	8,949,500	8,770,700
2	Legal & General Assurance Society *Viscount Caldecote*	3,071,500	2,612,600	—	—	N/A	2,671,200
3	Commercial Union Assurance Co. *Sir Francis Sandilands*	2,278,200	1,972,700	—	—	2,358,500	1,975,200
4	Standard Life Assurance Co. *A. M. Hodge*	1,986,442	1,808,064	—	—	1,895,700	1,453,878
5	Norwich Union Assurance Group *D. E. Longe*	1,492,706	1,282,893	—	—	—	—
6	Guardian Royal Exchange Assurance *J. E. H. Collins*	1,297,300	1,477,300	—	—	2,979,100	2,568,900
7	Scottish Widows' Fund & Life Ass. Society *E. H. M. Clutterbuck*	1,089,257	932,919	—	—	979,246	705,046
8	Eagle Star Insurance Co. *Sir Denis Mountain*	1,049,100	932,100	—	—	2,394,900	1,605,300
9	Pearl Assurance Co. *F. L. Garner*	1,024,406	922,086	3,671,600	3,320,100	684,371	544,917
10	Royal Insurance Co. *D. Meinertzhagen*	917,922	765,871	—	—	1,139,200	946,300
11	Sun Life Assurance Society *P. G. Walker*	887,031	754,986	—	—	1,023,000	767,000
12	Co-operative Insurance Society *H. W. Whitehead*	792,219	719,045	—	—	819,401	729,106
13	Equity & Law Life Assurance Society *P. D. J. H. Cox*	717,331	631,189	4,524,130	4,209,212	925,395	796,331
14	Friends' Provident Life Office *E. W. Phillips*	665,825	590,655	—	—	945,000	695,000
15	Hambro Life Assurance *J. M. Clay*	646,224	508,448	2,700,000	1,900,000	1,028,000	730,000
16	Sun Alliance & London Insurance *Lord Aldington*	592,600	394,400	—	—	872,529	637,075
17	Scottish Amicable Life Assurance Society *J. A. Spens*	580,165	495,055	N/A	2,527,445	831,426	763,792
18	General Accident Fire and Life Ass. Corpn. *G. R. Simpson*	538,540	484,442	—	—	1,992,200	1,165,900
19	Abbey Life Assurance Co. *R. F. Richardson*	504,321	414,736	—	—	—	—
20	Phoenix Assurance Co. *J. O. Hambro*	492,700	411,900	—	—	1,739,100	1,123,900
21	General Medical & General Life Ass. Soc. *D. S. Morpeth*	441,486	367,068	2,672,239	2,174,800	926,529	513,100
22	Liverpool Victoria Friendly Society *E. Robertson*	439,848	410,396	—	—	169,367	157,078
23	Royal London Mutual Insurance Society *B. G. Skinner*	391,525	363,665	N/A	1,108,312	214,200	196,300
24	Britannic Assurance Co. *J. F. Jefferson*	382,835	347,676	1,263,322	1,100,452	293,078	232,152
25	Provident Mutual Life Assurance Association *D. L. M. Robertson*	360,540	307,465	—	—	638,562	464,380

NOTE: N/A Not available.

Depend on us...

Royal Insurance covers the world, with a premium income in 1978 in excess of £1,200 million – approximately 75% of this written outside the U.K. in over 80 countries and 16 languages.

Fair dealing, unrivalled service and security are the hallmarks of Royal Insurance worldwide.

U.K. Head Office:
New Hall Place,
Old Hall Street,
Liverpool L69 3EN.

Chief Administration:
Bow Bells House,
Bread Street,
London EC4M 9ER.

Royal Insurance
looks after you. Fast

11b Insurance companies - Non-life

Rank	Name—*Chairman*	PREMIUM INCOME Latest year £000	Previous year £000	GROSS INVESTMENT INCOME Latest year £000	Previous year £000	UNDERWRITING PROFIT Latest year £000	Previous year £000
1	Royal Insurance Co. *D. Meinertzhagen*	1,220,135	1,235,476	122,504	113,694	25,401	15,155
2	Commercial Union Assurance Co. *Sir Francis Sandilands*	1,100,700	1,072,500	143,300	127,700	2,900	Loss 20,900
3	General Accident Fire and Life Ass. Corpn *G. R. Simpson*	745,793	674,582	88,284	75,316	1,079	6,304
4	Guardian Royal Exchange Assurance *J. E. H. Collins*	619,700	591,500	77,100	65,300	4,800	Loss 6,600
5	Sun Alliance & London Insurance *Lord Aldington*	520,700	465,500	59,900	53,400	Loss 4,900	1,100
6	Prudential Corporation *R. H. Owen*	394,400	358,400	45,300	35,600	Loss 9,300	Loss 12,500
7	Eagle Star Insurance Co. *Sir Denis Mountain*	363,900	315,000	49,500	39,600	Loss 10,100	Loss 4,300
8	Phoenix Assurance Co. *J. O. Hambro*	337,600	323,000	47,200	41,600	Loss 2,700	Loss 1,000
9	Norwich Union Insurance Group *D. E. Longe*	154,413	125,869	23,596	20,150	1,569	5,468
10	Legal & General Assurance Society *Viscount Caldecote*	131,000	123,200	21,200	16,700	Loss 6,000	Loss 3,900
11	Co-operative Insurance Society *H. W. Whitehead*	106,749	90,625	12,228	10,631	Loss 1,196	2,821
12	Cornhill Insurance Co. *D. W. G. Sawyer*	89,532	76,441	9,351	7,247	Loss 1,250	381
13	National Employers' Mutual Gen. Ins. Assn *M. H. R. King*	82,361	78,292	10,880	8,863	71	Loss 1,747
14	Provincial Insurance Co. *C. F. E. Shakerley*	73,076	63,647	6,471	5,768	Loss 1,071	Loss 1,243
15	Excess Insurance Group *W. L. Samengo-Turner*	66,525	63,127	10,948	12,044	Loss 5,645	Loss 3,811
16	Municipal Mutual Insurance *Sir Frank Marshall*	64,155	52,955	10,763	8,074	Loss 1,864	Loss 1,844
17	Iron Trades Employers Insurance Association *D. Rebbeck*	64,073	52,471	10,165	6,539	Loss 1,193	Loss 1,440
18	National Farmers' Union Mutual Ins. Soc. *R. Cary*	63,649	53,745	8,045	6,779	1,875	2,115
19	Minster Insurance Co. *D. S. A. Pearce*	51,005	43,020	7,611	7,033	Loss 1,879	Loss 1,666
20	Pearl Assurance Co. *F. L. Garner*	41,514	36,390	5,810	5,340	Loss 3,818	Loss 3,466
21	National Insurance & Guarantee Corpn *E. Carter*	25,897	19,644	2,722	2,166	Loss 284	Loss 755
22	Orion Insurance Co. *Sir Antony Part*	25,009	26,479	5,574	4,886	Loss 546	Loss 256
23	Dominion Insurance Co. *J. R. Johnstone*	23,145	22,460	4,148	3,334	Loss 2,069	Loss 2,223
24	United Friendly Insurance Co. *R. C. Balding*	23,042	16,910	1,026	843	156	350
25	Norwich Winterthur Reinsurance Corpn *D. E. Longe*	19,798	12,507	3,378	2,179	1,365	Loss 869

Bain Dawes

12 Other financial institutions

Rank	Name	Chairman	NET PROFIT AFTER TAX Latest year £000	Previous year £000	*Equity mkt. cap. £m
1	First National Finance Corpn	J. P. R. Glyn	17,025	Loss 4,109	8.7
2	Mercantile Credit Co.	A. Victor Adex	11,866	8,937	—
3	United Dominions Trust	L. C. Mather	11,300	3,900	44.9
4	Lombard North Central	Earl of Crawford and Balcarres	9,495	6,218	—
5	Yorkshire Bank	J. P. R. Glyn	7,047	6,449	—
6	Agricultural Mortgage Corpn	J. P. R. Glyn	2,878	2,536	—
7	John James Group of Companies	J. James	2,631	2,269	22.7
8	Cattle's (Holdings)	R. Waudby	1,066	804	9.3
9	H.F.C. Trust	I. Martindale	701	193	—
10	Goode Durrant & Murray Group	L. E. Robinson	489	Loss 3,289	6.0
11	London Scottish Finance Corpn	R. H. Landman	462	242	4.0
12	Britannia Arrow Holdings	G. Rippon	258	Loss 3,742	14.3
13	Ionian Securities	E. M. Behrens	Loss 13	51	—

NOTE: *At 13 July 1979.

13 Mining finance

Rank	Name—Chairman	Headquarters	*CAPITAL EMPLOYED Latest year £000	Previous year £000	NET PROFIT BEFORE INTEREST AND TAX Latest year £000	Previous year £000	**Equity mkt. cap. £m
1	Anglo-American Corpn of South Africa H. F. Oppenheimer	Johannesburg	2,700,136	1,878,527	168,677	130,576 p.a.	728.8
2	Federale Mynbou Beperk C. B. Coetzer	Johannesburg	704,793	595,111	103,938	78,641	—
3	Consolidated Gold Fields Lord Erroll of Hale	London	635,900	526,600	99,400	73,800	316.0
4	Anglo-American Gold Investment Co. J. Ogilvie Thompson	Johannesburg	602,621	409,108	34,448 p.a.	23,627	384.2
5	Charter Consolidated M. B. Hofmeyr	London	444,927	382,838	51,547	48,815	142.6
6	Gold Fields of South Africa A. Louw	Johannesburg	348,946	231,255	24,933	13,624	275.2
7	Selection Trust J. P. Du Cane	London	288,700	238,814	25,800	26,900 p.a.	149.6
8	Johannesburg Consolidated Investment Co. Sir Albert Robinson	Johannesburg	260,672	222,920	39,850	31,096	106.6

NOTES: *Total tangible assets less current liabilities (excluding bank loans and overdrafts) but including investments at market value.
**As at 13 July 1979.
South African companies converted at R1.8325 to £1.

Facts and figures don't always speak for themselves.

Your company's results – and future prospects – have to be communicated and interpreted to a wide audience.

To the City, shareholders, employees, financial press, the public at large.

As a leading financial advertising and PR agency, we know a thing or two about getting company results read – and remembered.

How your Chairman's Statement can be made to come across with clarity and conviction.

What a healthy injection of creative design will do for your Report and Accounts.

The kind of lively communication needed to put your employees in the picture.

Or the ways in which corporate campaigns can help small names grow big, and big names bigger.

And that's only half the story. Our Public Relations department also has a vital part to play in keeping the press up to date with what you're doing – and why.

It all adds up to a complete service called Streets Financial.

Now, what about seeing how we'd make your facts and figures speak up loud and clear?

Ring Jem Miller or Mike Lomax on 01-353 1090.

Streets Financial Limited

18 Red Lion Court, Fleet Street, London EC4A 3HT. Telephone 01-353 1090. Telex 21827.

14 Property companies

Rank	Name—Chairman	*CAPITAL EMPLOYED		GROSS RENTS		NET PROFIT BEFORE INTEREST AND TAX		**Equity mkt. cap. £m
		Latest year £000	Previous year £000	Latest year £000	Previous year £000	Latest year £000	Previous year £000	
1	Land Securities Investment Trust *Lord Samuel of Wych Cross*	1,175,112	870,998	59,240	56,258	54,570	48,337	608·6
2	English Property Corporation —	653,498	723,840	73,279	75,952	63,452	61,517	—
3	MEPC *Sir Gerald Thorley*	542,571	530,799	44,148	55,386	34,454	42,223	244·7
4	Town & City Properties *J. M. Sterling*	336,093	365,180	35,197	34,033	11,194	13,583	47.2
5	Hammerson Property & Investment Trust *S. Mason*	205,693	209,941	35,153	33,909	22,536	21,818	134.8
6	Slough Estates *G. N. Mobbs*	199,113	192,798	17,627	15,205	15,201	13,912	163.3
7	St. Martins Property Corporation *F. M. Al-Sabah*	171,144	163,071	8,835	9,753 p.a.	10,899	9,622 p.a.	—
8	British Land Co. *J. Ritblat*	169,995	165,281	14,458	15,725	13,981	14,279	56.8
9	Stock Conversion & Investment Trust *R. Clark*	135,885	130,627	8,837	7,681	7,710	6,273	108.5
10	Bernard Sunley Investment Trust *D. C. G. Jessel*	134,444	118,860	6,222	5,505	9,442	7,445	61.3
11	Haslemere Estates *F. E. Cleary*	128,548	109,797	10,109	8,643	7,853	6,899	72.5
12	Laing Properties *Sir Kirby Laing*	126,947	—[1]	15,107	—[1]	7,442	—[1]	80.8
13	Capital & Counties Property Co. *K. H. Wallis*	124,257	102,646	10,632	10,052	7,670	8,127	71·4
14	Brixton Estate *M. J. Verey*	119,975	87,525	8,117	6,180	5,385	2,631	53·7
15	Great Portland Estates *B. Samuel*	85,646	83,928	8,069	7,191	6,080	4,958	138·5
16	Daejan Holdings *L. L. Tobin*	73,563	80,244	7,962	7,561	7,587	7,966	23·8
17	Samuel Properties *Viscount Bearstead*	67,802	59,246	5,949	5,219	3,364	3,566	32·8
18	Scottish Metropolitan Property Co. *D. Walton*	62,539	45,290	3,146	2,792	3,067	2,813	38·4
19	Centrovincial Estates *J. Gold*	62,514	67,966	8,027	8,776	3,052	4,116	19·3
20	Berkeley Hambro Property Co. *J. O. Hambro*	57,028	65,887	5,747	6,265	5,052	5,803	30·4

NOTES: *Total tangible assets less current liabilities (other than bank loans and overdrafts and future tax).
**At 13 July 1979.
[1]Incorporated December 1977.

The property investment chain

Our investment team offers a strong link
between your funds and a sound property investment.

Close analysis of the letting and capital markets
in the U.K. has led to a *performance conscious*
sales, purchase and portfolio management service.
In development, too, important public and
private sector programmes have resulted from our
advice in planning, costing, funding and letting.

Hampton & Sons

6 Arlington Street, London SW1A 1RB
Tel: 01-493 8222 Telex: 25341

15 Investment trusts

Rank	Name—Chairman	Investments at market value £000	NET REVENUE BEFORE INTEREST AND TAX		*Equity market cap. £m.
			Latest year £000	Previous year £000	
1	Globe Investment Trust—A. F. Roger (Governor)	332,464	**18,785**	17,427	185·1
2	Industrial & General Trust—Sir Anthony G. Touche	205,109	**9,367**	8,506	118·7
3	Foreign & Colonial Investment Trust Co.—D. A. H. Baer	170,449	**7,894**	6,475	101·0
4	Alliance Trust Co.—D. F. McCurrach	161,746	**7,420**	6,619	104·3
5	Philip Hill Investment Trust—Sir Kenneth Keith	146,390	**8,179**	7,077	89·9
6	Witan Investment Co.—J. R. Henderson	141,036	**6,436**	5,163	72·9
7	Scottish Mortgage & Trust Co.—T. R. MacGregor	139,148	**6,447**	5,103	74·3
8	British Assets Trust—J. C. R. Inglis	134,107	**5,710**	5,121	66·0
9	British Investment Trust—F. B. Harrison	123,930	**5,874**	5,322	85·5
10	Atlas Electric & General Trust—Sir Anthony G. Touche	121,312	**5,312**	4,547	70·2
11	Scottish Investment Trust Co.—A. Grossart	112,758	**5,075**	4,194	80·5
12	Mercantile Investment Trust—G. J. A. Jamieson	106,191	**6,025**	5,422	60·4
13	Scottish United Investors—R. C. Smith	104,393	**4,123**	3,627	62·1
14	Edinburgh Investment Trust—I. R. Guild	99,724	**4,230**	3,970	67·2
15	Scottish Eastern Investment Trust—A. L. McClure	98,089	**4,869**	4,245	65·5
16	London Trust Co.—E. D. G. Davies	93,985	**4,502**	3,936	50·9
17	United States Debenture Corpn.—W. M. Cunningham	89,420	**4,818**	4,389	59·5
18	Border & Southern Stockholders Trust—C. A. McLintock	88,891	**3,111**	2,886	54·0
19	Anglo-American Securities Corpn.—G. J. A. Jamieson	88,678	**4,102**	3,172	51·1
20	Drayton Premier Investment Trust—P. Shelbourne	78,220	**4,382**	4,228	48·3
21	Investors Capital Trust—C. F. Sleigh	76,961	**3,449**	3,089	44·5
22	United British Securities Trust—Lord Wyfold	75,866	**3,246**	2,979	54·5
23	Scottish Western Investment Co.—J. A. Lumsden	75,508	**3,063**	2,604	43·6
24	Scottish National Trust Co.—R. F. Denholm	75,349	**3,010**	2,695	43·3
25	Clydesdale Investment Co.—J. A. Lumsden	74,031	**2,630**	2,315	39·9
26	Drayton Consolidated Trust—P. Shelbourne	73,275	**3,521**	3,542	39·5
27	Monks Investment Trust—M. Hamilton	69,514	**3,311**	2,734	36·5
28	Scottish American Investment Co.—P. W. Turcan	69,424	**4,210**	3,399	46·4
29	Lake View Investment Trust—C. A. McLintock	68,088	**2,632**	2,134	41·1
30	Guardian Investment Trust Co.—M. B. Baring	65,846	**3,010**	2,846	40·8
31	Rothschild Investment Trust—J. Rothschild	65,656	**5,047**	6,211	54·2
32	Trustees Corporation—Sir Anthony G. Touche	65,561	**3,066**	2,727	43·7
33	Great Northern Investment Trust—Viscount Weir	65,371	**3,817**	3,225	47·5
34	Scottish Northern Investment Trust—R. J. C. Fleming	63,200	**2,980**	2,465 p.a.	35·9
35	Stockholders Investment Trust—C. A. McLintock	62,401	**2,225**	1,845	35·4
36	American Trust Co.—A. L. McClure	62,229	**2,960**	2,621	34·3
37	Whitbread Investment Co.—F. O. A. G. Bennett	62,141	**3,314**	3,038	45·4
38	Sphere Investment Trust—C. M. Hughes	60,945	**2,553**	2,136	34·2
39	Continental and Industrial Trust—A. L. Hood	57,871	**2,732**	2,336	34·3
40	Securities Trust of Scotland—J. G. Wallace	57,457	**2,848**	2,559	34·2
41	Second Alliance Trust Co.—D. F. McCurrach	54,028	**2,179**	2,055	34·1
42	Northern American Trust Co.—I. R. Guild	52,636	**2,321**	2,157	27·8
43	Merchants Trust—M. W. Jacomb	51,724	**2,882**	2,383	36·0
44	London & Provincial Trust—Lord Wyfold	51,312	**2,117**	1,833	32·4
45	Hambros Investment Trust—J. O. Hambro	51,310	**2,708**	2,581	28·0
46	Raeburn Investment Trust—D. Meinertzhagen	47,740	**2,409**	2,306	30·6
47	Caledonian Trust Co.—J. A. Lumsden	47,550	**1,628**	1,525	25·1
48	Atlantic Assets Trust—J. V. Sheffield	47,288	**1,829**	1,738	27·8
49	Drayton Commercial Investment Co.—P. Shelbourne	46,983	**2,679**	2,505	27·7
50	Aberdeen Trust—J. S. R. Cruikshank	46,222	**2,223**	2,048	30·3

NOTES: *At 13 July 1979.

It has everything you could unreasonably demand.

When you pay over £9000 for a motor car, there are one or two things you should be able to take for granted.

The first is a measure of exclusivity.

What pleasure is there in owning a car that could be mistaken for one costing £2000 less than you paid?

The second is a fitting level of equipment to match the price.

Being asked to agonize over a list of options can be both tiresome and inappropriate.

On both counts, you'll find the new Vauxhall Royale saloon a refreshing change.

It costs £9428 and there isn't a cheaper version even if you wanted one.

There are just two options available: manual transmission at no additional cost (automatic transmission is standard) and air conditioning for a further £770.

Everything else you could possibly wish for is standard equipment.

The engine is a 2.8 litre, six cylinder unit that carries the Royale to a top speed of 115 mph. (Manufacturer's figures.)

And because it develops maximum torque at just 3400 rpm, there is no sense of strain or urgency, even under hard acceleration.

Inside, the appointments are a Puritan's nightmare.

All seats are covered in crushed velour with individual head restraints.

The driver's seat adjusts for height as well as for reach and rake.

There is central locking for the doors, a steel sunroof and radio/stereo cassette player with three loudspeakers.

The steering column is tiltable and the steering is, of course, powered.

The tinted windows are electrically operated and so is the boot release.

While a brilliantly engineered suspension and superbly aerodynamic body shape make the Royale uncannily quiet at any speed.

Outside, you'll find the same meticulous attention to detail and finish.

Double-skinned metallic paint, alloy wheels and a headlamp wash/wipe system.

And styling that is a welcome relief from the Pan-European designs that are becoming daily more common.

Ask your nearest Vauxhall dealer to give you a demonstration run in a Royale.

We think you'll find it's one of the best appointed luxury cars on the road.

ROYALE SALOON £9428, COUPÉ £9776. PRICES CORRECT AT TIME OF GOING TO PRESS, INCLUDE CAR TAX AND VAT. DELIVERY AND NUMBER PLATES EXTRA.

16 Largest building societies

Rank	Name	TOTAL ASSETS		LIQUID ASSETS		RESERVES	
		Latest year £000	Previous year £000	Latest year £000	Previous year £000	Latest year £000	Previous year £000
1	Halifax	7,602,681	6,508,587	1,383,375	1,282,957	220,377	184,366
2	Abbey National	6,254,360	5,413,528	1,096,668	1,126,609	235,081	200,325
3	Nationwide	3,303,437	2,804,016	589,261	558,899	118,462	107,296
4	Leeds Permanent	2,239,193	1,891,831	433,467	365,633	67,490	57,556
5	Woolwich Equitable	2,089,540	1,772,871	365,805	327,424	73,129	58,368
6	Anglia Hastings and Thanet*	1,423,844	1,265,006	249,963	274,063	58,638	49,584
7	Alliance	1,413,624	1,277,854	270,500	306,181	46,271	41,169
8	Leicester	1,253,168	1,120,879	222,174	243,779	45,197	38,493
9	Provincial	1,235,594	1,085,548	223,040	264,905	50,538	43,829
10	Britannia	1,084,758	965,230	238,751	267,869	44,958	38,730
11	Bradford & Bingley	1,028,218	874,911	195,997	200,278	42,192	37,446
12	Burnley	671,324	594,610	126,519	131,275	28,845	25,374
13	Bristol & West	652,875	569,186	173,489	178,419	26,563	19,787
14	Gateway	597,965	538,297	102,215	108,265	22,976	20,551
15	Cheltenham & Gloucester	575,912	504,961	123,022	125,692	23,253	19,763
16	Huddersfield & Bradford	545,652	497,554	95,357	114,327	24,468	20,925
17	Northern Rock	499,057	435,066	93,729	96,769	17,557	15,388
18	Town & Country	263,956	235,872	47,612	58,545	16,566	14,140
19	Coventry Economic	245,409	210,883	39,988	38,890	9,406	8,636
20	South of England	239,286	213,911	39,725	45,407	10,606	9,594
21	Midshires†	235,273	197,654	43,942	43,876	12,366	10,487
22	Guardian	234,616	207,734	53,670	57,849	13,678	11,035
23	Derbyshire	224,278	192,191	41,138	42,277	7,693	7,037
24	West Bromwich	216,275	181,484	50,684	51,133	9,250	7,964
25	Chelsea	202,445	189,687	32,856	44,298	8,413	7,561
26	Leeds & Holbeck	185,071	168,712	32,761	36,701	6,729	5,962
27	Portman	176,031	159,773	31,221	33,839	9,491	8,251
28	Skipton	165,944	150,813	34,925	36,751	7,157	6,404
29	Principality	149,314	124,070	30,893	26,513	7,128	5,934
30	Staffordshire	132,987	111,774	35,250	31,415	4,813	4,251
31	Bridgwater	132,923	117,571	29,686	32,928	5,302	4,610
32	Heart of England	128,894	109,069	24,974	22,439	5,229	4,592
33	Birmingham	114,003	101,719	20,776	22,666	6,127	5,785
34	London Goldhawk	113,948	98,989	25,395	28,227	4,667	4,377
35	Nottingham	108,672	90,578	19,914	22,212	6,276	5,338
36	Liverpool	106,599	90,774	17,183	21,880	4,685	3,907
37	Cheshire	97,233	79,802	17,521	18,117	4,558	3,884
38	Lambeth	96,652	80,984	19,343	17,323	4,975	4,248
39	Sunderland & Shields	95,139	81,839	16,239	16,022	4,524	3,881
40	Hearts of Oak & Enfield	90,571	81,151	17,047	19,510	3,681	3,292
41	Property Owners	90,026	79,534	19,924	23,530	3,545	3,074
42	National Counties	88,779	81,070	16,459	15,352	8,494	7,442
43	Sussex County	88,485	75,004	18,659	19,934	3,170	2,710
44	Sussex Mutual	77,901	65,366	22,657	17,592	3,779	2,991
45	Eastbourne Mutual	77,170	65,042	16,825	19,420	2,490	2,180
46	Norwich	75,571	68,370	14,209	15,796	3,285	3,037
47	Cumberland	72,605	63,122	14,323	13,322	3,651	3,117
48	Newcastle Upon Tyne Permanent	70,066	61,814	10,629	14,617	2,941	2,335
49	City of London	68,352	60,603	13,370	15,826	2,809	2,426
50	Dunfermline	67,489	58,845	13,080	14,314	2,536	2,191

NOTES: * Previous year figures are combined figures of Anglia B.S. and Hastings and Thanet B.S.
† Previous year figures are combined figures of Midshires B.S. and Wolverhampton & Mercia B.S.

17 The 500 leading European companies

Rank	Name	Country	Main activity	Turnover 1978 £m	Turnover 1977 £m	Reported profits 1978 £m
1	Royal Dutch Petroleum Co.	N	Oil and petroleum	13,767·0	13,640·0	1,868·4
2	Veba AG	G	Holding co. (electricity, chemicals, transport)	8,403·6	7,382·5	264·6
3	Philips' Lamps Holding	N	Electrical products	8,124·0	7,752·3	312·3
4	Siemens AG	G	Electrical and general engineering, electronics	7,819·2	6,791·8	443·5
5	Fiat	I	Motor vehicles, ships engines, diesel trains and aeroplanes	7,772·2	6,804·1	N/A
6	Volkswagenwerk AG	G	Motor vehicle manufacturers	7,203·2	6,509·9	592·5
7	Compagnie Française des Pétroles	F	Holding co. (oil, petroleum)	6,625·1	6,287·1	1,006·8
8	ENI	I	Holding co. (petroleum, chemicals, engineering, textiles, etc.)	6,577·8	5,704·8	207·2
9	Daimler-Benz AG	G	Motor vehicle and engine manufacturer	6,532·6	6,278·2	796·5
10	Hoechst AG	G	Chemicals, dyes, plastics, etc.	6,520·4	6,279·8	337·5
11	Renault—Régie Nationale des Usines	F	Autombile production	6,470·6	5,791·8	N/A
12	BASF AG	G	Chemical products	6,267·9	6,248·2	309·6
13	Bayer AG	G	Chemical products	6,155·3	5,766·0	334·8
14	Nestlé SA	Sw	Holding co. (chocolate, milk and food products)	5,920·6	6,089·4	392·4
15	Unilever NV	N	Food products, detergents, animal feedstuffs, toilet preparations	5,794·3	5,627·6	270·6
16	PSA Peugeot-Citroën	F	Automobiles, engines	5,624·7	4,927·7	334·8
17	Thyssen AG	G	Iron and steel	5,178·4	5,313·6	95·7
18	SNEA—Société Nationale Elf Aquitaine	F	Petrol, oil, natural gas, sulphur	4,827·5	4,483·2	466·7
19	Compagnie Générale d'Electricité	F	Holding co. (electrical engineers)	4,210·0	3,844·0	22·0
20	Saint Gobain-Pont à Mousson	F	Construction materials	4,023·9	3,744·6	154·4
21	OIAG—Oesterreichische Industrie Verwaltungs AG	A	State industrial holding co.	3,952·0	3,671·7	0·1
22	AEG—Telefunken	G	Electrical engineering	3,850·7	3,799·7	(70·9)
23	Petrofina SA	B	Oil exploration	3,788·0	3,581·7	267·8
24	RWE—Rheinisch Westfälisches Elektrizitätswerk AG	G	Generation and distribution of electricity	3,517·7	3,265·5	323·8
25	Montedison SpA	I	Chemicals and pharmaceuticals	3,417·2	3,237·9	(132·0)
26	Mannesmann	G	Pipe mills and steel processing	3,415·2	3,157·5	160·9
27	Ruhrkohle AG	G	Coal mining	3,366·0	2.958·0	53·8
28	Schneider SA	F	Holding co. (heavy industry, iron and steel)	3.317·6	2,894·1	N/A
29	Esso AG	G	Oil producers	3,254·9	3,287·1	137·2
30	Pechiney Ugine Kuhlmann	F	Holding co. (chemicals, aluminium, etc.)	3,247·1	3,055·5	N/A
31	Nederlandse Gasunie NV	N	Purchase and sale of natural gas	3,138·0	3,175·9	23·3
32	Deutsche Shell AG	G	Oil and petroleum	3,047·1	3,014·7	140·5
33	Rhône Poulenc SA	F	Holding co. (chemical and pharmaceutical products)	2,995·1	2,777·8	28·0
34	Karstadt AG	G	Department stores	2,890·2	2,857·8	35·1
35	Opel (Adam) AG	G	Car manufacturers	2,867·9	2,470·9	N/A
36	Ford Werke AG	G	Car manufacturers	2,823·5	2,739·4	311·9
37	Gutehoffnungshütte Aktienverein	G	Holding co. (shipbuilding, iron and steel trades, etc.)	2,737·5	2,653·8	79·0
38	Estel NV	N	Steel	2,725·1	2,522·1	82·0
39	Ciba-Geigy AG	Sw	Chemicals, pharmaceuticals, dyes, etc.	2,706·7	3,012·4	N/A
40	Thomson-Brandt	F	Electrical engineers	2,688·0	2,315·5	28·1
41	Akzo NV	N	Holding co. (chemicals, fibres, etc).	2,653·2	2,595·3	43·0
42	Bosch (Robert) GmbH	G	Electronic engineers & auto-electrical mnfctrs	2,592·5	2,469·1	N/A
43	Finsider	I	Holding co. (iron & steel)	2,562·3	2,303·6	(291·5)
44	Esso SAF	F	Oil producers	2,547·1	2,379·2	25·3
45	Aral AG	G	Petroleum	2,545·5	2,497·4	5·6
46	DSM NV	N	Chemical products	2,488·8	2,521·2	(0·4)
47	BBC AG - Brown, Boveri & Cie	Sw	Electrical engineering	2,455·2	2,481·5	N/A
48	Pirelli-Dunlop Union SpA	I	Rubber products	2,394·4	2,033·8	92·1
49	KF/Konsum	S	Wholesale & retail distributors	2,343·8	2,209·2	6·9
50	Michelin & Cie	F	Holding co. (tyres)	2,314·2	2,051·6	128·4

NOTES: The following letters are used to indicate countries: A - Austria; B - Belgium; D - Denmark; F - France; Fin - Finland; G - Germany; I - Italy; L - Luxembourg; Lie - Liechtenstein; N - Netherlands; No - Norway; S - Sweden; Sp - Spain; Sw - Switzerland.
Exchange rates used as at 31-12-78: Austria - 27.225; Belgium - 58.70; Denmark - 10.355; Finland - 7.9475; France - 8.50; Germany - 3.71; Holland - 4.02; Italy - 1690.0; Liechtenstein - 3.30; Luxembourg - 58.70; Norway - 10.205; Spain - 142.85; Sweden - 8.73; Switzerland - 3.30.
N/A Not available.

Rank	Name	Country	Main activity	Turnover 1978 £m	Turnover 1977 £m	Reported profits 1978 £m
51	Migros-Genossenschafts-Bund	Sw	Department stores & supermarkets	**2,210·2**	2,191·3	**53·9**
52	Volvo AB	S	Motor vehicles, marine industrial & aero engines, etc.	**2,191·6**	1,852·0	**54·4**
53	SHV Holdings NV	N	Shipping, natural gas, oil & transport	**2,139·1**	2,065·3	**49·7**
54	Flick (Gruppe Friedrich)	G	Holding co. (iron, steel, mechanical engineering)	**2,055·1**	1,795·4	**109·0**
55	Deutsche Spar-Zentrale	G	Wholesale distributors and supermarkets	**2,032·9***	1,964·2**	N/A
56	Schickedanz Group	G	Mail order	**2,005·4**	1,981·1	**32·6**
57	Metallgesellschaft AG	G	Non-ferrous metals	**1,918·2**	1,886·8	**26·4**
58	Salzgitter AG	G	Iron & steel manufacturers	**1,812·4**	1,730·1	**(6·3)**
59	Kaufhof AG	G	Department stores	**1,812·2**	1,752·0	**40·6**
60	Deutsche BP AG	G	Petroleum & natural gas	**1,792·5**	1,725·1	**6·2**
61	BMW-Bayerische Motorenwerke AG	G	Motor & motor cycle manufacturers	**1,767·4**	1,490·7	**143·0**
62	STET - Societa Finanziaria Telefonica	I	Electrical machinery, apparatus & supplies	**1,762·9***	1,427·1**	N/A
63	Voest Alpine AG	A	Iron & steel	**1,715·3**	1,612·5	N/A
64	Charbonnages de France	F	Coal mining	**1,708·9**	1,382·6	**33·8**
65	Carrefour	F	Hypermarkets	**1,708·5**	1,466·7	**51·5**
66	IBM Deutschland GmbH	G	Data processing	**1,703·5**	1,720·0	N/A
67	BSN-Gervais Danone	F	Food products	**1,692·7**	1,515·6	**33·3**
68	Reemtsma Cigarettenfabriken GmbH	G	Cigarette & drinks manufacturers	**1,688·4**	1,693·3	**61·9**
69	Solvay & Cie.	B	Chemicals & plastics	**1,620·5**	1,582·1	**55·5**
70	Cockerill	B	Steel manufacturers	**1,612·7**	N/A	**(128·5)**
71	Shell Française	F	Petroleum products	**1,591·9**	1,466·8	**(22·0)**
72	Deutsche Texaco AG	G	Oil refinery	**1,586·3**	1,528·6	**97·5**
73	Italsider SpA	I	Iron & steel	**1,537·2**	1,329·9	**(204·3)**
74	Henkel KgaA	G	Detergents & cleaning agents	**1,510·0**	1,445·6	**46·8**
75	Esso Italiana	I	Oil, petroleum	**1,499·8**	N/A	**519·0**
76	Alusuisse	Sw	Aluminium	**1,499·3**	1,648·9	**28·5**
77	Ruhrgas AG	G	Gas supply	**1,480·7**	1,268·7	**117·2**
78	Hoffmann La Roche (F.) & Co. AG	Sw	Chemicals & pharmaceuticals	**1,467·0**	1,662·6	**61·0**
79	Creusot-Loire SA	F	Iron & steel	**1,455·8**	1,242·8	**40·2**
80	Mobil Oil AG	G	Oil & natural gas	**1,455·5**	1,354·4	N/A
81	East Asiatic Co. Ltd.	D	Ship owners, global traders, plantation owners & forest developers	**1,432·1**	1,791·3	**26·8**
82	GB Inno BM SA	B	Supermarkets & department stores	**1,404·8**	1,275·7	**24·6**
83	Electrolux Aktiebolag	S	Refrigerators, cleaning office machines	**1,377·2**	1,058·3	**77·2**
84	Degussa	G	Precious metals, chemical & furnace construction	**1,367·1**	1,200·8	**36·1**
85	Deutsche Lufthansa AG	G	Airline operator	**1,345·7**	1,238·0	**35·5**
86	Saab-Scania Aktiebolag	S	Vehicles, aircraft, electronics, etc.	**1,333·5**	1,236·7	**38·2**
87	IBM France	F	Computers	**1,302·9**	1,160·2	N/A
88	Sandoz AG	Sw	Dyestuffs, pharmaceuticals, chemicals etc.	**1,302·1**	1,446·4	**47·3**
89	Sacilor—Acieries et Laminoirs	F	Iron & steel	**1,295·3**	1,148·4	**(132·4)**
90	BAYWA AG	G	Agricultural products & machinery	**1,250·2**	1,196·2	**6·9**
91	Ahold N.V.	N	Supermarkets, food manufacturers	**1,288·8**	1,029·3	**22·3**
92	ICA—Koncernen	S	Food, restaurants, consumer goods	**1,210·0***	N/A	**9·7***
93	Krupp (Fried.) Hüttenwerke AG	G	Iron & steel production	**1,196·0**	1,218·6	**(4·6)**
94	Mobil Oil Française	F	Oil refinery & distribution	**1,144·3***	1,015·0**	—
95	Klöckner Werke AG	G	Iron and steel producers, heavy engineering	**1,144·0**	1,110·9	**(9·7)**
96	ASEA	S	Electric power equipment	**1,124·2**	1,113·2	**34·0**
97	SKF Group (AB Svenska Kullagerfabriken	S	Roller bearings	**1,092·0**	916·8	**29·6**
98	Edeka Zentrale AG	G	Consumer goods	**1,078·4**	933.7	**6·7**
99	SNAM SpA	I	Wholesale of motor vehicles, fuel & gasoline, water & land transport	**1,074·8**	947·1	**53·0**
100	Sulzer (Gebruder) AG	Sw	General engineering	**1,054·9**	1,061·4	N/A

NOTES: *1977 figures; **1976 figures.

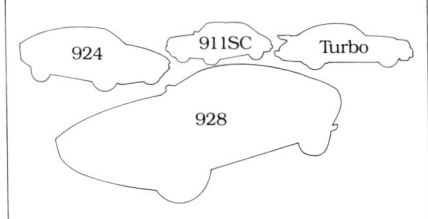

PORSCHE

Some people are never satisfied.

Porsche, for instance.

They couldn't simply be content with creating the most enduring and beloved sports car the world has ever known. The Porsche 911.

They had to keep on improving it. Refining its power, flexibility, reliability and roadholding. And adding even more luxury.

Did that satisfy them? Hardly. Because their attention next turned to the incredible potential of turbocharging.

And so was born the Porsche Turbo, the ultimate performance roadcar. A car which has drained motoring journalists dry of superlatives.

Now were Porsche satisfied?

Not yet. The designers, engineers and technicians of Porsche's research centre at Weissach were, in fact, already busy with Projects 928 and 924.

Two very different versions of the Porsche ideal. Front mounted, water cooled engines and sleek, new shapes.

First off the mark was the 2 litre 924 bringing Porsche motoring within reach of many more people.

Next came the car voted Car of the Year 1978, the 4.5 litre 928 V-8 luxury sports coupé. Said to be the car by which others will be judged for the next decade.

924, 911SC, 928, Turbo. Whichever you choose, Porsche believe you'll be well satisfied.

As for Porsche themselves: they will never be satisfied.

Porsche Cars Great Britain Limited, Richfield Avenue, Reading, RG1 8PH. Tel: 0734 595411.
For Tourist, NATO, Diplomatic and Personal Export Enquiries. Tel: 01-568 1313. The present Porsche line-up consists of ten models: the four cylinder 924 series including the 924 Turbo; the six cylinder 911 series; the eight cylinder 928 series and the Turbo. For further information and details of leasing facilities contact your nearest official Porsche centre.

South East: A.F.N. Ltd., Isleworth. Tel: 01-560 1011. A.F.N. Ltd., Guildford. Tel: 0483 38448. Charles Follett Ltd., Mayfair. Tel: 01-629 6266. Malaya Garage (Billingshurst) Ltd., Billingshurst. Tel: 040 381 3341. Maltin Car Concessionaires Ltd., Henley-on-Thames. Tel: 04912 78111. Motortune Ltd., Kensington. Tel: 01-581 1234. **South West:** Dick Lovett (Specialist Cars) Ltd., Wroughton. Tel: 0793 812387. **South:** Heddell and Deeks (Motors) Ltd., Bournemouth. Tel: 0202 510252. **Midlands:** Swinford Motors (Continental) Ltd., Stourbridge. Tel: 038 482 3047. Roger Clark (Cars) Ltd., Narborough. Tel: 0533 848270. Gordon Lamb Ltd., Chesterfield. Tel: 0246 451611. **East Anglia and Essex:** Lancaster Garages (Colchester) Ltd., Colchester. Tel: 0206 48141. **North West:** Ian Anthony Sales (Knutsford) Ltd. Tel: 0565 52737. **North East:** JCT 600 Ltd., Yeadon. Tel: 0532 502231. **North:** Parker and Parker Ltd., Kendal. Tel: 0539 24331. Gordon Ramsay Ltd., Newcastle upon Tyne. Tel: 0632 812829/814383. Gordon Ramsay Ltd., Bishop Auckland. Tel: 0388 5601. **Scotland:** Glen Henderson Motors Ltd., Ayr. Tel: 0292 81531. Glen Henderson Motors Ltd., Glasgow. Tel: 041-943 1155. Glen Henderson Motors Ltd., Edinburgh. Tel: 031-225 9266. **Northern Ireland:** Isaac Agnew Ltd. (Retail), Glengormley. Tel: 02313 7111. Isaac Agnew Ltd., Belfast. Tel: 0232 663231. **Channel Islands:** Jones Garage, St. Saviour, Jersey. Tel: 0534 26156.

Building costs won't stop going up.

But you __can__ control them.

No one's going to stop building costs going up for a while yet. But contrary to the impression you may have got from certain well-publicised contracts, costs *can* be kept under control – and a lot of the people who know how to do it are working for Bovis.

Bovis save you money in two ways; by not wasting time and by technical ingenuity. When we re-constructed half of the former Biba building in Kensington for Marks & Spencer we finished in time for Christmas 1977, *over a year* earlier than orthodox methods would have achieved.

The architects for the IBM building at Greenford thought the job nearly impossible, but perhaps Bovis could do it. The go-ahead came on January 16, 1977; we were on site by February 1, delivered the first phase a month early and the whole £4 million worth in just 13 months.

What Bovis contribute is, above all, management. If you would like to know how our methods could save *you* money, get in touch with John Gillham on 01-422 3488.

Rank	Name	Country	Main activity	Turnover 1978 £m	Turnover 1977 £m	Reported profits 1978 £m
101	Ericsson (Telefonaktiebolaget L.M.)	S	Electrical engineering & telecommunications	1,033·3	897·2	62·0
102	Oerlikon Bührle Holding AG	Sw	Holding co. (general engineering)	1,021·9	816·5	69·1
103	OMV AG	A	Petroleum products	1,012·8	924·7	34·5
104	Horten AG	G	Department stores	977·3	891·0	15·8
105	Lyonnaise des Eaux et de L'Eclairage	F	Public utilities	976·3	832·4	29·8
106	Nouvelles Galeries Réunis	F	Department stores	946·0	831·6	13·1
107	Bertelsmann AG	G	Publishers	935·8	766·4	52·6
108	Saarbergwerke	G	Coal & electric power	928·8	1,029·9	N/A
109	Casino	F	Food manufacturers and distributors	927·2	805·9	25·5
110	Olivetti & Cia SpA	I	Business machinery & systems manufacturers	920·6	807·8	N/A
111	Vereinigte Industrie Unternehmungen AG	G	Holding co. (electricity, aluminium & chemicals)	916·0	946·6	28·0
112	Klöckner Humboldt Deutz AG	G	General engineering	908·2	959·0	37·9
113	Deutsche Babcock AG	G	General engineering	905·0	803·4	30·9
114	Gevaert Photo-Produkten NV	B	Photographic equipment	901·8	873·3	12·4
115	Ogem Holding BV	N	Industrial holding co.	892·6	871·9	14·1
116	Skanska Cementgjuteriet	S	Builders	873·1	749·3	31·5
117	Wolff AG (Otto)	G	Iron & steel production	858·4	785·1	13·4
118	Internatio-Muller NV	N	Holding co.	854·9	819·9	10·5
119	VEW—Vereinigte Elektrizitätswerke Westfalen AG	G	Electricity supply	847·2	758·1	75·5
120	Beijerinvest AB	S	Holding co. (industrial investment)	840·4	814·6	8·0
121	Neste Oy	Fin	Oil & gas	826·3	778·7	16·5
122	SAS	S	Airline	807·5	630·5	12·7
123	Compania Telefonica Nacional de España	Sp	Telephone & data transmission service	806·4	629·3	178·9
124	Snia Viscosa	I	Textiles, chemicals & engineering	804·2	676·7	N/A
125	CEPSA	Sp	Oil refining	803·4*	652·7**	16·2*
126	Métallurgie Hoboken Overpelt	B	Non-ferrous metals	801·4	720·1	6·1
127	Grundig AG	G	Electronic equipment	795·1	741·2	62·3
128	Société Internationale Pirelli SA	Sw	Holding co. (cables, tyres & rubber articles)	791·2	897·0	9·5
129	Radar SA	F	Holding co. (supermarkets)	789·7	694·7	9·4
130	Lafarge	F	Cement production	770·0	743·6	45·0
131	Printemps SA	F	Department stores	767·1	702·1	8·9
132	Systembolaget AB	S	Beer, wine, etc.	761·2	678·4	18·8
133	Haniel & Cie. (Franz)	G	Petroleum products	760·2	694·8	30·3
134	Standard Elektrik Lorenz AG	G	Electrical engineering	753·9	737·2	20·2
135	Avions Marcel Dassault-Breguet Aviation	F	Aircraft	743·7	670·2	56·8
136	CFAO—Compagnie Française de L'Afrique Occidentale	F	Holding co. (industrial)	743·0	673·8	25·9
137	Brinkmann (Martin) AG	G	Tobacco	742·8	732·3	20·1
138	Saba (J. S.) AB	S	Wholesale of consumer goods	736·3	595·5	2·6
139	Cebeco	N	Wholesale trade	734·7*	578·2**	5·2*
140	Chimique Routière et d'Entreprise Générale	F	Civil engineering	729·4	717·6	9·0
141	Delhaize Frères et Cie	B	Supermarkets	728·8	553·6	12·8
142	Preussag AG	G	Coal, oil & non-ferrous metals	723·5	705·9	18·4
143	Neckermann Versand KGaA	G	Mail order house & department stores	722·1	795·1	(8·0)
144	Chemische Werke Hüls AG	G	Petrochemicals	720·8	737·5	N/A
145	Union Explosives Rio Tinto SA	Sp	Chemicals, industrial explosives, etc.	719·5*	596·6**	10·3*
146	SOK—Suomen Osuuskauppojen Keskuskunta	Fin	Co-operative wholesalers	718·2*	694·7**	1·6*
147	Intercom	B	Electricity & gas production & distribution	716·1	680·7	64·4
148	Enterprise Minière et Chimique	F	Mining & metals	713·8	519·0	1·8
149	Thyssen Bornemisza NV	N	Cement, machinery, transport equipment, water transport, general wholesale trade	711·2	766·1	31·3
150	Kon. Volker Stevin NV	N	Civil engineering	705·0	N/A	29·1

NOTES: *1977 figures; **1976 figures.

Rank	Name	Country	Main activity	Turnover 1978 £m	Turnover 1977 £m	Reported profits 1978 £m
151	KLM - Royal Dutch Airlines	N	Air transport	704·4	683·9	20·4
152	Stahlwerke Röchline Burbach	G	Steel	700·6	481·4	N/A
153	Chargeurs Réunis SA	F	Holding co. (transport)	690·4	619·5	14·7
154	ENSIDESA - Empresa Nacional Siderurgica SA	Sp	Iron & steel	683·3	583·4	(85·5)
155	Hachette (Librairie) SA	F	Publishers	681·2	664·1	31·2
156	Holzmann (Philipp) AG	G	Civil engineering & construction co.	680·5	690·2	20·0
157	SCOA	F	International wholesale & retail distribution	676·1	771·9	4·4
158	Swissair	Sw	Airline	675·5	718·7	20·2
159	Norsk Hydro A/S	No	Producers of nitrogen & magnesium products & plastics	670·1	506·2	24·1
160	SEAT	Sp	Vehicle manufacturers	669·8	582·9	(72·5)
161	Televerket	S	Telephones, telegraphy, broadcasting	665·9	567·1	14·5
162	Hapag-Lloyd AG	G	Shipping	661·3	590·4	18·5
163	L'Oréal	F	Hair products & cosmetics	653·4	565·9	48·1
164	Heineken NV	N	Holding co. (brewers, etc.)	652·5	604·0	55·4
165	Arbed	L	Iron & steel producers	638·3	574·6	(26·3)
166	Liebherr Group	G	Manufacture of plant & construction machinery	628·0	528·3	N/A
167	Générale d'Entreprises	F	Civil engineering	624·1	465·9	54·6
168	Rijn Schelde Verolme Machinefabrieken	N	Shipbuilding & mechanical engineering	621·5	647·5	(14·7)
169	Sandvik AB	S	Iron & steel	619·9	517·4	27·7
170	Hollandsche Beton Groep NV	N	Holding Co. (building and civil engineering)	617·8	607·4	21·8
171	Swedish Match Co.	S	Building and interior products, matches, packaging materials	613·3	576·9	(2·5)
172	Wessanen NV	N	Food manufacturer	612·6	549·8	8·4
173	Office Commercial Pharmaceutique (O.C.P.)	F	Pharmaceutical distributors	612·2	514·4	4·8
174	Boehringer Ingelheim Gruppe	G	Pharmaceuticals	610·5*	592·5**	61·2*
175	Beghin-Say	F	Paper, sugar refinery	605·1	511·5	14·6
176	Schering AG	G	Chemicals and pharmaceuticals	599·9	574·8	57·9
177	VAW—Vereinigte Aluminium Werke AG	G	Aluminium production	599·4	576·7	(1·2)
178	Nedlloyd Groep NV	N	Shipping	598·5	578·1	11·1
179	Grånges Aktiebolag	S	Iron and steel mining	588·2	617·2	(7·2)
180	SCA—Svenska Cellulose AB	S	Chemical pulp, paper, timber, chemical products	587·4	526·9	23·4
181	'Austria' Tabakwerke AG	A	Tobacco	571·5	N/A	N/A
182	Alfa-Laval AB	S	General engineering	571·2	482·1	24·3
183	Ferodo (SA Française du)	F	Motor components	571·1	498·4	26·9
184	Messerschmitt-Boelkow-Blohm GmbH	G	Transport equipment	570·6	485·5	21·9
185	IBM Italia	I	Computers	566·5	488·8	90·5
186	Holderbank Financière Glaris SA	Sw	Holding co. (cement)	565·3	594·9	35·2
187	Dragados y Construcciones SA	Sp	Builders and civil engineers	563·0	509·8	11·2
188	KBB NV—Koninklijke Bijenkorf Beheer	N	Holding co. (shops and department stores)	557·2	512·4	10·2
189	Comptoirs Modernes	F	Supermarket and food retailers	554·2	321·1	11·6
190	United Breweries Ltd.	D	Breweries	544·7	497·6	20·2
191	Atlas Copco AB	S	Compressed-air equipment	543·2	476·2	39·9
192	Zahnradfabrik Friedrichshafen AG	G	Vehicle components producers	539·1	512·9	N/A
193	Alitalia	I	Airline	537·6	484·3	10·9
194	Swedyards	S	Shipbuilding	533·8	N/A	211·8
195	Vereinigte Edelstahlwerke	A	Steel	528·9*	525·3**	N/A
196	Pernod Ricard SA	F	Holding co. (wines and spirits)	527·3	461·2	40·0
197=	Honeywell Bull	F	Business machines, etc.	524·3	445·7	27·2
197=	Strabag-Bau AG	G	Building and construction	524·3	487·6	15·9
199	Poclain	F	Manufacturers of excavators	523·5	209·0	1·4
200	Freudenberg & Co.	G	Holding co. (leather, rubber and chemicals)	517·5	490·8	N/A

NOTES: *1977 figures; **1976 figures.

There is not another organisation in the World that is just like yours – ASK ALTERGO.

An Altergo consultant will not try to tell you how to run your business, but they will talk your language, and they will, almost certainly, have experience of and know how computers are being used in organisations similar to your own.

Altergo Consultancy makes available to you a resource made valuable by its scarcity – a vast collective experience of applying high technology in the realisation of business objectives.

Typically, an Altergo consultant is a graduate business analyst with a sound knowledge of computing applied to specific industrial or commercial sectors – Banking, Insurance, Retailing, Government, Petro-Chemical, etc.

The best way to find out what an Altergo consultant can do for you is to meet one.

Call Altergo – 01-734 9681 Ext. 81.

altergo

38 Soho Square
London W1V 5DF.

Rank	Name	Country	Main activity	Turnover 1978 £m	Turnover 1977 £m	Reported profits 1978 £m
201	Polygram	N	Publishing, printing and allied industries, electrical apparatus and machinery, business services and supplies	517·3*	490·0**	N/A
202	Continental Gummiwerke AG	G	Manufacturers of tyres, and industrial rubber articles	516·2	500·8	7·7
203	BPA—Byggproduktion AB	S	Civil engineers	510·3*	324·4**	0·4*
204	Industrie A. Zanussi SpA	I	Electrical machinery apparatus and supplies	503·0	355·0	1·0
205	Douwe Egberts BV	N	Coffee, tea and tobacco	502·0	483·5	31·6
206	Otra NV	N	International traders	499·0	503·4	1·1
207	Bayernwerk AG	G	Electricity	497·0*	392·6**	36·1*
208	OK-Oljekonsumenternas Förbund	S	Wholesale and retail of cars, hotels and boarding houses and water transport	493·6	447·9	1·4
209	Linde AG	G	Refrigeration equipment, chemical engineering and machinery	492·0	449·5	28·2
210	API—Anonima Petroli Italiana SpA	I	Petroleum refining	487·4	437·5	0·3
211	Havas (Agence)	F	Advertising and tourism	487·0	417·6	8·8
212	Euromarché	F	Supermarkets and hypermarkets	482·2	370·2	8·5
213	Hankkija	Fin	Wholesale co-operative	479·3	413·2	1·4
214=	Andreae—Noris Zahn	G	Pharmaceuticals	478·7	455·1	5·9
214=	EBES	B	Electricity production and distribution	478·7	438·5	N/A
216	Mjolkcentralen Arla	S	Food manufacturers	476·4	415·2	6·3
217	Dyckerhoff & Widmann AG	G	Construction and cement production	470·1	454·7	N/A
218	Axel Springer Verlag AG	G	Printing and publishing	465·6	442·0	8·9
219	Roussel Uclaf SA	F	Pharmaceutical and biological products	464·5	414·6	N/A
220	Bouygues SA	F	Building constructors	464·1	354·1	14·0
221	Redoute à Roubaix SA	F	Mail order	460·5	387·1	N/A
222	Fougerolle	F	Public works, road works and civil engineering	457·4	363·3	N/A
223	Tabacofina SA	B	Holding co. (tobacco)	454·9	422·0	13·6
224	Dumes	F	Building and construction	452·9*	377·8**	22·5*
225	Routiers Colas	F	Civil engineering	452·1	413·7	15·1
226	Docks de France	F	Supermarket and hypermarket operators	450·0	388·8	7·6
227	Dillinger Hüttenwerke AG	G	Iron, steel and ferro-alloys	448·4	395·3	10·2
228	Dollfus-Mieg et Cie. SA	F	Holding co. (textiles)	447·7	402·8	2·0
229	Nederlandse Spoorwegen NV	N	Railways	444·1	421·1	(0·6)
230=	Carl-Zeiss-Stiftung	G	Holding co. (glass and optical equipment)	441·6	414·0	13·4
230=	Rheinische Braunkohlenwerke AG	G	Coal, electricity	441·6*	418·1**	45·3*
232	Bührmann Tetterode NV	N	Holding co. (paper manufacturers)	439·5	388·7	20·8
233	Steag AG	G	Electricity, gas and steam supply and construction	438·9	414·1	14·5
234	Eschweiler Bergwerks Verein	G	Coal production	438·4	342·3	(3·0)
235	Grands Travaux de Marseille	F	Civil engineering	436·7	391·1	16·5
236	E. Merck	G	Chemical and pharmaceutical manufacturers	436·3	397·2	6·3
237	Valmet Oy	Fin	Machinery and transport equipment	434·8*	432·7**	(0·4)*
238	Verenigde Machinefabrieken Stork NV	N	Engineers	432·3	440·3	(2·4)
239	VFW—Fokker mbH (Zentralgesellschaft)	G	Aircraft manufacturer, etc.	426·3	448·1	2·1
240	A. Ahlström Osakeyhtiö	Fin	Pulp, paper and timber production	424·8	N/A	5·3
241	HEW—Hamburgische Elektrizitäts Werke AG	G	Electricity and heat distribution	423·9	408·8	53·8
242	Rütgerswerke AG	G	Raw material processors	423·2	540·2	14·0
243	Norddeutsche Affinerie	G	Smelting and refining of non-ferrous and precious metals	421·9	415·9	15·3
244	Poliet	F	Holding co. (building materials)	420·7	418·0	10·3
245	Hochtief AG	G	Civil engineering and construction	420·5	436·5	35·6
246	Chevron Oil Belgium NV	B	Petroleum products	420·0	425·9	1·0
247	Cit-Alcatel	F	Telecommunication systems	417·1	380·6	21·4
248	Ballast-Nedam Groep NV	N	Builders, constructors and engineers	417·0	283·2	7·9
249=	AGA Aktiebolag	S	Gas, batteries, radiators and electronics	416·3	279·8	24·0
249=	Steyr Daimler Puch AG	A	Motor vehicle and engine manufacturers	416·3	387·2	9·7

NOTES: *1977 figures; ** 1976 figures.

We're very accomplished in obtaining the lowdown on European stocks and shares.

The Extel® European Company Card Service gives you all the figures and facts that matter - in English - on some 700 large firms quoted on the Bourses. It's the safe, easy way to keep abreast of all that's going on across the Channel.

Write or ring for complete details. *Toute de suite,* monsieur. You don't know what you might be missing.

Extel Statistical Services Limited
the <u>fact</u> getters

37-45 Paul Street, London EC2A 4PB · Phone 01-253 3400 · Telex 263437

® *Extel is the registered trade mark of The Exchange Telegraph Company Limited.*

Rank	Name	Country	Main activity	Turnover 1978 £m	Turnover 1977 £m	Reported profits 1978 £m
251	Nordwestdeutsche Kraftwerke AG	G	Electricity production and distribution	416·1	384·2	46·5
252	PWA-Papierwerke Waldhof Aschaffenburg AG	G	Chemical pulp and paper manufacturers and converters	411·5	413·8	16·6
253	La Rinascente	I	Department stores	410·0	359·7	0·5
254	Kügelfischer Georg Schafer & Co.	G	Ball and roller bearings	409·1	403·7	12·2
255	Compagnie Générale des Eaux	F	Water purification and distribution	408·4	366·7	25·2
256	Société Auxiliaire d'Entreprises	F	Civil engineering	406·6	316·8	9·4
257	Bekaert SA	B	Holding co. (wire and wire products)	404·0	384·0	31·2
258	Royal Bos-Kalis Westminster Group NV	N	Dredging co.	401·7	329·6	16·0
259	ABV—Vagförbättringar AB	S	Machinery	400·0	375·0	1·8
260	Energie Versorgung Schwaben AG	G	Electricity supply and distribution	397·0	368·7	14·2
261	Carnaud SA	F	Iron	395·8	331·6	10·3
262	SNECMA	F	Aircraft engines	395·2*	396·2**	11·2*
263	Esselte AB	S	Printing, publishing and packaging	392·1	280·2	15·0
264	Radiotechnique (La)	F	Radios, televisions and electrical equipment	390·5	361·1	29·3
265	Fichtel & Sachs AG	G	Vehicle components	390·1	371·8	24·0
266	Lauritzen Group	D	Shipping co.	389·1	368·0	27·5
267	Usines Chausson (SA des)	F	Motor components	388·7	337·8	(4·8)
268	Fischer (Georg) AG	Sw	Machinery and castings	388·5	424·2	(2·4)
269	Sidmar	B	Iron and steel	375·0	326·6	0·6
270	Hagemeyer NV	N	Cosmetics, pharmaceuticals, and electrical engineering	372·8	394·5	(0·4)
271	DCGG—Deutsche Continental Gas Gesellschaft	G	Gas and electrical production and supply	370·9	350·4	17·0
272	Interfood SA	Sw	Holding co. (confectionery)	370·3	362·4	N/A
273	Deli Mij NV	N	Wholesale trade (timber, tobacco and commodities)	368·3	431·3	8·5
274	Wacker Chemie GmbH	G	Industrial chemicals and plastics	365·7	350·3	17·9
275	Badenwerk AG	G	Electricity supply	365·2	335·1	29·8
276	Enso Gutzeit Osakeyhtiö	Fin	Wood and paper	364·5	315·0	3·9
277	Svenska Flaktfabriken AB	S	Industrial ventilation, heating and air conditioning equipment	359·4	316·3	6·8
278	Beiersdorf AG	G	Pharmaceuticals, cosmetics, surgical products and toiletries	357·6*	322·4**	N/A
279	O & K Orenstein & Koppel AG	G	General engineering	354·2	304·5	10·3
280	Cedis	F	Supermarkets	352·5	309·0	10·6
281	Sachs AG	G	Transport equipment	349·6*	295·1**	N/A
282=	Olida et Caby Associés SA	F	Foods	344·4	316·4	4·7
282=	Smidth (F.L.) & Co	D	Engineering	344·4	333·3	28·2
284	Bewag Berliner Kraft und Licht (Bewag) AG	G	Electricity production and distribution	342·1	320·0	40·4
285	Ferrostaal AG	G	Iron and steel; acquisition of companies in the steel industry	341·9*	264·1**	N/A
286	Babcock-Fives (Compagnie Industrielle et Financière)	F	Holding co. (mechanical, structural and electrical engineers)	341·2	223·5	17·0
287	Rauma-Repola Oy	Fin	General engineering	341·0	336·0	7·0
288	Buderus AG	G	Iron and steelworks	340·8	309·9	1·2
289	UNERG	B	Gas, electricity, etc.	340·3	319·4	25·8
290	Stora Kopparbergs	S	Mining and steel	340·2	475·9	10·5
291	Compagnie Financière Lesieur	F	Holding co. (fats and oils)	338·8	331·5	10·9
292	Deutsche Marathon Petroleum GmbH	G	Refining and wholesale of petroleum	337·7	436·8	N/A
293	UTA-Union de Transports Aériens	F	Airline	336·7	291·7	7·8
294	Schindler Holding AG	Sw	Holding co. (general engineering)	336·5	357·5	13·5
295	Boliden AB	S	Mining, metallurgy and chemicals	335·4	320·6	6·0
296	Générale Sucrière	F	Sugar refineries	335·2	245·0	7·5
297	Iberduero SA	Sp	Electricity	333·8	292·9	103·6
298	Telefonbau und Normalzeit	G	Electrical machinery, apparatus and supplies	329·7	307·4	34·8
299	Heraeus GmbH	G	Precious metals, industrial instruments	329·2	272·6	22·3
300	Sodra Skogsägarna	S	Wood and paper	329·0	306·5	(3·9)

NOTES: *1977 figures; **1976 figures.

PILKINGTON

Top left. Float glass   Top right. High technology safety windscreens   Bottom left. Cemfil glass fibre used to manufacture glass reinforced cement   Bottom right. Photochromic glass

Five portraits of the company

Financial Highlights	1979	1978
	£m	£m
Sales to outside customers	548.8	469.5
Total Group profit before taxation (including licensing income of £379m)	90.3	71.7
Group profit after taxation	47.6	35.4
Dividends	9.8	7.2
Profit retained in business	35.9	26.9
Earnings per share	36.7p	27.5p
Dividends per share (net)	7.9p	5.8p

Above, four of our main products.

To the left, the summarised results of the year to March 31st, 1979.

Behind all five portraits, a group that's a world leader in the manufacture and marketing of advanced glass products; a group that earned £38 million in licensing income from overseas; a group that is firmly based in established markets, and well placed to benefit in new ones.

How's that for enterprise!

Rank	Name	Country	Main activity	Turnover 1978 £m	Turnover 1977 £m	Reported profits 1978 £m
301	Borregaard A/S	No	Holding co. (paper and chemicals)	326·6	290·3	(2·5)
302	Varta AG	G	Holding co. (batteries and plastics)	325·6	321·2	15·2
303	Euroc AB	S	Cement production	323·2	280·7	13·5
304	Schmalbach Lubeca GmbH	G	Manufacturers of packaging materials	322·4	350·4	2·7
305	Matra	F	Manufacture of aircraft, motors and components	321·1	247·4	18·3
306	Molkerei Zentrale Süd GmbH & Co. KG.	G	Milk and milk products	320·5	275·5	0·2
307	Dansk Shell	D	Petroleum	320·4	287·5	13·1
308	Sommer Allibert	F	Holding co. (wall and floor coverings, plastic products, etc.)	320·3	246·4	8·4
309	Bofors AB	S	Arms, tanks and steel products	319·3	266·4	4·4
310	Svenska Esso AB	S	Petroleum	318·2	292·7	6·1
311	Nokia AB (Oy)	Fin	Pulp, paper, power, etc.	317·8	292·2	6·0
312	Diehl KG	G	Data systems, clocks and defence products	317·0	328·8	N/A
313	Viniprix	F	Supermarkets	316·2	324·9	4·4
314	Kymi Kymmene	Fin	Paper, engineering and chemicals	314·3	264·1	N/A
315	Hidroelectrica Española SA	Sp	Electric power production and distribution	312·8	N/A	89·7
316=	OCE—Van der Grinten	N	Office equipment and materials	310·1	292·6	17·6
316=	Potin (Félix) SA	F	Holding co. (foodstuffs, retailing)	310·1	295·8	N/A
318	Kemanobel AB	S	Chemicals	310·0	259·4	12·3
319	Bilfinger & Berger Bau AG	G	Building and civil engineering contractors	308·0*	303·5**	N/A
320	Pressbyraforetagen AB	S	Wholesale and retail of consumer goods	307·6	280.5	0·7
321	Porsche AG	G	Motor vehicles	302·7	270·2	7·5
322=	UCB SA	B	Chemical and pharmaceutical manufacturers	302·1	292·7	2·6
322=	Semperit AG	A	Tyres, rubber goods and plastics	302·1*	293·5**	(5·9)*
324	Meneba	N	Holding co. (flour millers, etc.)	301·9	300·8	0·9
325	Superfos A/S	D	Fertilisers	301·7	276·8	16·8
326	Dortmunder Union Schultheiss Brauerei AG	G	Brewers	300·4	293·2	13·6
327	Campenon-Bernard SA	F	Holding co. (civil engineering)	300·3*	240·9**	2·1*
328	Elkem Spigerverket A/S	No	Ferro-alloys, steel, etc.	300·2	261·1	2·1
329	Chemie Linz	A	Chemicals	299·1	281·0	2·4
330=	Grands Magasins Jelmoli SA	Sw	Department stores and mail order houses	298·9	298·4	14·9
330=	Landis & Gyr AG	Sw	Electrical equipment	298·9	313·9	19·1
332	Cellulose du Pin SA	F	Wood pulp and paper	298·6	308·2	N/A
333	Akergruppen	No	Shipbuilding	297·2	272·9	(0·4)
334	Usego Trimerco Holding AG	Sw	Holding co. (food industry)	297·1	295·7	(0·8)
335	Ford Motor Company (Belgium) SA	B	Motor manufacturers	294·7	272·4	16·7
336	Motor Iberica SA	Sp	Motor vehicles	292·9	233·8	N/A
337	DAF Trucks	N	Commercial vehicles	292·3	299·4	(8·3)
338	Van Leer BV (Royal Packaging Industries)	N	Fabricated metal products	291·5	276·4	16·0
339	Uddeholms Aktiebolag	S	Steel, paper and chemicals	290·6	297·8	2·9
340	AHV—Altos Hornos de Vizcaya SA	Sp	Iron and steel	290·2*	248·3**	N/A
341	SAGEM	F	Electrical and electronic equipment	290·1	N/A	15·4
342	Métallurgique Hainaut-Sambre (Sté.)	B	Iron and steel	287·9	220·5	(48·6)
343	Energieversorgung Weser-Ems AG	G	Electricity supply	287·5	262·8	22·2
344	Wella AG	G	Hair products	286·8	265·0	N/A
345	Maizena GmbH	G	Food and starch manufacturers	285·9	278·0	N/A
346	PRB	B	Polyurethane chemicals	284·2	283·8	7·9
347	Lefebvre (Jean) Entreprise	F	Civil and public works contractors	282·9	250·1	8·9
348	Hunter Douglas NV	N	Building products etc.	281·9	246·8	13·4
349	Publicis SA	F	Holding co. (advertising and public relations consultants)	278·8	250·8	N/A
350	Société Génerale de Fonderie	F	Heating, air conditioning, sanitary and kitchen equipment	277·9	261·8	(5·2)

NOTES: *1977 figures; **1976 figures.

Rank	Name	Country	Main activity	Turnover 1978 £m	Turnover 1977 £m	Reported profits 1978 £m
351	Dansk Esso A/S	D	Petroleum products	276·9	280·1	6·9
352	CEM—Compagnie Electro-mécanique	F	Electrical engineering	276·5	249·9	N/A
353	Lonza AG	Sw	Chemical manufacturers and electricity supply works	274·5	309·4	N/A
354	Stadtwerke Köln GmbH	G	Suppliers of gas, electricity and public transport	274·3	254·1	6·4
355	Boehringer Mannheim GmbH	G	Pharmaceuticals	273·1	252·8	27·3
356	VNU—Verenigde Nederlandse Uitgevers Bedrijven BV	N	Publishing and printing	272·8	248·1	20·6
357	Grünzweig+Hartmann und Glasfaser AG	G	Building materials	272·5	282·0	N/A
358	Wärtsilä AB (Oy)	Fin	Pottery, glass, iron, and steel, shipbuilding	272·0	237·4	3·2
359	Allgäuer Alpenmilch AG	G	Milk products	271·6	262·0	17·1
360	Gist-Bricades NV	N	Chemicals and pharmaceuticals	270·4	248·4	9·2
361	Kléber Colombes	F	Tyres, aircraft and motor components	269·4	250·5	11·5
362	Fromageries Bel-La Vache qui Rit	F	Dairy products	264·9	249·8	N/A
363	Incentive AB	S	Metal products and machinery	264·7	239·0	6·3
364	Mo Och Domsjö Aktiebolag	S	Forest products	262·5	229·6	11·2
365	Von Roll AG	Sw	General engineering	259·7	265·5	N/A
366	Pierrefitte-Auby	F	Holding co. (chemicals, fertilisers)	259·5*	220·5**	2·5
367	Lainière de Roubaix	F	Holding co. (wool textile manufacturers and merchants)	256·2	265·3	(1·2)
368	Ardal A/S	No	Aluminium	254·3	225·5	1·6
369	Merlin Gerin	F	Electrical engineers	254·0	212·3	10·2
370	Olympia Werke AG	G	Office machinery	251·2	246·7	N/A
371	Pricel	F	Holding co. (textiles)	248·7	244·8	13·0
372=	Compagnie Générale de Radiologie	F	X-ray equipment	248·5*	N/A	N/A
372=	Société Bic	F	Pen distributors	248·5	229·8	30·9
372=	Vowerk & Co. KG	G	Holding co. (electrical appliances, carpets)	248·5	251·8	N/A
375	CM Industries	F	Holding co. (pharmaceuticals)	247·5	165·4	6·7
376	Borsumii Wehry N.V.	N	Consumer goods	245·3	228·9	8·0
377	PLM—Aktiebolaget Platmanufactur	S	Metal, plastic and glass containers	243·0	235·3	5·8
378	International Sleeping Car and Tourism Co.	B	Transport, hotels, restaurants and tourism	242·7	228·9	5·7
379	Société des Ciments Française SA	F	Cement production	238·5	221·3	5·0
380	Schuitema NV	N	Retail sale of food, etc.	237·3	191·3	1·3
381	Österreichische Electrizitätswirtschafts AG	A	Gas and electricity production and supply	235·5	211·0	(5·8)
382	Magazine zum Globus AG	Sw	Department stores	234·9	232·1	2·5
383	Hutchinson Mapa	F	Rubber products	234·7	222·3	3·0
384	NKL—Norges Kooperative Landsforening	No	Wholesale co-operative	233·2*	271·6**	4·1*
385	Moulinex	F	Household appliances	230·6	199·0	9·7
386	Maisons Phénix	F	Building and construction	229·1	203·0	27·4
387	Italcementi Fabriche Riunite Cemento SpA	I	Cement manufacturer	228·8*	179·2**	4·8*
388	OBAG—Energieversorgung Ostbayern AG	G	Electricity production and distribution	228·5	156·5(a)	25·2
389	Bell AG	Sw	Meat processing and canned meats	227·0	230·3	N/A
390	Compagnie Optorg	F	International traders	226·9	217·6	4·2
391	Broström Shipping Co. Ltd	S	Shipping	226·7	229·1	(2·0)
392	Nixdorf Computer AG	G	Computers	226·1*	184·8**	N/A
393	Kvaerner Industrier A/S	No	Holding co. (shipbuilding)	225·6	235·0	2·6
394	Moët-Hennessy S.A.	F	Champagne, brandy and perfume	225·5	180·0	21·0
395	SCAC	F	Fuel trading	225·2*	200·2**	1·4*
396	Billerud Uddeholm	S	Manufacturers of pulp, paper and timber	225·1	166·5	7·5
397	IBM Sweden	S	Computers	224·6	183·7	29·8
398	Danske Sukkerfabrikker A/S	D	Sugar producers	223·9	168·8	14·0
399	Hilti AG	Lie	Fabricated metal products	223·0	N/A	N/A
400	ALTANA Industrieaktien und Anlagen AG	G	Holding co. (pharmaceuticals, dietetics, etc.)	222·0	217·2	14·6

NOTES: *1977 figures; **1976 figures.
(a) 9 months.

Enterprises
Hamlet

Producers of International Commercials

For Show-Reels contact
Harry Brooks or Diana Hayward
at 46 Lowndes Square London SW1
01-235-1811

Rank	Name	Country	Main activity	Turnover 1978 £m	Turnover 1977 £m	Reported profits 1978 £m
401	Compagnie Générale Maritime	F	Shipping	221·8*	261·3**	N/A
402	Acciaiere e Ferriere Lombarde Falck	I	Iron and steel	221·3	182·7	1·7
403	Rautaruukki Oy	Fin	Iron and steel	221·2	148·0	5·4
404	Télémécanique Electrique	F	Electrical engineering	221·1	205·0	14·2
405	Outokumpu Oy	Fin	Metal production	221·0	173·7	1·4
406	Economats du Centre	F	Food chain	220·8	196·4	3·9
407	Elektrizitäts Aktiengesellschaft Mitteldeutschland	G	Electricity supply	220·2	199·6	14·8
408	FECSA—Fuerzas Electricas de Cataluna SA	Sp	Electricity production and distribution	219·3	178·6	34·9
409	Wieland-werke AG	G	Non-ferrous metals	218·9*	190·8**	N/A
410	Papeteries de Belgique SA	B	Paper and cardboard manufacturers	218·6	213·7	N/A
411=	Didier Werke AG	G	Refractory products	218·3	229·1	10·7
411=	Dragages et Travaux Publics (Entreprises)	F	Builders and civil engineers	218·3	214·2	7·6
413	Eisen und Metall AG	G	Iron and steel	217·7	200·4	0·4
414	Danfoss A/S	D	Engineering	217·2	208·7	27·8
415	Neunkirchener Eisenwerk AG	G	Iron, steel and fertilisers	215·3	166·3	(16·2)
416	Galerias Preciados	Sp	Department stores	214·8	178·1	(1·5)
417	Isar-Amperwerke AG	G	Electricity generation and distribution	214·1*	208·6**	N/A
418	Lyon Alemand Louyot (Comptoir)	F	Precious metals, electrical appliances, electronics, telephones	212·9	165·1	0·6
419=	Hussel Holding AG	G	Holding co. (wholesale and retail)	212·4	198·8	7·5
419=	Züblin AG (Ed)	G	Civil engineering	212·4	204·6	3·2
421=	Union Carbide Belgium NV	B	Industrial chemicals, plastics	212·1	221·9	7·6
421=	Knorr-Bremse	G	Light engineering	212·1	216·2	N/A
423	Rheinmetall Berlin AG	G	Holding co. (engineering)	211·9	197·7	8·5
424	Dalmine SpA	I	Manufacturers of steel and tubular products	211·0*	231·0**	(21·9)*
425	Gerresheimer Glas AG	G	Glass manufacture	210·7	214·1	(5·3)
426	Blohm & Voss	G	Shipbuilding and repair	210·6	170·6	8·5
427	Braun AG	G	Consumer goods	209·2	218·9	N/A
428=	Pelikan AG	G	Office equipment, etc.	209·1	N/A	10·1
428=	Süddeutsche Zucker AG (Sudzucker)	G	Sugar refineries	209·1	297·4	9·4
430	Luossavaara Kiirunavaara AB	S	Metal production	208·8	185·9	(23·3)
431	Ruhrchemie AG	G	Chemicals	208·6	203·1	1·7
432	Borel (Jacques) International	F	Restaurateurs, caterers	208·1	188·2	(9·7)
433	Yhtyneet Paperitehtaat	Fin	Paper manufacturers and forestry	207·3	181·0	3·9
434	Bredero NV	N	Building and construction	206·5	184·8	4·5
435	Flachglas AG	G	Glass manufacturers	206·3	198·0	19·5
436	Eridania Zuccherifici	I	Sugar production	205·4	156·1	6·9
437	Aussedat Rey	F	Paper manufacturers	204·5	N/A	(0·1)
438	KNP-Koninklijke Nederlandse Papier-fabricken N.V.	N	Paper production	204·3	179·2	5·8
439	Klein, Schanzlin & Becker AG	G	Pumps, valves and compressors	204·1	198·3	6·4
440	Holmens Bruk AB	S	Paper and wood production	203·4	164·1	4·1
441=	Gelder Papier (Van)	N	Paper manufacturers	202·2	210·6	8·1
441=	Voith Beteiligungen GmbH	G	Engineering	202·2	179·5	8·4
443	Kemira Oy	Fin	Chemicals	200·2	165·7	2·1
444	International Service System A/S	D	Security maintenance	198·3	170·9	7·4
445	Norcem A/S	No	Plastics, glass and cement production	197·7	166·5	4·5
446	Dyckerhoff Zementwerke AG	G	Cement producers	197·5	186·6	6·5
447	SEB SA	F	Holding co.	197·1	189·8	14·5
448	Felten & Guilleaume Carlswerk AG	G	Holding co. (electrical engineering)	196·2	184·1	N/A
449	SSIH—Sté. Suisse pour l'Industrie Horlogère SA	Sw	Holding co. (horological products)	195·6	184·8	0·6
450	Wayss & Freytag AG	G	Civil engineers	195·1	151·8	1·9

NOTES: *1977 figures; **1976 figures.

Aurora
Holdings Limited

An international group involved in precision engineering and the manufacture of special steels.

Rank	Name	Country	Main activity	Turnover 1978 £m	Turnover 1977 £m	Reported profits 1978 £m
451	Salamander AG	G	Footwear manufacturers	194·9	182·4	7·6
452	Cros SA	Sp	Chemicals	194·0*	178·2**	N/A
453	DBA	F	Manufacturers of equipment for motor and aircraft industry	193·3	290·0	(6·4)
454=	Bazar de l'Hôtel de Ville	F	Department stores	192·6	163·7	6·5
454=	Kempense Steenkolenmijnen NV	B	Coal production	192·6	201·9	(0·3)
456	Nordostschweizerische Kraftwerke AG	Sw	Electricity production and distribution	192·3	184·5	7·7
457	Monberg & Thorsen A/S	D	Chemicals, building and construction	191·2	137·5	4·3
458=	Dunlop AG	G	Tyres	190·6	191·8	N/A
458=	Philipsons Automobil AB	S	Vehicle distributor	190·6	171·0	12·7
460	Club Mediterrannée SA	F	Hotel and holiday village operators	190·2	159·1	N/A
461	Thomassen & Drijver Verblifa N.V.	N	Tin boxes and packing materials	189·9	198·1	11·5
462	Iggesund Bruk AB	S	Forestry and timber	187·8	156·7	5·5
463	Compagnie Française des Ferrailles	F	Railways	187·1	185·1	2·7
464	Burmeister & Wain A/S	D	Shipbuilders	186·2*	211·4**	8·0*
465	Triumph-Adler Group	G	Computers and office machinery	186·0*	177·9**	8·6*
466	Goldschmidt (Th.) AG	G	Organic metals and chemicals	185·9	178·1	5·3
467	Kodak AG	G	Films and cameras	185·5	165·8	11·0
468	Dornier GmbH	G	Machinery, transport equipment	185·2	N/A	N/A
469=	Heidelberger Zement AG	G	Cement and concrete products	184·3	169·9	24·5
469=	United Steamship Co. (DFDS A/S)	D	Freight and passenger shipping services	184·3	180·1	17·5
471	Pakhoed Holding NV	N	Holding co. (tank storage, transport properties)	184·0	102·9	3·4
472	Siab Byggen AB	S	Building and construction	183·7*	144·6**	0·4*
473	Norsk Shell A/S	No	Petroleum products	182·5	165·1	0·6
474	Kone Oy	Fin	Textiles, metals and machinery	181·8	163·9	5·2
475	KNSM Group NV	N	Shipping	181·6	185·0	1·2
476	Stadtwerke Hannover AG	G	Gas, electricity supply	179·5	167·1	9·9
477=	Fagersta AB	S	Iron and steel	178·8	159·1	4·9
477=	Rochette Cenpa SA	F	Paper and wood pulp	178·8	192·3	N/A
479	Bilspedition (AB Godstrafik &)	S	Transport and haulage	178·7*	149·9**	1·2*
480	Skanska Andelsslakterier	S	Food manufacturer	178·6	160·5	0·7
481	Bols (Erven Lucas)	N	Liqueurs and spirits	178·4	155·3	11·9
482	Pompey (Cie. Industrielle et Financière de)	F	Iron and steel	178·3	169·3	7·4
483	Fabrique Nationale Herstal SA	B	Small arms, ammunition and machinery	177·9*	139·7**	6·1*
484	Grands Moulins de Paris SA	F	Flour milling and animal feedstuffs	174·3	155·2	1·6
485	SAT (SA de Télécommunications)	F	Telecommunications	173·9	159·2	10·2
486	Bremer Vulkan Schiffbau und Maschinenfabrik	G	Shipbuilding and repair	172·1	214·0	2·5
487	Darty et Fils (Ets)	F	Domestic electrical appliances	170·2	137·0	12·1
488	Korf Stahl AG	G	Holding co. (iron and steel)	169·0*	168·9**	(9·2)*
489	Société de Prayon	B	Production of zinc, etc.	168·8	N/A	(7·2)
490	Locabail (Cie. pour la Location d'Equipements Professionels)	F	Leasing of commercial and industrial equipment	168·4	150·0	0·1
491	Heidelberger Druckmaschinen AG	G	Office machinery	168·0*	127·7**	N/A
492	Rousselot SA	F	Chemicals, polymers and adhesives	167·2	170·1	6·8
493	Perrier (Source)	F	Holding co. (mineral waters, milk products)	167·0	107·3	8·2
494=	DLW AG	G	Floor coverings	166·5	136·1	16·6
494=	Magneti Marelli SpA. (Fabbrica Italiana)	I	Electrical engineering	166·5	149·3	1·5
496	Tampella (Oy) AB	Fin	Forest products, pulp and paper	165·9	166·5	0·5
497	Petrochim SA	B	Petroleum and coal products	164·4*	208·7**	1·6*
498	Elsevier—NDU NV	N	Publishers and printers	162·8	147·5	10·1
499	ESAB	S	Engineering	161·6	149·0	2·4
500	Lech-Elektrizitätswerke AG	G	Generation and distribution of electricity	161·2	142·4	24·4

NOTES: *1977 figures; **1976 figures.

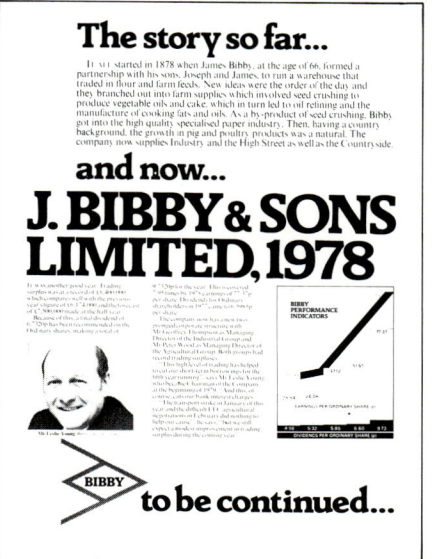

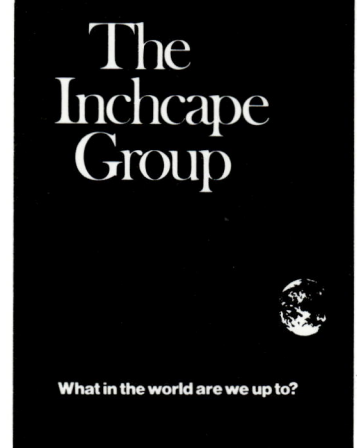

Bank of Boston House, 5 Cheapside, E.C.2.

If banking is a service business, then it should be on service that you judge a bank.

We've spent 57 years in the City, building an organisation to cater for the toughest judge of all: the financial professional.

That's why The Bank of Boston in London offers a surprising depth of service to international customers—including an active foreign exchange dealing department and the facilitating of investments in the U.S.

Why we have unusually good representation in 40 countries.

Why our two hundred people in London aim at the highest standards (if you give the best service, you have the best bank).

And it works.

We are one of the top ten US international banks, and a major force in correspondent banking.

And six out of the top ten companies in the prestigious "The Times One Thousand" are our customers.

Do you put a premium on service too?
We look forward to meeting you.

Boston. The bank for financial professionals.

BANK OF BOSTON
THE FIRST NATIONAL BANK OF BOSTON

Bank of Boston House, 5 Cheapside, London EC2P 2DE (Tel: 01-236 2388). Also at: 31 Lowndes Street, Belgravia, London SW1X 9HX (Tel: 01-235 9541).

ARGENTINA; AUSTRALIA; BAHAMAS; BOLIVIA; BRAZIL; CHANNEL ISLANDS; DOMINICAN REPUBLIC; FRANCE; GERMANY; HAITI; HONG KONG; IRAN; JAPAN; LEBANON; LUXEMBOURG; MEXICO; PANAMA; SINGAPORE; SPAIN; U.K.; U.S.A.; URUGUAY; VENEZUELA.

18 The 100 leading American companies

Rank (sales)	Name	Sales £000	*CAPITAL EMPLOYED £000	Rank	NET INCOME Latest year £000	Previous year £000
1	Exxon Corpn	29,407,676	13,572,695	1	**1,271,660**	1,124,432
2	General Motors Corpn	29,097,273	9,457,002	2	**1,614,544**	1,536,072
3	Ford Motor Co.	19,691,221	5,773,421	6	**731,285**	769,900
4	Mobil Corpn	16,883,716	6,208,406	5	**518,071**	459,902
5	Texaco	13,166,504	6,910,732	3	**392,342**	409,616
6	Standard Oil Co. of California	11,094,510	5,074,050	7	**508,978**	461,954
7	International Business Machines Corpn	9,700,191	6,885,860	4	**1,431,627**	1,251,600
8	Gulf Oil Corpn	9,155,218	4,944,886	9	**364,055**	346,105
9	General Electric Co.	9,045,587	4,244,943	13	**565,965**	500,840
10	Sears, Roebuck & Co.	8,259,734	4,287,341	12	**424,127**	385,678
11	Standard Oil Co. (Indiana)	7,427,986	4,960,540	8	**495,415**	475,074
12	International Telephone & Telegraph Corpn	7,023,900	4,466,691	11	**304,594**	258,794
13	Chrysler Corpn	6,267,633	2,064,987	25	**Loss 94,166**	57,439
14	Atlantic Richfield Co.	5,862,989	4,734,817	10	**370,188**	322,870
15	Safeway Stores	5,776,352	858,622	70	**67,250**	47,085
16	K Mart Corpn	5,382,828	1,586,755	39	**158,189**	139,417
17	Shell Oil Co.	5,091,627	3,931,653	14	**374,467**	338,324
18	United States Steel Corpn	5,085,491	3,908,963	15	**111,380**	63,468
19	J. C. Penney Co.	4,991,370	1,508,227	44	**127,028**	135,773
20	E. I. Du Pont de Nemours & Co.	4,871,338	3,049,730	19	**362,214**	250,880
21	Conoco	4,458,635	2,560,531	21	**207,728**	175,182
22	Western Electric Co.	4,382,389	2,232,277	24	**258,290**	225,556
23	Tenneco	4,032,678	3,403,061	16	**214,475**	196,525
24	Procter & Gamble Co.	3,727,850	1,756,367	33	**235,493**	212,387
25	Union Carbide Corpn	3,622,000	2,876,447	20	**181,475**	177,241
26	Kroger Co.	3,602,840	451,329	90	**38,935**	27,913
27	Goodyear Tire & Rubber Co.	3,446,831	1,760,006	32	**104,074**	94,710
28	Great Atlantic & Pacific Tea Co.	3,437,882	354,392	93	**Loss 24,018**	1,469
29	Beatrice Foods Co.	3,437,291	N/A	—	**120,129**	101,962
30	Sun Co.	3,418,819	1,982,897	27	**168,171**	166,582
31	Caterpillar Tractor Co.	3,322,610	1,746,174	36	**260,637**	204,856
32	Eastman Kodak Co.	3,227,671	2,406,945	22	**415,273**	296,145
33	Philips Petroleum Co.	3,220,703	2,310,279	23	**326,995**	237,902
34	Dow Chemical Co.	3,170,003	3,061,542	18	**264,745**	255,760
35	International Harvester Co.	3,067,241	1,324,227	49	**85,919**	93,769
36	Westinghouse Electric Corpn	3,066,759	1,440,709	47	**112,024**	115,420
37	Philip Morris	3,052,566	1,741,632	37	**188,048**	154,148
38	R. J. Reynolds Industries	3,047,797	1,754,919	34	**203,383**	194,914
39	RCA Corpn	3,037,901	1,500,817	45	**128,133**	113,681
40	Union Oil of California	2,917,799	2,031,359	26	**175,944**	153,832
41	United Technologies Corpn	2,883,589	1,194,467	52	**107,764**	90,195
42	Occidental Petroleum Corpn	2,877,724	1,641,029	38	**3,084**	70,763
43	Bethlehem Steel Corpn	2,846,577	1,808,630	30	**103,601**	Loss 206,282
44	F. W. Woolworth Co.	2,808,791	923,852	64	**59,970**	42,297
45	Xerox Corpn	2,716,327	1,950,938	28	**213,968**	187,149
46	Esmark	2,681,940	640,985	82	**36,866**	30,823
47	Kraft	2,609,550	737,637	77	**84,685**	70,931
48	Rockwell International Corpn	2,609,044	872,811	69	**96,237**	66,321
49	Boeing Co.	2,514,325	791,577	73	**148,614**	82,982
50	Ashland Oil	2,497,373	899,411	66	**112,656**	75,602

NOTES: *Total tangible assets less current liabilities (other than bank loans and overdrafts).
N/A Not available.
Converted at US$2.17275 to £1.

Rank (sales)	Name	Sales £000	*CAPITAL EMPLOYED		NET INCOME	
			£000	Rank	Latest year £000	Previous year £000
51	Federated Department Stores	2,487,456	923,341	65	**91,081**	90,468
52	General Foods Corpn	2,474,378	712,004	78	**78,014**	81,619
53	LTV Corpn	2,421,142	N/A	—	**18,227**	Loss 27,329
54	Standard Oil Co. (Ohio)	2,392,228	3,135,022	17	**207,205**	83,329
55	American Brands	2,382,559	646,045	81	**97,360**	72,618
56	Monsanto Co.	2,309,838	1,872,236	29	**139,271**	126,844
57	Marathon Oil Co.	2,257,364	1,301,276	50	**103,633**	90,650
58	Firestone Tire & Rubber Co.	2,245,127	1,166,126	53	**Loss 68,255**	50,719
59	Amerada Hess	2,163,674	1,003,034	61	**65,547**	82,329
60	Minnesota Mining & Manufacturing Co.	2,145,514	1,477,105	46	**259,111**	190,057
61	Cities Service Co.	2,145,162	1,533,172	43	**54,309**	96,744
62	Lucky Stores	2,144,015	293,822	96	**37,004**	28,205
63	Winn-Dixie Stores	2,045,452	248,958	97	**38,709**	32,401
64	Georgia-Pacific Corpn	2,026,464	1,350,823	48	**138,994**	120,585
65	Greyhound Corpn	2,006,143	531,844	87	**26,857**	37,982
66	Armco Steel Corpn	2,005,424	1,087,008	57	**91,273**	55,152
67	Coca-Cola Co.	1,996,510	799,602	72	**172,451**	150,142
68	Colgate-Palmolive Co.	1,984,607	813,079	71	**80,806**	73,879
69	Gulf & Western Industries	1,984,562	1,535,422	42	**83,082**	69,187
70	W. R. Grace & Co.	1,983,472	1,086,516	58	**78,427**	64,653
71	Sperry Rand	1,923,516	1,245,290	51	**103,156**	81,288
72	Deere & Co.	1,912,302	1,140,034	55	**121,879**	117,658
73	International Paper Co.	1,910,114	1,565,251	41	**107,790**	107,560
74	McDonnell Douglas Corpn	1,900,946	585,936	85	**74,148**	56,591
75	Ralston Purina Co.	1,867,863	670,533	80	**71,154**	65,677
76	Aluminum Co. of America	1,864,826	1,567,046	40	**143,919**	89,840
77	American Can Co.	1,832,240	780,394	74	**55,045**	52,468
78	Continental Group	1,815,165	1,044,575	60	**58,083**	66,183
79	Borden	1,750,114	676,134	79	**62,514**	58,391
80	Weyerhaeuser Co.	1,748,678	1,773,706	31	**170,815**	139,865
81	TRW	1,743,067	627,797	83	**80,195**	70,978
82	Pepsico	1,737,258	741,494	76	**103,909**	86,222
83	National Steel Corpn	1,726,113	1,077,021	59	**51,720**	27,672
84	American Stores Co.	1,720,232	182,225	98	**12,241**	11,883
85	Getty Oil Co.	1,692,203	1,750,406	35	**150,846**	14,269
86	Litton Industries	1,681,376	616,084	84	**41,810**	25,731
87	Bendix Corpn	1,668,623	568,128	86	**59,648**	54,355
88	Signal Companies	1,643,908	764,975	75	**73,962**	46,718
89	Honeywell	1,632,862	889,150	67	**83,535**	61,816
90	Consolidated Foods Corpn	1,627,231	461,090	89	**46,316**	40,533
91	Jewel Companies	1,618,388	313,095	95	**18,935**	12,404
92	Johnson & Johnson	1,609,635	880,750	68	**137,641**	113,827
93	Lockheed Corpn	1,603,958	349,925	94	**29,870**	25,498
94	Republic Steel Corpn	1,601,407	969,913	62	**51,126**	18,884
95	Champion International Corpn	1,599,422	1,109,767	56	**93,774**	63,797
96	Allied Chemical Corpn	1,504,064	1,141,708	54	**55,340**	62,249
97	Inland Steel Co.	1,494,883	963,909	63	**72,862**	40,411
98	General Mills	1,492,579	430,422	91	**62,501**	53,864
99	CBS	1,491,938	499,237	88	**91,165**	83,768
100	Raytheon Co.	1,490,877	365,985	92	**69,053**	52,118

NOTES: *Total tangible assets less current liabilities (other than bank loans and overdrafts).
N/A Not available.
Converted at US$2.17275 to £1.

FOR FAST FINANCIAL INFORMATION ON ANY COMPANY...

...ANYWHERE IN THE WORLD

Jordans can offer you the most flexible service in the business.

Whether you need facts from the Registries in London, Cardiff or Edinburgh or in-depth information on overseas companies, our experts are on the spot.

And that means a fast, accurate service which helps you make the right decisions — quickly.

Jordan & Sons Ltd
Jordan House
Brunswick Place
London N1 6EE
Telephone 01-253 3030
Telex 261010

44 Whitchurch Road
Cardiff CF4 3UQ
Telephone 0222-371901
Telex 49167

Jordans

19 The 50 leading Japanese companies

Rank	Company	Head office	SALES		NET PROFIT	
			Latest year £000	Previous year £000	Latest year £000	Previous year £000
1	Toyota Motor	Toyota	5,527,787	4,832,247	245,588	246,625
2	Nippon Steel	Tokyo	5,094,957	4,912,672	95,504	33,470
3	Nissan Motor	Tokyo	4,871,563	4,744,230	138,258	170,391
4	Tokyo Electric Power	Tokyo	3,853,960	3,736,093	174,391	158,653
5	Nippon Oil	Tokyo	3,404,131	3,765,723	12,646	30,957
6	Matsushita Electric Industrial	Osaka	3,375,039	3,029,603	120,055	102,653
7	Hitachi	Tokyo	3,187,846	2,932,583	79,278	66,395
8	Mitsubishi Heavy Industries	Tokyo	2,692,422	2,912,845	20,424	31,749
9	Tokyo Shibaura Electric	Kawasaki	2,618,845	2,240,646	40,978	29,390
10	Nippon Kokan	Tokyo	2,441,666	2,538,363	21,806	10,997
11	Kansai Electric Power	Osaka	2,358,541	2,297,652	96,872	111,265
12	Sumitomo Metal Industries	Osaka	2,174,002	2,058,300	32,203	11,364
13	Kawasaki Steel	Kobe	2,029,388	1,974,773	36,807	14,382
14	Daiei	Osaka	1,986,207	1,850,629	14,836	12,638
15	Mitsubishi Electric	Tokyo	1,974,049	1,673,029	30,627	20,612
16	Honda Motor	Tokyo	1,947,793	1,794,372	33,797	36,978
17	Chubu Electric Power	Nagoya	1,872,129	1,845,274	90,587	92,074
18	Kobe Steel	Kobe	1,867,069	1,759,696	28,904	14,847
19	Maruzen Oil	Osaka	1,858,148	2,064,127	247	663
20	Kirin Brewery	Tokyo	1,660,600	1,413,772	39,354	34,923
21	Ishikawajima-Harima Heavy Industries	Tokyo	1,474,437	1,612,353	4,139	12,106
22	Toyo Kogyo	Hiroshima	1,449,512	1,326,851	5,565	2,397
23	Mitsubishi Oil	Tokyo	1,433,947	1,584,053	16,923	34,784
24	Taisei	Tokyo	1,381,278	1,170,836	16,125	16,072
25	Nippon Electric	Tokyo	1,299,768	1,137,350	16,076	14,847
26	Daikyo Oil	Tokyo	1,299,550	1,299,231	3,143	6,807
27	Nippon Express	Tokyo	1,289,683	1,186,025	10,648	9,383
28	Kajima	Tokyo	1,215,620	1,110,042	28,180	27,793
29	Isuzu Motors	Tokyo	1,208,841	989,985	28,372	13,056
30	Shimizu Construction	Tokyo	1,178,146	1,113,932	15,677	19,261
31	Kyushu Electric Power	Fukuoka	1,158,731	1,128,779	42,636	49,576
32	Tohoku Electric Power	Sendai	1,136,304	1,117,535	54,817	50,746
33	Toa Nenryo Kogyo	Tokyo	1,125,987	1,304,283	37,016	41,681
34	Sanyo Electric	Osaka	1,114,243	1,123,808	23,962	23,081
35	Showa Oil	Tokyo	1,087,926	1,167,983	7,328	7,364
36	Mitsubishi Chemical Industries	Tokyo	1,086,425	1,153,878	4,832	10,695
37	Taiyo Fishery	Tokyo	1,064,946	1,096,775	2,222	2,220
38	Kawasaki Heavy Industries	Kobe	1,059,033	1,195,502	Loss 12,446	20,450
39	Nippon Mining	Tokyo	1,037,326	1,127,136	1,935	6,566
40	Ito-Yokado	Tokyo	1,025,257	818,967	16,701	13,546
41	Kubota	Osaka	1,019,979	978,980	41,628	39,489
42	Ohbayashi-Gumi	Osaka	1,018,543	1,087,818	9,069	10,272
43	Seiyu Stores	Tokyo	1,017,554	937,907	7,221	5,899
44	Japan Air Lines	Tokyo	993,113	919,483	6,137	17,191
45	Mitsukoshi	Tokyo	991,210	952,792	22,574	21,761
46	Jusco	Osaka	939,442	800,076	13,193	10,072
47	Fujitsu	Kawasaki	931,195	818,205	22,665	17,312
48	Sumitomo Chemical	Osaka	918,589	944,680	8,224	2,822
49	Chugoku Electric Power	Hiroshima	913,489	887,552	54,116	45,592
50	Tokyo Gas	Tokyo	904,917	887,024	28,080	30,336

NOTE: Converted at 473.5 Yen to £1.

A General Aviation＊ Limited Edition

There's only one general aviation company that can offer the serious purchaser so much under one roof. CSE.

Arguably considered to be the biggest and best of its kind anywhere in the world.

CSE are sole distributors for Piper, Embraer and Gates Lear aircraft, of Bell Textron helicopters, and of leading makes of engines, propellers, simulators, avionics and components.

We offer the most comprehensive maintenance facilities this side of the Atlantic. Also the Oxford Air Training School, one of the largest for training pilots for airlines and governments all over the world.

CSE — a sound investment.

CSE Aviation Limited, Oxford Airport, Kidlington, Oxford OX5 1RA England.

＊*General Aviation—everything to do with flying (except military and major airlines) including executive jet and piston engined aircraft, and helicopters.*

20 The 30 leading Canadian companies

Rank	Name	Sales £000	*Capital employed £000	NET INCOME Latest year £000	Previous year £000
1	General Motors of Canada	3,045,213	N/A	**80,059**	71,244
2	Ford Motor Company of Canada	2,708,775	399,566	**14,987**	14,474
3	Canadian Pacific	2,609,840	2,765,850	**134,439**	94,601
4	Imperial Oil	2,236,640	1,117,283	**123,841**	113,981
5	Geo. Weston	2,065,789	346,726	**19,963**	10,837
6	Gulf Canada	1,839,874	837,034	**72,136**	72,964
7	Alcan Aluminium	1,634,956	1,369,556	**133,191**	92,742
8	Bell Canada	1,206,636	3,585,930	**170,550**	131,726
9	Massey-Ferguson	1,153,813	645,785	**Loss 101,246**	12,905
10	Chrysler Canada	1,138,680	N/A	**Loss 12,123**	3,798
11	Canadian National Railway Co.	1,132,064	N/A	**32,393**	N/A
12	Shell Canada	1,070,795	853,993	**59,712**	60,974
13	Seagram Co.	1,045,948	877,447	**41,682**	40,075
14	Canada Packers	919,151	N/A	**8,245**	7,144
15	Transcanada Pipelines	856,489	606,112	**37,507**	33,991
16	Inco	821,571	1,419,203	**30,688**	39,384
17	Macmillan Bloedel	790,737	496,776	**39,813**	23,908
18	Texaco Canada	750,183	582,952	**58,313**	14,460
19	Steel Co. of Canada	700,321	640,751	**47,413**	35,577
20	Noranda Mines	666,967	749,726	**53,526**	28,308
21	Moore Corporation	609,072	316,180	**39,456**	35,819
22	Northern Telecom	593,398	350,681	**37,225**	32,275
23	ITOL	576,700	288,600	**44,100**	38,400
24	Air Canada	521,628	N/A	**18,728**	7,890
25	Abitibi Paper Co.	511,023	352,385	**31,020**	14,951
26	Canada Development Corpn	505,836	N/A	**14,361**	N/A
27	Domtar	489,414	275,845	**24,967**	10,586
28	Molson Companies	472,041	150,789	**17,384**	12,204
29	Imasco	458,105	181,323	**22,247**	16,990
30	Genstar	450,815	441,407	**32,186**	25,411

NOTES: *Total tangible assets less current liabilities (excluding bank loans and overdrafts).
N/A Not available.
Converted at CAN$2.5355 to £1 and US$2.17275 to £1.

21 The 20 leading Australian companies

Rank	Name	Turnover £000	*Capital employed £000	NET PROFIT AFTER TAX Latest year £000	Previous year £000
1	Broken Hill Proprietary Co.	1,226,198	1,564,171	**43,707**	33,071
2	Woolworths	900,921	128,321	**17,669**	14,855
3	G. J. Coles & Co.	802,835	194,118	**19,551**	16,265
4	Elder Smith Goldsbrough Mort	719,860	169,392	**5,236**	4,499
5	Conzinc Riotinto of Australia	604,340	908,956	**39,278**	40,252
6	Myer Emporium	552,180	223,345	**20,143**	23,547
7	CSR	502,531	536,322	**28,736**	20,058
8	Amatil	493,802	186,739	**15,095**	12,536
9	ICI Australia	423,210	306,286	**24,913**	17,046
10	Australian Consolidated Industries	353,428	252,930	**11,878**	8,886
11	Dunlop Australia	298,983	128,233	**8,014**	8,743
12	Ansett Transport Industries	263,706	97,233	**9,476**	8,870
13	Burns, Philip & Co.	257,748	189,846	**6,320**	3,059
14	Carlton and United Breweries	254,006	124,470	**10,243**	8,860
15	Thomas Nationwide Transport	239,198	119,712	**7,345**	7,457
16	Grace Bros. Holdings	208,190	76,075	**6,466**	5,621
17	Ampol Petroleum	203,165	143,400	**5,527**	5,139
18	David Jones	**196,948	110,878	**2,760**	3,954
19	Philips Industries Holdings	196,837	83,326	**Loss 1,669**	521
20	Australian National Industries	195,196	72,699	**7,623**	4,554

NOTES: *Total tangible assets less current liabilities (excluding bank loans and overdrafts).
**Australian Group sales.
Converted at A$1.936 to £1.

Have you been in touch with British Vita today?

The answer's almost certainly 'yes' since the British Vita Group is an international leader in polymer technology. The Group includes Vitafoam polyurethane foams, Caligen polyester foams, Vitacom rubber compounds, Vitalay carpet underlays, Vitaluxan fibres, Vitapruf coated fabrics, Vitamol rubber mouldings. For the consumer, there's Vitaluxe sleep, leisure and furniture ranges, plus Swimsafe, the ideal swimming aid for children.

The principal markets for all these products are furniture, bedding, household textiles, transportation, engineering and rubber.

With its headquarters at Middleton, Manchester, the British Vita Group has more than 60 operations in 23 countries. Today, as always, the key to Vita's world-wide success lies in constant product development and quality, based on proven experience in polymer technology and engineering.

That's why we believe you must have been in touch with British Vita today!

vita **a vital part of World industry.**
British Vita Company Limited
Middleton Manchester M24 2DB
Tel: 061-643 1133
Telex: 667722

22 The 20 leading South African companies

Rank	Name	*Capital employed £000	Turnover £000	NET PROFIT AFTER TAX Latest year £000	Previous year £000
1	Barlow Rand	624,778	886,174	51,866	42,123
2	Rembrandt Group	531,937	N/A	42,541	38,659
3	South African Breweries	409,635	779,252	26,859	24,207
4	AECI	341,228	383,902	31,269	20,300
5	Anglo-American Industrial Corpn	260,423	267,764	28,600	20,732
6	South African Marine Corpn	224,780	119,644	10,077	12,268
7	Tiger Oats & National Milling Company	186,608	420,394	13,709	12,210
8	Huletts Corpn	173,176	183,871	8,807	7,107
9	Premier Milling Co.	135,646	372,123	11,940	11,450
10	Tongaat Group	134,545	126,052	8,051	6,011
11	Sentrachem	131,769	101,710	11,380	10,030
12	Anglo-Alpha Cement	127,396	64,284*	3,314	4,003
13	Highveld Steel & Vanadium Corpn	127,164	94,396	11,460	11,318
14	Anglo-Transvaal Industries	117,889	235,599	6,733	4,734
15	OK Bazaars (1929)	108,575	295,083	6,921	6,922
16	Federale Volksbeleggings	103,202	98,582	3,978	4,548
17	Pretoria Portland Cement Co.	101,191	71,362	4,550	6,426
18	Triomf Fertilizer Investments	100,726	139,986	790	Loss 2,601
19	Sappi	95,790	111,939	7,882	6,971
20	C. G. Smith Sugar	95,716	101,501	8,298	7,446

NOTES: * Adjusted to an annual rate.
N/A Not available.
Converted at R1.8325 to £1.

23 The 20 leading companies in the Republic of Ireland

Rank	Name	Turnover £000	*Capital employed £000	NET PROFIT BEFORE TAX AND INTEREST Latest year £000	Previous year £000
1	Jefferson Smurfit Group	190,986	80,798	17,299	17,847
2	Cement-Roadstone Holdings	173,460	181,051	21,795	16,208
3	Esso Teoranta	151,820[2]	20,456	5,791	777
4	Irish Shell	143,099[1]	33,474	4,329	6,936
5	Waterford Glass	116,727	64,528	11,586	10,346
6	Irish Sugar Company	105,831	46,340	5,148	4,819
7	Carroll Industries	99,015[3]	26,089	5,052	5,402
8	Brooks Watson Group	88,847	15,923	2,790	2,303
9	R. & H. Hall	88,625	24,414	2,483	2,013
10	Irish Distillers Group	69,779	51,443	8,812	6,771
11	Youghal Carpets (Holdings)	65,744	21,252	2,618	251
12	Ranks (Ireland)	38,796	15,564	1,081	2,364
13	Clondalkin Mills Group	35,594	11,367	2,650	3,080
14	Abbey	31,739	19,814	3,235	2,388
15	Independent Newspapers	30,762	9,641	3,279	2,112
16	W. & R. Jacob & Company	30,502	13,519	481	212
17	Concrete Products Of Ireland	28,936	13,477	2,756	2,451
18	Arnott & Co., Dublin	28,249	13,855	2,537	2,026
19	H. Williams & Company	28,009	1,803	482	547
20	McInerney Properties	27,778	4,837	1,493	1,155

NOTES: Figures are in Irish currency.
Due to delays in receipt of information as a result of the Irish postal strike, some of the figures in this table may not be completely up to date.
* Total tangible assets less current liabilities (excluding bank loans and overdrafts and future tax).
[1] Including sales taxes and excise duties. [2] Including customs and excise duties and VAT [3] Excluding export duty.

A little light relief

It's no joke when your company stationery looks flat and dull. It's not funny when print costs go through the roof. How can Selwyn make you smile again? Well – the cartoon is just for starters.

Selwyn Thermography is a unique print process designed to give stationery a lift. Quality relief printing in any colour from the smallest type to the company symbol. It's fast and a quick change of copy is no problem. It's virtually half the price of die stamping too! If your stationery needs a little light relief send today for our free brochure and samples, and include your letterheading for a free quotation.

SELWYN
THERMOGRAPHY

The Selwyn Press, Northern Way, Bury St. Edmunds, Suffolk IP32 6NR. Tel: (STD 0284) 62201.
Our clients include Rolls Royce, Richard Costain Ltd, Kelloggs, Whitbread, Brooke Bond, Oxo, Harrods, Shell, Bland Payne.

127

COMPANY INFORMATION- FAST!

Same day searches from the Companies Registries in London, Cardiff and Edinburgh.

Phone Derek Stevenson on 01·251 4941

or Telex 23678

 **Company Information Services**

ICC House, 81 City Road, London EC1Y 1BD

A member of the ICC Group of Companies Publishers of over 200 Business Ratio Reports and Financial Surveys on UK Industry and Commerce

24   Foreign banks in Britain[*]

American Banks

Allied Bank International
American Express International Banking Corporation
American National Bank and Trust Co. of Chicago
Amex Bank Ltd.
Amex International Ltd.
Bank of America International Ltd.
Bank of America (Jersey) Ltd.
Bank of America National Trust and Savings Association
The Bank of California N.A.
The Bank of New York
The Bank of Tokyo Trust Company
Bankers Trust Co.
Bankers Trust International Ltd.
Carolina Bank
Chase Bank (C.I.) Ltd.
Chase Manhattan Bank N.A.
Chase Manhattan Ltd.
Chemical Bank
Citibank N.A.
Citibank (C.I.) Ltd.
Citicorp International Bank Ltd.
City National Bank of Detroit
Continental Illinois Ltd.
Continental Illinois National Bank and Trust Co. of Chicago
Crocker National Bank
The Detroit Bank and Trust Company
The Fidelity Bank
First Chicago Ltd.
First City National Bank of Houston
First City National Bank of Houston
First International Bancshares Ltd.
First National Bank in Dallas
First National Bank in St Louis
The First National Bank of Boston
The First National Bank of Boston (Guernsey) Ltd.
The First National Bank of Chicago
The First National Bank of Chicago (C.I.) Ltd.
First Pennsylvania Bank N.A.
First Wisconsin National Bank of Milwaukee
Girard Bank
Harris Trust and Savings Bank
Irving Trust Co.
Manufacturers Hanover Ltd.
Manufacturers Hanover Bank (Guernsey) Ltd.
Manufacturers Hanover Trust Co.
Marine Midland Bank
Marine Midland Bank Ltd.
Mellon Bank N.A.
Merrill Lynch International Bank
Morgan Guaranty Trust Co. of New York
National Bank of Detroit
North Carolina National Bank
The Northern Trust Co.
Rainier National Bank
Republic National Bank of Dallas
Seattle – First National Bank
Security Pacific National Bank

Texas Commerce Bank N.A.
Texas Commerce International Bank Ltd.
United California Bank
Wells Fargo Bank N.A.
Wells Fargo Ltd.
Western Trust & Savings Ltd.

Japanese Banks

The Bank of Tokyo Ltd.
The Bank of Yokohama Ltd.
The Dai-Ichi Kangyo Bank Ltd.
The Daiwa Bank Ltd.
The Fuji Bank Ltd.
The Hokkaido Takushaku Bank Ltd.
The Industrial Bank of Japan Ltd.
The Kyowa Bank Ltd.
The Long-Term Credit Bank of Japan Ltd.
The Mitsubishi Bank Ltd.
The Mitsubishi Trust and Banking Corporation
The Mitsui Bank Ltd.
The Mitsui Trust and Banking Corporation
The Nippon Fudosan Bank
The Saitama Bank Ltd.
The Sanwa Bank Ltd.
The Sumitomo Bank Ltd.
The Sumitomo Trust and Banking Co. Ltd.
The Taiyo Kobe Bank Ltd.
The Tokai Bank Ltd.
The Toyo Trust and Banking Co.
The Yasuda Trust and Banking Co. Ltd.

Other Overseas Banks

Afghan National Bank Ltd.
African Continental Bank Ltd.
Algemene Bank Nederland N.V.
Allied Arab Bank
Amsterdam-Rotterdam Bank N.V.
Arab Bank Ltd.
Australia and New Zealand Banking Group Ltd.
Australia and New Zealand Banking Group (C.I.) Ltd.
Banca Commerciale Italiana
Banca Nazionale del Lavoro
Banco Central S.A.
Banco de Bilbao
Banco de la Nacion Argentina
Banco de Santander
Banco de Vizcaya
Banco di Roma
Banco do Brasil S.A.
Banco do Estado de São Paulo S.A.
Banco Español en Londres S.A.
Banco Mercantil de São Paulo S.A.
Banco Real S.A.
Banco Totta & Acores

[*] At 1 June 1979.

Bangkok Bank Ltd.
Bank Julius Baer International Ltd.
Bank Brussels Lambert (U.K.)
Bank Bumiputra Malaysia Berhab
Bank für Gemeinwirtschaft AG
Bank Hapoalim B.M.
Bank Leumi (U.K.) Ltd.
Bank Melli Iran
The Bank of Adelaide
Bank of Baroda
Bank of Ceylon
Bank of China
Bank of Credit and Commerce International S.A.
Bank of Cyprus (London) Ltd.
Bank of India
Bank of Montreal
Bank of New South Wales
Bank of New Zealand
The Bank of Nova Scotia
The Bank of Nova Scotia (C.I.) Ltd.
Bank of Tehran
Bank Sadarat Iran
Bank Sanaye Iran
Bank Sepah Iran
Banque Belge Ltd.
Banque Belgo-Zairoise S.A.
Banque Canadienne Nationale
Banque de l'Indochine et de Suez
Banque de Paris et des Pays-Bas
Banque Nationale de Paris Ltd.
Bayerische Landesbank Girozentrale
Bayerische Vereinsbank
Bilbao International Bank Ltd.
The British Bank of the Middle East Ltd.
Canadian Imperial Bank of Commerce
Central Bank of India
Chase & Bank of Ireland (International) Ltd.
Commercial Bank of Australia Ltd.
The Commercial Bank of Korea Ltd.
Commercial Bank of the Near East Ltd.
The Commercial Banking Co. of Sydney Ltd.
Commerzbank A.G.
Commonwealth Trading Bank of Australia
Crédit Industriel et Commercial
Crédit Lyonnais
Crédit Suisse
Credito Italiano
Deutsche Bank A.G.

Discount Bank (Overseas) Ltd.
Dow Banking Corporation
Dresdner Bank A.G.
French Bank of Southern Africa Ltd.
Ghana Commercial Bank
Habib Bank Ltd.
The Hanil Bank Ltd.
Havana International Bank Ltd.
The Hongkong & Shanghai Banking Corporation
The Hongkong & Shanghai Banking Corporation (C.I.) Ltd.
Hungarian International Bank Ltd.
Investitions-und-Handels-Bank A.G.
Korea Exchange Bank
Korea First Bank
London and Continental Bankers Ltd.
Malayan Banking Berhad
Mercantile Bank Ltd.
Moscow Narodny Bank Ltd.
The Muslim Commercial Bank Ltd.
National Bank of Abu Dhabi
The National Bank of Australasia Ltd.
National Bank of Greece
National Bank of Nigeria Ltd.
National Bank of Pakistan
Nedbank Ltd.
Oversea-Chinese Banking Corporation Ltd.
Overseas Union Bank Ltd.
Philippine National Bank
Punjab National Bank
Qatar National Bank S.A.Q.
Rafidain Bank
The Royal Bank of Canada
The Royal Bank of Canada (Channel Islands) Ltd.
Schlesinger Ltd.
Société Générale
Sonali Bank
State Bank of India
Swiss Bank Corporation
The Thai Farmers Bank Ltd.
Toronto-Dominion Bank Ltd.
Trade Development Bank
Union Bank of Switzerland
United Bank Ltd.
United Commercial Bank
United Overseas Bank Ltd.
Westdeutsche Landesbank Girozentrale
Zambia National Commercial Bank
Živnostenská Banka National Corporation

* At 1 June 1979.

Finding the answers takes time.

Handling information is a complex business. Our time could save yours; we have the information and the skills. These have been built up during the last twelve years inside and outside The Thomson Organisation Ltd.

The needs and requirements of our clients from publishing, advertising, manufacturing and finance are very different. We cater specifically for their needs; from simple population statistics to an involved economic forecast, from quick queries over the 'phone to more detailed reports and analysis.

What are your needs and how can we be of service to you?

Contact Christine Hull, Manager, The Times Information and Marketing Intelligence Unit, New Printing House Square, London WC1X 8EZ. Tel: 01-837 1234. Ext. 501.

The Times Information and Marketing Intelligence Unit.

Alphabetical index to listed companies

For Unit Trusts appearing without addresses, see addresses of the parent companies indicated on page 84

Banco de Vizcaya 129
75-79 Coleman St., London EC2R 6BL
Banco di Roma 129
14-18 Eastcheap, London EC3M 1JY
Banco de Brasil SA 129
P.O. Box 131, 16-17 King St.,
London EC2P 2NA
Banco do Estado de São Paulo SA 129
Plantation House, 31-35 Fenchurch St.,
London EC3M 3NA
Banco Espanol en Londres SA 129
London Fruit Exchange, Brushfield St.,
London EC1
Banco Mercantil de São Paulo SA 129
Stock Exchange, London EC2N 1HH
Banco Real SA 129
Bucklersbury House, 3 Queen Victoria
St., London EC4N 8EL
Banco Totta & Acores 129
3 Abchurch Yard, London EC4
Bangkok Bank Ltd. 130
59 Gresham St., London EC2V 7HB
The Bank of Adelaide 130
11 Leadenhall St., London EC3
Bank of America Intl. Ltd. 129
St. Helen's, 1 Undershaft, London EC3
Bank of America (Jersey) Ltd. 129
11 Esplanade, St. Helier, Jersey, CI
Bank of America National Trust and 129
Savings Assoc.
P.O. Box 407, 27-29 Walbrook St.,
London EC4P 4HN
Bank Julius Baer Intl. Ltd. 130
3 Lombard St., London EC3
Bank of Baroda 130
31 King St., London EC2
Bank Brussels Lambert (U.K.) 130
St. Helen's, 1 Undershaft,
London EC3P 3EY
Bank Bumiputra Malaysia 130
64 Maril Lane, London EC4
The Bank of California 129
1 Cornhill, London EC3V 3PY
Bank of Ceylon 130
48 Moorgate, London EC2
Bank of China 130
111 Cannon St., London EC4
Bank of Credit and Commerce 130
International S.A.
60 Mark Lane, London EC3
Bank of Cyprus (London) Ltd. 130
27 Charlotte St., London W1
Bank für Gemeinwirtschaft 130
Bucklersbury House, Cannon St.,
London EC4
Bank Hapoalim B.M. 130
22 Lawrence Lane, London EC2
Bank of India 130
Kent House, Telegraph St.,
London EC2
Bank Leumi (U.K.) Ltd. 130
7 Woodstock St., London W1
Bank Melli Iran 130
113 Leadenhall St., London EC3
Bank of Montreal 130
47 Threadneedle St., London EC2
Bank of New South Wales 130
29 Threadneedle St., London EC2
The Bank of New York 130
147 Leadenhall St., London
EC3V 4PN
Bank of New Zealand 130
1 Queen Victoria St., London EC4
The Bank of Nova Scotia 130
62 Threadneedle St., London EC2
The Bank of Nova Scotia (C.I.) Ltd. 129
62 Threadneedle St., London EC2
Bank Saderat Iran 130
Plantation House, Mincing Lane,
London EC3
Bank Sanaye Iran 130
12 Eastcheap, London EC3
Bank of Scotland 77
The Mound, Edinburgh EH1 1YZ
Bank Sepah-Iran 130
3 Eastcheap, London EC3
Bank of Tehran 130
48 Gresham St., London EC2
The Bank of Tokyo Ltd. 129
24 Moorgate, London EC2
Bank of Tokyo and Detroit (Intl.) 82
18 Finsbury Circus, London EC2M 7BR
The Bank of Tokyo Trust Co. 129
2nd Floor, Northgate House,
20-24 Moorgate, London EC2
The Bank of Yokohama 129
10 Eastcheap, London EC3
Bankers Trust Co. 129
9 Queen Victoria St., London
EC4P 4DB
Bankers Trust Intl. Ltd. 129
56 New Broad Street, London EC2
Banking Insurance and Finance Union 16
Sheffield House, Portsmouth Rd., Esher,
Surrey
Sidney C. Banks 56
29 St. Neot's Rd., Sandy, Beds
SG19 1LD
Banque Belge Ltd. 130
9 Norton Folgate, London E1
Banque Belgo-Zairoise S.A. 130
48 Moorgate, London EC2
Banque Canadienne Nationale 130
72 Basinghall St., London EC2
Banque de l'Indochine et de Suez 130
64 Bishopsgate, London EC2

Banque de Paris et des Pays-Bas 130
Moor House, London Wall,
London EC2
Banque Nationale de Paris Ltd. 130
Plantation House, Mincing Lane,
London EC3
Barclays Bank 77
54 Lombard St., London EC3P 3AH
Barclays Bank International 82
54 Lombard St., London EC3P 3AH
Barclays Unicorn 84
Unicorn House, 252 Romford Road,
London E7 9JB
*Barclaytrust Investment Fund 84
(Income)
Baring Brothers 80
88 Leadenhall St., London EC3A 3DT
Charles Barker ABH Intl. 56
30 Farringdon St., London EC4A
Barker & Dobson Group 56
217-219 Kensington High St.,
London W8
Barlow Rand 126
Barlow Park, Katherine St.,
Sandton 2196
Augustus Barnett & Son 52
Barnett House, Backchurch Lane,
London E1 1BR
Barr & Wallace Arnold Trust 50
21 The Calls, Leeds LS2 7ER
Barratt Developments 42
Wingrove House, Ponteland Road,
Newcastle-upon-Tyne NE5 3DP
Barretts & Baird (Wholesale) 68
The Abattoir, Harvil's Hawthorn,
West Bromwich, W. Midlands
Barrow Hepburn Group 60
73 South Audley Street, London
W1Y 6JR
Bartella 62
122 Chancery Lane, London WC2A 1PP
Arthur Bartfield Group 62
Brooks Wharf, 48 Upper Thames St.,
London EC4V 3DE
Barton & Sons 56
Neville House, 42 Hagley Rd.,
Birmingham B16 8PE
BASF AG 99
D 6700 Ludwigshafen am Rhein
BASF United Kingdom 48
P.O. Box 4, Earl Road, Cheadle Hulme,
Cheadle, Cheshire SK8 6QG
Bass 30
30 Portland Pl., London W1N 3DF
Bassett, Geo., Holdings 44
Livesey St., Owlerton, Sheffield S6 2AP
BAT Industries 30
P.O. Box 345, Windsor House,
50 Victoria St., London SW1H 0NL
Bath and Portland Group 44
20 Manvers St., Bath BA1 1LX
Batleys of Yorkshire 54
977 Leeds Rd., Huddersfield HD2 1UN
Bayer AG 99
5090 Leverkusen-Bayerwerk
Bayer UK 44
Bayer House, Richmond, Surrey
TW9 1ST
Bayerische Landesbank Girozentrale 130
99 Bishopsgate, London EC2
Bayerische Vereinsbank 130
40 Moorgate, London EC2
Bayernwerk AG 106
8 München 2, Blutenbergstr. 6
BAYWA AG 100
Arabellastr. 4, 8000 München 81
Bazar de l'Hôtel de Ville 116
55 rue de la Verrerie, Paris 4e
BBA Group 42
Whitechapel Road, Cleckheaton,
West Yorkshire BD19 6HP
BBC AG-Brown, Boveri & Cie 99
CH-5401 Baden, Hasselstr.
Beatrice Foods 119
120 South La Salle St., Chicago,
Illinois 60603
Beattie, James 64
71-78 Victoria St., Wolverhampton
WV1 3PQ
Beecham Group 32
Beecham House, Great West Rd.,
Brentford, Middlesex TW8 9BD
Beghin-Say 104
59239 Tumeries, Lille
Beiersdorf AG 108
Unnastrasse 48, 2000 Hamburg 20
Beijerinvest AB 103
Birger Jarlsgatan 6, S-103 97 Stockholm
Bejam Group 44
1 Garland Rd., Honeypot Lane,
Stanmore, Middx. HA7 1LE
Bekaert S.A. 108
L. Bekaertstraat 1, 8550 Zwevegem
Bell, Arthur 40
Cherrybank, Perth PH2 0NG
Bell AG 112
Elsasserstr. 187, Postfach 261, 4002 Basel
Bell Canada 124
1050 Beaver Hall Hill, Montreal,
Quebec H3C 3G4
Bell & Howell 68
Lennox Rd., Basingstoke, Hants
Bellway Holdings 62
Dobson House, The Regent Centre,
Gosforth, Newcastle-upon-Tyne NE3 3LT

Bemrose Corporation 56
Waygoose Dr., Derby DE2 6XP
Bendix 120
Bendix Center, Southfield, Mich. 48076
Bentalls 56
Wood Street, Kingston-upon-Thames,
Surrey KT1 1TX
Berec Group 38
Ever Ready House, 1255 High Rd.,
Whetstone, London N20 0EJ
Berisford, S. & W. 30
Berisford House, Mark Lane,
London EC3R 7QJ
Berkeley Hambro Property Co. 92
51 Bishopsgate, London EC2N 3AJ
Berry Bros. & Rudd 68
3 St. James's St., London, S.W.1.
Bertelsmann AG 103
Carl-Bertelsmann Strasse 270, Postbox
5555, 4830 Gütersloh
Bestobell 44
Stoke House, Slough, Bucks SL2 4HS
Bethlehem Steel 119
Bethlehem, Pennsylvania 18016
Bewag-Berliner Kraft und Licht AG 108
Stauffenbergerstr. 26, 1000 Berlin 30
Bibby, J. 40
Richmond House, 1 Rumford Place,
Liverpool L3 9QQ
BICC 30
21 Bloomsbury St., London
WC1B 3QN
Bilbao International Bank Ltd 130
25 Hill St., St. Helier, Jersey
Bilfinger & Berger Bau AG 110
Carl-Reiss-Platz 1-5, Postfach 51 60,
6800 Mannheim 1
Billerud Uddeholm 112
P.O. Box 60, S-66100 Säffle
Billington, Edward 46
Cunard Building, Liverpool L3 1EL
Bilspedition AB 116
Mölndalsvägen 85, 412 85 Göteborg
Percy Bilton 62
Bilton House, Ealing, London W5 2TL
Birmid Qualcast 38
Dartmouth Rd., Smethwick, Warley,
W. Midlands B66 1BW
Birmingham B.S. 96
42-44 Waterloo St., Birmingham
B2 5QB
Biro Bic 68
Whitby Ave., London NW10
Bishop's Stores 42
Stonefield Way, Ruislip, Middlesex
HA4 0JR
Bison Group 52
Haigh Park Rd., Stourton, Leeds
LS10 1RU
BL 30
Nuffield House, 41-46 Piccadilly,
London W1V 0BD
Black and Decker 46
Cannon Lane, Maidenhead, Berks
Black & Edgington 54
Industrial Estate, Port Glasgow,
Renfrewshire PA14 5XN
B. H. Blackwell 68
50 Broad St., Oxford
Blackwood Hodge 36
25 Berkeley Square, London W1A 4AX
Blagden & Noakes (Holdings) 52
16 Hatton Garden, London EC1N 8FJ
Blohm & Voss 114
Hermann-Blohm-Str. 3, 2000 Hamburg 11
Blue Circle Industries 34
Portland House, Stag Pl., London
SW1E 5BJ
Blyth, Greene, Jourdain & Co. 64
Plantation House, Fenchurch St.,
London EC3M 3EE
BMW-Bayerische Motorenwerke AG 100
Petuelring 130, 8000 München 40
BOC Intl. 30
Hammersmith House London W6 9DX
Bodycote International 64
104 Stamford St., Manchester M16 9LR
Boehringer Ingelheim Gruppe 104
6507 Ingelheim, Bingerstr. 172
Boehringer Mannheim GmbH 112
6800 Mannheim 31, Sandhoferstr. 116
Boeing 119
7755 East Marginal Way South,
Seattle, Washington 98124
Bofors 110
S 69020 Bofors (Varmland)
Boliden AB 108
Sturegatan 22, S-11485 Stockholm
Erven Lucas Bols 116
Lucas Bolsstraat, Nieuw-Vennep,
Amsterdam
Booker McConnell 32
Bucklersbury House, 83 Cannon St.,
London EC4N 8EJ
Boot, Henry 46
Banner Cross Hall, Ecclesall Rd.
South, Sheffield S11 8PD
Booth, Alfred 62
34 St. James's St., London SW1A 1JA
Booth (International Holdings) 62
Trent Bridge Leather Works,
Nottingham NG2 3BT
Boots Pure Drug Co. 30
1 Thane Road West, Nottingham
NG2 3AA

Borden (UK) 60
St. Christopher Works, N. Baddesley,
Southampton
Borden Inc. 120
277 Park Avenue, N.Y., N.Y. 10017
Border & Southern Stockholders Trust 94
Winchester House, 77 London Wall,
London EC2N 1DH
Jacques Borel Intl. SA 114
Tour Maine-Montparnasse, 33
Ave du Maine, 75755 Paris
Borg-Warner 44
P.O. Box 18, Letchworth, Herts
SG6 1NH
Borregaard A.S. 110
Sarpsborg 1701
Borregaard Industries 42
Norway House, 21-24 Cockspur St.,
London, S.W.1
Borsumij Wehry NV 112
Den Haag, Carnegielaan 1
Borthwick, Thomas 32
Priory House, St. Johns Lane,
London EC1M 4BX
Bos Kalis Westminster 44
Westminster House, Blackwest, Alton,
Hants GU34 4PU
Robert Bosch GmbH 99
D-7 Stuttgart 1, Gerlingen-Schillerhöhe,
Robert-Bosch-Platz 1
Boston Trust and Savings 78
Boston House, Lower Dagnall St.,
St. Albans, Herts AL3 4PG
Boustead 66
14-15 Conduit St., London W1R 9TG
Bouygues 106
381 ave du Général de Gaulle,
92140 Clamart (Hauts-de-Seine)
Bowmaker 78
Bowmaker House, Christchurch Rd.,
Bournemouth BH1 3LG
Bowater Corpn. 30
Bowater House, Knightsbridge,
London SW1X 7LR
Bowater-Scott Corporation 44
Bowater House, Knightsbridge, London
SW1X 7LR
Bowring, C. T. 30
The Bowring Building, Tower Place,
London EC3P 3BE
Bowthorpe Holdings 56
Gatwick Rd., Crawley, West Sussex
RH10 2RZ
BPA-Byggproduktion AB 106
Tegnerg 23, Box 45126, 104 30 Stockholm
BPB Industries 36
Ferguson House, 15-17 Marylebone Rd.,
London NW1 5JE
BPM Holdings 54
28 Colmore Circus, Birmingham
B4 6AX
Braby, Leslie 64
Cowley Mill Rd., Uxbridge,
Middx UB8 2QG
Bradford & Bingley B.S. 96
Main St., Bingley, W. Yorkshire
BD16 2LW
Braid Group 64
82 Derby Rd., Liverpool L20 8LR
H. Brammer & Co. 62
Station House, Stamford New Road,
Altrincham, Cheshire WA14 1EP
Braun AG 114
6000 Frankfurt (Main) 19,
Rüsselheimerstr. 22
Bredero NV 114
P.O. Box 74, Kromme Niellwegracht 66,
3500 AB Utrecht
Bremer Vulkan Schiffbau und 116
Maschinenfabrik
Lindenstr. 110, Postfach 70 02 40,
2820 Bremen-Vegesack
Bridgwater B.S. 96
1 King Sq., Bridgwater TA6 3DF
Bridon 38
Warmsworth Hall, Doncaster,
South Yorks DN4 9JX
Brinkmann (Martin) AG 103
Dötlingerstr. 1-12, 2800-Bremen 1
Brintons 58
16 Exchange St., Kidderminster,
Worcs DY10 1AG
Bristol & West B.S. 96
GPO Box 27, Broad Quay, Bristol 1
BS9 7AX
Britannia Arrow Holdings 90
3 London Wall Bldgs, London Wall,
London EC2M 5QL
Britannia B.S. 96
P.O. Box 20. Newton House, Leek,
Staffs ST13 5RG
Britannia Lead 44
Adelaide House, King William St.,
London EC4R 9DX
Britannia Trust Management Ltd. 84
3 London Wall Bldgs., London Wall,
London EC2M 5QL
Britannic Assurance 86
Moor Green, Moseley, Birmingham
B13 8QF
British Aerospace 77
Brooklands Rds., Weybridge, Surrey
KT13 0SJ
British Aircraft Corpn. (Holdings) 32
100 Pall Mall, London SW1Y 5HR

134

140

141

Printed in Great Britain by
WATERLOW (DUNSTABLE) LIMITED

Insuring projects like The Queen's Award

These are only a selection from a long list of insurance and reinsurance projects handled by the C. E. Heath Group around the world.

A high proportion of the premiums involved have been channelled through the London insurance market.

This has helped the Group's overseas currency earnings to be doubled over a three-year period, and has resulted in our gaining The Queen's Award for Export Achievement.

Jack-up drilling rig "Interocean 11" on the Barge "Genmark 105" under tow on a 15,000-mile voyage from Japan to Mexico, which was completed in 77 days.

C. E. Heath has placed in London and world-wide markets the liability and property insurance cover of the Port Authority of New York and New Jersey including the World Trade Centre complex.